NORTH KOREA

Series Editor
Sonia Ryang, University of Iowa

New Asian Anthropology offers a forum for theoretical debate and empirical contributions toward a new anthropology of Asia. Books in the series provide critiques of existing studies and frameworks, and draw on radically new ethnographical data. Proposed subject matter ranges from fieldwork methodology to epistemology to fresh interpretations of the classics. The geographical area is broadly defined as Asia, including the Middle East, Central Asia, South Asia, Southeast Asia, East Asia, and diasporic Asia. The series provides a forum for dialogue among indigenous Asian and non-Asian anthropologists and other social scientists who address anthropological issues.

Titles in Series:

Writing Selves in Diaspora: Ethnography of Autobiographics of Korean Women in Japan and the United States, by Sonia Ryang
North Korea: Toward a Better Understanding, edited by Sonia Ryang

NORTH KOREA
Toward a Better Understanding

Edited by
Sonia Ryang

LEXINGTON BOOKS

A DIVISION OF
ROWMAN & LITTLEFIELD PUBLISHERS, INC.
Lanham • Boulder • New York • Toronto • Plymouth, UK

LEXINGTON BOOKS

A division of Rowman & Littlefield Publishers, Inc.
A wholly owned subsidary of The Rowman & Littlefield Publishing Group, Inc.
4501 Forbes Boulevard, Suite 200
Lanham, MD 20706

Estover Road
Plymouth PL6 7PY
United Kingdom

British Library Cataloguing in Publication Information Available

Library of Congress Cataloging-in-Publication Data

North Korea : toward a better understanding / edited by Sonia Ryang.
    p. cm. — (New Asian Anthropology)
 Includes bibliographical references.
 ISBN-13: 978-0-7391-3205-0 (cloth : alk. paper)
 ISBN-10: 0-7391-3205-9 (cloth : alk. paper)
 ISBN-13: 978-0-7391-3206-7 (pbk. : alk. paper)
 ISBN-10: 0-7391-3206-7 (pbk. : alk. paper)
 ISBN-13: 978-0-7391-3207-4 (electronic)
 ISBN-10: 0-7391-3207-5 (electronic)
 1. Korea (North)—Relations—Japan. 2. Japan—Relations—Korea (North) 3. Korea
(North)—Relations—United States. 4. United States—Relations—Korea (North) I.
Ryang, Sonia.
 JZ1748.A57J9 2009
 327.5193—dc22   2008031242

Printed in the United States of America

Contents

Acknowledgments

THIS VOLUME WAS BORN as a result of a conference entitled *North Korea: Policy, Modernity, Fantasy—International Conference*, held at the University of Iowa in October 2007. As the organizer of the conference, I had the privilege to invite participants whom I regard to be the world's top scholars in their academic field. Presenters included (in the order of appearance) Gavan McCormack, Charles K. Armstrong, Steven Chung, Michael Doveton, Hyun Ok Park, Peter Beck, Tessa Morris-Suzuki, and myself. Discussants were Jeff Baron, Scott Schnell, Adrienne Hurley, and Jae-on Kim. First of all, I'd like to thank the presenters, discussants, and members of the audience of the conference.

Many members of the University of Iowa community, anchored in the International Programs and Center for Asian and Pacific Studies, came to the conference and contributed to discussion in meaningful ways. The president of the University of Iowa, Dr. Sally Mason, warmly welcomed the participants in person, emphasizing the importance that the growth of Korean studies would play in the university's overall academic achievement. The associate provost and dean of International Programs, Professor William Reisinger, also endorsed the significance of the conference in his opening remarks.

I'd like to thank conference fund providers, University of Iowa International Programs Major Project Grant, Association for Asian Studies Northeastern Council Conference Grant, and University of Iowa Center for Asian Studies Grant. Particularly, I wish to acknowledge that the University of Iowa International Programs press and event coordination offices provided an admirable support throughout for the successful execution of the conference. I'd like to make a special mention of Heidi Vekemans for her competent support.

Michael Schiffer of The Stanley Foundation, Iowa, has helped the organization of the conference both materially and intellectually. I am deeply grateful for all individuals and organizations whose contribution and participation made the conference, and subsequently this volume, into a successful endeavor.

Sonia Ryang

Introduction

North Korea: Going Beyond Security and Enemy Rhetoric

Sonia Ryang

1. Beyond Securitization

STANDING ON THE EDGE OF LAKE CHEON ATOP Mt. Paekdu, which traverses the Korean-Chinese border, the first word that came to my mind was "sacred." It was 1981, more than a quarter of a century ago. North Korea was still a rather tightly closed country—today's North Korea looks wide open to the outside world when compared with those days. Lake Cheon's awe-inspiring and breathtaking expanse of aquamarine water was, indeed, a sanctuary for North Koreans themselves. The proud faces of the North Korean guides on the Revolutionary Pilgrimage Tour are still vivid in my memory as they emphasized the divine nature of Mt. Paekdu, where Kim Il Sung had waged guerilla warfare against the Japanese, an event that had come to represent the quintessential origin story and national identity of modern-day North Korea. A soldier or two stood here and there by the lake, their boredom leading them to kill time by watching us from afar, these visitors from Japan. With this memory still in my mind, it is hard to imagine, as is often reported, that these soldiers today are ordered to shoot on the spot anyone illegally crossing the border in search of food and work in China.

While I do not claim to have known North Korea well in 1981, there does not seem to be any better way of knowing it today, either. Despite recurring news headlines referring to nuclear crises, famine and food shortages, natural disasters, and human rights violations, we seem to be lacking any reasonably concrete knowledge about this nation, and we are left with a variety of judgmental and at times derogatory labels. As the labels have multiplied during the last decade or so, especially following the displays of hostility by the United States and Japan since 2002, the world remains without a reliable and tangible understanding of the functional mechanisms of government, economic life, political structure, culture, value system, dominant ideology and discourse, and process of social reproduction in North Korea.

This predicament calls a number of questions to mind: What does it mean to think about North Korea, and how are we to understand it? Do concerns about North Korea become legitimate only when they are posited as national security questions? Do we only need to know "nuclear North Korea," and not "cultural North Korea," "social North Korea," or "ethnic North Korea"?[1] Academic discourse on North Korea is still dominated by the Cold War–driven area studies model, which aggressively gives priority to security-related works. This cluster of discourses is full of speculations based on pseudo-game-theory computations, forecasting what North Korea might or might not do in certain given scenarios, which have been reinforced by the post-9/11 U.S. global war against terror. Often these discourses go not far beyond psychological crystal ball reading—attempting, as it were, to calculate North Korea's intentions or figure out the "North Korean mind."

Aside from these analyses, current English-language publications on North Korea include travelogues; picture books and journalistic reflections based on short-term stays in the country; syntheses of chronology, historiography, and historical interpretation; and tell-all exposés written by former (so-called) defectors and various temporary sojourners from the West (such as translators or diplomats who lived in North Korea).[2] While in different ways useful and informative, all of these works tend to be overshadowed by security-oriented studies, which are usually marketed as a more urgent field of investigation.

In light of the U.S. intellectual history of studying other cultures, this security-heavy trend when approaching North Korea is altogether understandable. During World War II, the United States faced Japan, a formidable opponent worthy of serious scrutiny under the rubric of wartime enemy studies. Prominent researchers and anthropologists in particular were mobilized by the Office of Strategic Services (today's Central Intelligence Agency) and the Office of War Information in order to determine exactly what this enigmatic enemy was about: the mentality that lay behind the radical practice of *kamikaze* suicide bombing, seemingly in total disregard of international war conventions then in practice among Western nations, and the logic behind what appeared as almost masochistic self-discipline and cruelty toward others needed to be captured and represented in a language familiar to the West.[3]

Considering that the United States has again been experiencing a wartime mentality since the launch of military incursions in Afghanistan and Iraq during the opening years of the twenty-first century, now revamped as elements of a technically eternal and unlimited global war against terror (there being no judicial or legislative mechanism to cancel this war under the existing U.S. system), the resemblance between the discourse of WWII enemy studies—encompassing psychological, historical, and ethnological analyses—and today's North Korean studies (albeit with its heavy inclination toward security studies) emerges rather clearly.

Yet, the United States is not actually at war with North Korea. No *kamikaze* bomber from North Korea has hit U.S. soil or attacked U.S. forces. No Pearl Harbor–style surprise attack has ever come from North Korea. No example of espionage by North Korean secret agents on U.S. soil has ever been disclosed. Why, then, does North Korea continue to be portrayed so intensely as a hostile entity by academics and other commentators representing various interests and bodies? This practice corresponds to what Hazel Smith calls the "securitization" of discourse on North Korea. By this, she means that "the scholarly discourse has become partisan, contributing to the escalation of conflict rather than the analysis of it."[4] The "securitization" of studies of North Korea is curious, given the dire situation within the country since the mid-1990s: famine and starvation that have resulted in malnutrition among an entire generation of young North Koreans and provoked a wave of economic migration across the Chinese border that continues to this day.[5] Nevertheless, more words have been printed in relation to security, military strategy, and game-plan scenarios, that is, fictive projections, than about anything else. Why?

It is important to remember, in this context, that North Korea and the United States fought against each other in a real war more than a half century ago. Commonly referred to as "the forgotten war" in the United States, the Korean War (1950–1953) opposed North Korea (with Chinese backing) with U.S. and South Korean forces in the name of the United Nations. In North Korean rhetoric, that war was, and still is, always described as the one against the "U.S. imperialist-invader wolves." For a long time, Bruce Cumings's monumental study, *The Origins of the Korean War* (in two volumes), remained the most thorough, well-researched, broadly read and disseminated book written in English on this war, although the fiftieth anniversary of the ceasefire has led to a surge of books related to this conflict in recent years.[6] We use the term ceasefire because the war was never officially ended. Technically speaking, therefore, long before 9/11, the United States and North Korea were warring parties, and this status continues today.

It is interesting to note that, in contrast to the attention paid to Japan during World War II, little attempt was made at understanding Koreans (and more specifically, North Koreans) by military or intelligence agencies during the Korean War. Furthermore, as stated above, not much attention was paid to this war at all for about one half of the century, either in official or lay circles.

Even more forgotten is the fact that the United States was one of the parties responsible for the arbitrary partitioning of Korea in 1945, which had been the victim of Japan's colonial rule. Having never fought against the Allies, Korea was arbitrarily severed into north and south in 1945, primarily due to rising U.S. concern over the looming rivalry with the Soviet Union in East Asia. This partition was to cost the Korean people the loss of millions of lives: one could argue that partition was eventually responsible for a fratricidal war, national division, and decades of confrontation between the two halves of Korea, involving mutual bickering, espionage, subversion, assassinations, and, above all, the separation of communities, neighbors, families, and friends.

The postwar occupation of (southern) Korea by the United States from 1945 to 1948, in contrast with the postwar occupation of Japan (1945–1952), was carried out in a crude fashion without careful planning. Few preliminary studies were conducted, and field officers to be stationed there were given little specialized preparatory education.[7] John Hodge, a general stationed in Okinawa, was one day ordered by General Douglas MacArthur to simply depart for Korea and run the southern half of the peninsula. What both the U.S. military and government were more conscious of was the emergence of a stark confrontation with the Soviet Union, which then occupied the northern half of Korea. Either way, Korea or the Koreans did not count as worthy even of humane treatment, let alone prior investigation aimed at deepening cultural understanding. Put bluntly, Koreans hardly figured as sufficiently human by the U.S. establishment in postwar strategic calculations in a climate of emerging Cold War tension.

This view—regarding Koreans as not sufficiently human—has continued in the United States as far as the North Koreans are concerned. (South Koreans have also become skeptical of the way in which they are viewed by U.S. forces, given the long-term heavy U.S. military presence in South Korea and the treatment of certain South Koreans, such as sex workers in *kijichon*, or camp towns, by U.S. military personnel.[8]) Occasionally, efforts to humanize North Koreans do take place, but they are characterized by pleas for humanitarian aid on the one hand and denunciation of the North Korean government's human rights violations on the other.

This is not to criticize or make light of these forms of humanizing engagement: they are essential in terms of securing the basic existence of so-called ordinary North Koreans. But do we know who these people are? What kind of relationship do these so-called ordinary North Korean citizens have with the leadership? I raise these questions, since humanitarian discourses are often founded on the premise of a dictatorial oppressor on one side and the vast majority of North Koreans—suffering, victimized, and exploited—on the other. Yet, there really is not enough serious research to enable this binary assumption to go beyond images and impressions. These are mainly images that we have created and impressions that we have adopted from the comfort zone of Western cultural values. Furthermore, just as the oppositional rhetoric of "the horrible dictator Saddam Hussein versus the victimized Iraqi people" served as justification for the U.S. invasion and continued occupation of Iraq, it is important to be wary that similar semantic tools could be deployed against North Korea. In a rhetorical simulation, one can hear the justifying voice: "In order to liberate twenty-three million North Koreans from the horrible dictator, we will invade North Korea. Along the way, a million or two may be killed by bombing and attacks, but such casualties are necessary for achieving peace." Thus, we return to the point, via humanitarian discourse, where North Koreans are seen as not sufficiently human.

The current state of discourses on North Korea displays an interesting deficit: why is it, for example, that despite hundreds, if not thousands, of Western visitors having visited North Korea in diverse capacities (as inspectors, investigators, researchers, aid workers, and tourists) since the mid-1990s, we are still lacking a consistent understanding of this nation? Even if we may not aspire to come up with a convenient bundle of North Korean national traits (as in the former Cold War approach), it seems that we lack a basic understanding of the culture of North Koreans. By this, I am not necessarily and simply referring to their daily lives, dietary customs, or sexual behavior—as in the cases of many so-called primitive peoples studied in such a manner by Western anthropologists. Neither do I intend to assert a crude empiricist equation of seeing with knowing: one can go to North Korea one thousand times and still not see anything. This, too, may not simply be a result of tight controls by North Korean authorities on which routes outside visitors may take and which sites they may visit. It may also reflect a lack of background knowledge of North Korea on the part of the visitor, who bends his or her vision through prejudice and presuppositions and, thus, perpetuates a vicious circle.

We are told, time and again, that North Koreans are loyal to their leader, that they would do anything, even die, for him, and that they are fiercely proud and nationalistic. But, equally, we are told that they are oppressed, suffering, and ready to rise against the evil dictator. What do we know beyond or between these opposing assumptions? We do not even know why and how they are like that and, indeed, even if they *are* like that. We are not well equipped with the conceptual tools that could lead us beyond the current securitization of our discourses on North Korea.

The anthropologist might say: "How can we know about these people when we cannot conduct fieldwork?" This is a valid concern. But it is also true that anthropologists have always studied peoples and cultures at great distances without ever having visited the places where they are found. The first example that should be remembered in this context is Ruth Benedict's *The Chrysanthe-mum and the Sword*. Written during World War II under the directive of the U.S. Office of War Information, this book became a postwar cultural recon-struction manual for the Japanese themselves. Even today, this book is one of the longest-selling classics in Japan's bookstores.[9] Conversely, one may conduct lengthy fieldwork in one place, only to come up with a body of material that appears to confirm previously assumed positions or, worse still, amounts to an uncritical reflection of colonial and other asymmetrical relations of power—as many classical Western anthropologists have done in parts of pre-independence Africa and Asia. In all fairness, we should be able to conduct viable empirical research on North Korea by relying on currently available written materials, published opus, visual data, and interviews, without necessarily having to go to North Korea, and without necessarily having to adopt a pronounced emphasis on security-related issues, as is the case with many recent studies.

2. History and the Never-Ending War

The foreground detailed above calls for some background information. Let me, therefore, start with a very brief review of the history of North Korea. As shown by authors such as Bruce Cumings, Charles K. Armstrong, Wada Ha-ruki, and Hyun Ok Park, the development of the northern half of the Korean peninsula into the form with which we are familiar today is the product of numerous factors closely related to the colonial history of Korea and Korean anti-Japanese resistance, as well as the postwar partition of Korea (one-sidedly) by the Allied Forces.[10] Prior to Japan's colonial takeover, the annexation *(hap-pyeong* in Korean; *heigō* in Japanese) of 1910, which lasted until 1945, Korea was ruled by the neo-Confucian court government of the Yi royal family. Re-ferred to as Choseon (1392–1905), the land of the morning calm, Korea had a nominal suzerain-vassal relationship with the Chinese emperor. In nominal terms, Korea belonged to the emperor's rule, in the sense that all its domestic decisions pertaining to the succession (such as the crown prince's matrimony or the enthronement of a new king, for example), required that a ceremonial entourage be sent to the emperor for his post-factum approval.

This nominal, yet long-lasting, connection with China presented an inter-esting obstacle when the Japanese emperor tried to lay claim to Korea in the late nineteenth century following the restoration of his power in 1867. For Koreans, there was only one emperor under heaven, that of China, and Japan's use of this title was a problem for them from the very beginning of their mod-ern contact with the country. Japan and Korea, to be sure, were no strangers to each other by the end of the nineteenth century. Japan's mediaeval warlord,

Toyotomi Hideyoshi, had dispatched a massive military force to Korea in 1592 in the hope of taking over Korea in order to use it as foothold for the conquest of Ming China. This war, referred to in Korea as *Imjinwaeran*, the Japanese disturbance of the year of Imjin (the Chinese classical calendar name for the year 1592), is remembered to this day (especially by older generations) with nationalistic emotional fervor, and is a focal point for anti-Japanese sentiment in South Korea. The character *wae*, referring to the Japanese, is conspicuously contemptuous of the Japanese, as its derogatory etymology ridicules their short physique.

The linkage between 1592 and 1910, the latter being the year in which Korea was annexed by Japan, is only one of many examples of so-called postcolonial re-linkages emphasized in the postliberation nationalist turn of denigrating and hating everything Japanese in South Korea. This does not apply in the case of North Korea, however. In the effort to start from pure ground zero, North Korea's historiography understates mediaeval history and even Japanese colonial rule. Instead, the modern history of North Korea emphasizes the birth of Kim Il Sung, *his* youth, *his* anti-Japanese guerrilla activities, and *his* role in helping liberate Korea from Japan. In some ways, Japan and the Japanese, Korea's colonial masters, are not accorded importance (nor viewed with noticeable hatred) in North Korea's postliberation historiography.

It is the United States that is treated in a much more emotional manner. This, needless to say, is related to the post–Korean War enmity against the "U.S. imperialist-invader wolves" or *seungnyangi mije chimryakja*. For instance, an important incident mentioned in modern history books in North Korea that took place prior to Kim's birth in 1912 is the capture of the USS *Sherman* in the Daedong River in Pyongyang. The story goes that Kim Il Sung's great-grandfather, Kim Eung U, was among the leaders in performing this heroic deed, and this episode is used to illustrate the historically long-held aggressive ambitions of the Americans toward Koreans. As such, the United States in North Korea plays a similar role to Japan in South Korea as a prime target of national hatred in the construction of a postcolonial national identity. But such an enterprise is not lacking a factual foundation. Only five years after the end of World War II and the partition of the nation, and only two years after the emergence of the northern half of Korea as the Democratic People's Republic of Korea, this young state had to face a formidable counterpart, the U.S.-led UN military force, in its armed intervention in South Korea. Many researchers (led by Cumings, among others) have already explored how the Korean War (1950) began, and how it came to a stalemate after three years without reaching an official conclusion.[11] I shall therefore eschew the details of the war and confine myself to emphasizing that, in North Korea, the Korean War is not remembered or classified as a civil war, but as an anti-invasion, anti-aggression war against U.S. imperialism. Even the participation of South Korea in this war against the North is downplayed: the enemy, in other words, is unequivocally the United States and the United States only.

Tour routes in North Korea can be roughly divided into three categories, in my view: revolutionary pilgrimage sites, sites of national achievement, and anti-American sites. Revolutionary pilgrimages consist of visits to sacred places related to the North Korean revolution, and would include mandatory bowing in front of the gigantic gold statue of Kim Il Sung in Pyongyang and visits to sites such as Kim Il Sung's childhood home, locations in which Kim Il Sung conducted guerilla operations against the Japanese, and the birthplace of Kim Jong Suk (Kim's first wife, Kim Jong Il's birth mother). After Kim Il Sung's death in 1994, such pilgrimages added a visit to Keumsusan Palace, where all memorabilia related to Kim (including the desk he used, the train he traveled in, and the vehicle he was chauffeured around in), as well as Kim's preserved body itself, is housed. In all of these spots, specially trained *haeseolweon* (tour tutors) accompany you, providing perfect recitals of the stories attached to each sacred site. The second category of tour includes visits to collective farms, factories, and schools, as well as recreational facilities such as amusement parks, restaurants, movie theaters, and tourist resorts, although these facilities are specially built and arranged for foreign dignitaries and the privileged to visit.

The third category of tour, importantly, includes visits to the War Victory Memorial Museum (*cheonseung kinyeongwan*), as North Koreans claim victory over the United States in the Korean War, yet also includes visits to the northern side of Panmunjeom, a town bisected by the Demilitarized Zone. Here, visitors are encouraged to chant anti-American slogans in groups, such as "Down with U.S. Imperialism!" (*Mijereul tadohaja!*) or "Let us get rid of U.S. Imperialism from South Korea and reunify our fatherland!" (*Mijereul namjoseoneseo moranaego choguegul tongilhaja!*).

If visitors have enough time, they will be taken to two small wooden warehouses (restored and rearranged as sites to be visited) standing side by side in the village of Sincheon, a village that was occupied by the U.S. Army during the Korean War following MacArthur's amphibious landing at Incheon in 1950 and the "rollback" of U.S. troops northward. Separately housing two hundred mothers and four hundred babies, American soldiers deprived them of water and starved them for days, in the end burning them all alive. Visitors will not miss seeing the *haeseolweon*'s face reddening with anger, voice trembling and fists curled up in indignation, as she (*haeseolweon* are usually women) tells you the story of this crime against humanity. As she describes how the U.S. soldiers took delight at the sight of dehydrated and crying babies longing for their mother's milk, how the mothers wanted to have their babies back so much that they were almost driven insane, and how the smell of burning human carcasses pervaded the entire area for weeks, one will see tears of anger in her eyes. Side by side with an emphasis on national achievement and reverence for the Great Leader, and despite its claim of victory over the United States in the Korean War, the visitor is regularly reminded that North Korea understands that it is currently at war with the United States.

Some argue that Kim Il Sung consciously used the Korean War and the temporary nature of the ceasefire to his political advantage, eliminating his opponents by making them responsible for the war. I am not interested in this kind of speculation. Rather, it is important to register, when trying to understand North Korea today, that almost its entire national being or raison d'être is founded upon the perception of its existence vis-à-vis hostile forces, foremost among them the United States. As Charles K. Armstrong argues in chapter 2 of this book, the point that North Korea professes to be in an ongoing war must not be underestimated in thinking about North Korea.

Following the ceasefire, the latter half of the 1950s and the 1960s were formidable years for North Korea: heightened tensions among the population were mobilized for the purposes of economic reconstruction and restructuring, including the nationalization and collectivization of agriculture, heavy and light industries, and key business sectors, enabling North Korea to make giant strides toward Socialist reforms, and allowing it to achieve, with apparent lightening speed, victory in the GNP statistical war with South Korea. South Korea suffered from a series of unstable governments until the military coup staged by the late President Park in 1972. That was also the year when North Korea declared its Socialist constitution, and the year in which it celebrated Kim Il Sung's sixtieth birthday, an important marker in the East Asian life cycle, symbolizing longevity and accomplishment.

With Kim's sixtieth birthday celebration, it appeared that North Korea had turned a significant corner in terms of positioning its leader. Kim became not only supreme commander of the military, head of state, and head of the party, but also everyone's creator and the end-point for their devotion; that is to say, personal ontological significance and meaning of life for North Koreans came to revolve around Kim's existence. As I argue in chapter 3 of this volume, the 1970s and 1980s witnessed the cultivation of a distinct form of life for North Koreans founded upon their relationship to the leader as individuals wholly accountable for their own conduct and their total loyalty to the leader under the rubric of the *juche* ideology invented by Kim (for more about *juche*, see chapters 2 and 3). The death of Kim Il Sung in 1994 did not fundamentally change the social structure, but the transition of power to his son Kim Jong Il resulted in certain readjustments that affected North Korea's international standing more than its internal social relations.

Whereas Kim Il Sung was known for his self-reliant style of governing and his leadership role among certain Asian and African nations and international leftist forces, especially in the periphery of the polarized Cold War geopolitical environment, his son Kim Jong Il enjoys almost no international credentials. While the elder Kim could lay claim to a personal history of having actually fought against the Japanese during the preliberation years, and served as the nation's supreme commander during the Korean War, the latter has no such military experience whatsoever. In contrast with the elder Kim's long-lasting and legendary leadership style of "on-the-spot guidance" during the arduous period of reconstruction in the aftermath of the Korean War (whether it is true or not that he used such a method being beside the point here), the younger Kim can trace no such footsteps of his own. The younger Kim's lack of experience in diplomacy and international relations resulted in his unsophisticated revelation of North Korea's past kidnappings of Japanese citizens to Koizumi Junichiro, then Japanese prime minister, who made the historic first visit to North Korea by a Japanese head of state in September 2002. The news—and the way it was revealed by Kim and broadcast in an overly dramatic fashion by the Japanese media—served both Koizumi (much loved by the Japanese people) and his short-lived successor Abe well by inflaming anti–North Korean sentiment. It is true that Kim Jong Il met with Kim Dae Jung in 2000 at the first-ever North–South Korean summit in history. However, it is also true that, despite a favorable climate following the end of the Cold War in Europe and increased debate and interest in South Korean civil society with regard to its northern neighbor (as discussed by Hyun Ok Park in chapter 5 of this volume), the younger Kim has not been able to fashion a viable and constructive policy vis-à-vis South Korea.

As we entered the new millennium, North Korea under Kim Jong Il became the object of worldwide concern with regard to its human rights and the possibility of social implosion resulting from natural disasters and famine on the one hand and the strain placed upon ordinary people by disproportionate government budgeting for nuclear weapons and missile projects on the other. As Tessa Morris-Suzuki argues in chapter 6 of this volume, North Korea's poor civil rights record and its suspected abuse and violation of basic human rights are attracting increasing awareness globally and counterproductively affecting its standing in the world. This is not, however, the one-sided result of wayward behavior by North Korea. As any sensible world-watcher knows, U.S.-led Western policy toward North Korea, particularly during the Bush presidency, has pushed an already isolated and helpless regime into an increasingly desperate corner. In chapter 1 of this volume, Gavan McCormack addresses issues pertaining to North Korea as it faces hostile U.S. and Japanese maneuvers from official and unofficial quarters.

3. Condemning the Evil

At the time of writing this Introduction, in late 2007, we are able to see that despite media hype relating to North Korean crises and the participation of some academics inside or outside the "Washington Beltway" in glossing media language, for now, the world has not yet seen many of the things that they have predicted: regime change, nuclear disaster, all-out war and mass destruction, waves of starving North Korean refugees pushing north or south across the country's borders, and scandalous international crimes such as massive currency counterfeiting, drug smuggling, summary executions, torture, and human trafficking. Instead, what we see today are scenes of talks, handshakes (albeit cursory), and smiling faces seated around the six-party negotiating table, which includes the two Koreas, Japan, China, the United States, and Russia.

Amidst this uncertainty, only one thing appears to be certain: that the United States, Japan, and the West in general do not wish to have North Korea as it is now. September 11, 2001, was, in many senses, a doomsday for North Korea, not simply because it was subsequently declared an "axis of evil" state, but, more importantly, because this characterization by U.S. president George W. Bush (2000–2008) was to set the pace of policymaking, public mediation, and academic depiction related to North Korea through its evocation of the country as an evil, backward, and hellish place. This constituted a shift from the ambivalence and uncertainty that previously dominated America's public discourse about this regime. Whereas, in the past, North Korea had been thought of as unknown, enigmatic, and impenetrable, now it had unquestionably become an evil enemy. As the reader will see in the following, this shift in the rhetorical approach to this regime was, unfortunately, often accompanied by a conspicuous absence of research on this regime, both in terms of quantity and quality. In other words, the declaration of North Korea as part of an axis of evil resulted not so much in increased efforts to get to know this nation, but rather in an intensification in the type of emotional and often unfounded labeling of this regime that we frequently see today.

In order to illustrate this point, I elect to look closely at clusters of rhetorical references that are embodied in *North Korea through the Looking Glass* by Kongdan Oh and Ralph Hassig (2000). I focus on this text not simply because it has been influential to some extent, but also because its publication predates the 9/11 attack and George Bush's "axis of evil" address, the outbreak of the Iraq War, and the eruption of intense hostility against North Korea in Japan following the revelation of North Korea's past kidnappings of Japanese citizens during the 1970s and 1980s. Its date of publication also roughly coincides with Madeleine Albright's visit to North Korea and the first North-South summit in Korea. Although written prior to the more serious North Korean nuclear and missile crises, one can see what Hazel Smith termed as "securitization" already occurring in this type of research monograph, in that the rhetoric here serves to escalate hostility and tension rather than analyzing the situation.

While critical of dismissing North Korea as a "rogue state," Kongdan Oh and Ralph Hassig write that "North Korea lives a schizophrenic existence in which dreams of creating a totalitarian Socialist utopian community under the stern but benevolent rule of a modern-day emperor are pursued with the calculations of domestic and international power politics" and "it [North Korea] is out of step with the world of the new millennium," "a country with no future."[12] The diagnostic language ("schizophrenia") aside, what exactly is "a totalitarian socialist utopian community"? What exactly should one assume when one is told that Kim Il Sung is a "modern-day emperor"? Further, it is assumed that readers agree upon the criteria constituting notions such as "emperor" and "utopia," with no further theoretical or interpretive ado.

Further into *North Korea through the Looking Glass*, the authors denounce North Korea for being a "nation of its own," as if to suggest that this is a negative trait. But which nation on earth does not try to be "its own"? And, looking at the passage below, which nation, aside from North Korea, does this remind us of?

> North Korea is a land of illusions. An ideology that places the leader above the people and the nation. An economy built on the assumption that people can lead selfless, communitarian lives. A ruler and his top policymakers who rarely travel outside the country or meet foreigners. A military that boasts of being the mightiest in the world. A social control system that seeks to keep 23 million people isolated from the outside world. And a foreign policy based on the premise that by threatening other nations North Korea can become a respected member of the international community.[13]

It does not take a particularly anti-U.S. reader to realize that each sentence quoted above fits the United States under George Bush. But, according to the authors, these are exclusively North Korean traits.

In 2000, the year that Oh and Hassig published their book, as the previous millennium came to an end and the current one began, media depictions of North Korea looked almost benign in comparison to those in the aftermath of 9/11 or, more precisely, Bush's January 29, 2002, State of the Union address that classed North Korea, along with Iraq and Iran, as part of an "axis of evil." Prior to this labeling, albeit with ups and downs along the way, North Korea had been making its way into the world as simply one among many uniquely strange and unquestionably disadvantaged nations, striving to survive in the rearranged global power framework of the post–Cold War era. Although the United States placed North Korea on the list of state sponsors of terrorism in 1988 following the involvement of North Korean secret agents in the destruction of (South Korean–owned) Korean Airlines Flight 858 in November 1987, North Korea enjoyed quite a positive standing during the 1990s, including its relations with the United States. In 1991, the Unites States withdrew its last remaining nuclear weapons from South Korea. This led to the North's ratification of the IAEA safeguards in 1992, resulting in its declaration that it had ninety grams of plutonium and seven nuclear reactor sites. While for the following two years, the dispute between North Korean authorities and IAEA inspectors over inaccuracies in North Korea's self-reporting weakened North Korea's international credibility, the historic visit by former U.S. president Jimmy Carter to North Korea opened up real possibilities for dialogue between the United States and the North.

Although Kim Il Sung's death in July 1994 somewhat threatened stability in the North and temporarily raised the possibility of uncertainty, in the summer and fall of that year, North Korea and the United States reached an "agreed framework" whereby North Korea would receive two light-water reactors of a kind unable to be deployed for military purposes, in addition to other assistance from the United States. The latter half of the 1990s was largely focused on negotiations about North Korea's missile proliferation, interrupted by severe natural disasters and food crises in North Korea starting from 1996, and aided by the ascendance of Kim Dae Jung, a former resistance leader, to the South Korean presidency in 1998. President Kim's "sunshine policy" toward the North generated considerable success in softening the tough attitude of the North (under Kim Jong Il) toward the outside world, resulting in the staging of a Korean North-South summit in Pyongyang in 2000, the first ever since national partition in 1945. It was also around this time that news about North Koreans crossing the Chinese border began to reach the outside world. Variously named as "refugees," "defectors," or "illegal migrants," news of their movements triggered international concern over the basic survival and human rights of the North Korean people.

Amidst the anxious attention being paid to the need for humanitarian aid to North Korea on one hand, and the need for verification of its plutonium waste in order to monitor its nuclear reactors on the other, Madeleine Albright, then secretary of state and the highest-serving U.S. government officer ever to visit North Korea, met Kim Jong Il in October 2000. Upon her visit, we were told that: "[Kim Jong Il] is amazingly well-informed and extremely well-read" and that he was "practical, thoughtful, [. . . and] has a sense of humor" and "can talk about almost any subject."[14] Even in the wake of the twin towers' fall in September 2001, North Korea did not quite yet register as an evil entity in U.S. public consciousness—the association between "Islamic evil" and "North Korean evil" was not immediately made.

However, by the time George Bush classed North Korea, together with Iraq and Iran, as part of "an axis of evil" in his State of the Union address on January 29, 2002, claiming that these nations were "seeking weapons of destruction" and that they posed "a grave and growing danger" to the United States, in a climate of heightened U.S. patriotism and zeal for an endless and limitless war against terror, North Korea was made unequivocally an enemy of the United States. Furthermore, this emotion-charged presidential address displayed an unquestionable hatred toward North Korea and other examples of what he called "terrorist" regimes on earth. In the terms of Bush's address, the world could be unambiguously divided into terrorist nations and nonterrorist nations. Nations such as North Korea "could provide [weapons of mass destruction] to terrorists, giving them the means to match their hatred." The crime of North Korea was that it was "a regime arming with missiles and weapons of mass destruction, _while starving its citizens,_" meaning that the current military crisis was brought about by the moral failure of a North Korean leadership that demanded sacrifices of the people and victimized them.[15]

There has been a patent moral agenda in denunciations of Kim Jong Il's character in the context of anti–North Korean discourse in the West. Oh and Hassig's work was no exception, and Bush's 2002 address, dubbing North Korea as evil, appeared to rely on pre-existing characterizations of Kim Jong Il as corrupt, unreliable, crazy, and weird, as found in Oh and Hassig. Despite Albright and her party witnessing him as otherwise, American public consciousness in the tense post-9/11, anti-terror climate opted to listen to morally debauched opinion related to Kim. Having said this, I must stress that the moral threat presented by Kim Jong Il was itself inconsistently perceived. According to Oh and Hassig, one of this dictator's various crimes was his bad manners, including his "habit of talking to elders with his hands in his pockets."[16] Further examples of supposed character defects include selfishness, greed, and corruption. Kim Jong Il is, we are told, awkward with people, has a bad temper, loves shooting and hunting and, above all, is overweight while his nation is gripped by famine.[17]

I am not here to defend Kim Jong Il's moral character, body size, food selection, or personal taste. Many world leaders are—just like anyone—fond of things that are strange to some (or many): U.S. vice president Dick Cheney (2000–2008) is known to be very fond of shooting and hunting, which became clear when the media discovered that he had accidentally shot and injured his hunting mate.[18] We have a president that has an enormous devotion for golf and his conspicuous way of personally contributing to the U.S. war effort (during which thousands of lives have been taken) is to cut down on his enjoyment of golf.[19] The habits of these leaders are hardly morally superior to those of Kim Jong Il or any other pundits. I have no way of knowing whether most world leaders weigh more or less than the average citizen of the nations they lead. No leader in the modern history of humanity has died of starvation because their people were starving, although there is the exception of Gandhi, who reduced his food intake drastically in the face of the nation's misfortune. My point is to assert that the characterizations of the personalities (let alone body weights) of individual leaders are irrelevant and that, furthermore, talking about these at length is counterproductive, as it prevents us from asking more important questions and may actually hinder attempts to find out what we need to know about the society concerned.

By presenting the problems North Korea faces and produces—including famine and the nuclear weapons program—as primarily generated by the character defects and moral failures of its leader, this body of discourse obscures historical realities. These include the fact that North Korea has been subject to a nuclear threat from the U.S. forces located in South Korea for over half a century, the fact that North Korea has never been allowed to enjoy peace in the sense that the Korean War has yet to officially end, and the fact that the end of the Cold War in Europe did not necessarily alter the state of tension and confrontation in northeast Asia. Furthermore, Japan has emerged in the immediate vicinity as a formidably hostile power. Anti-Korean sentiment there culminated in an explosion of North Korea–bashing on a national scale in the wake of the 2002 revelation that North Korea had kidnapped Japanese citizens during the 1970s and 1980s (as discussed extensively in chapters 1 and 6 in this volume by Gavan McCormack and Tessa Morris-Suzuki, respectively).

Similar types of disclaimers can be applied to overeager assertions or predictions that North Korea will collapse or mock guidelines on how to bring about such a collapse—as these so-called scenarios are artificial and based on one-sided moral judgments, ultimately having no real value other than giving North Korea–haters a false sense of triumph. In a further excerpt from Oh and Hassig, the authors write,

> Errors and lies impose consequences. Errors in principles and policies stifle growth. Lies multiply, one lie covering another, their aftereffects rippling through society and reverberating in time. Lies destroy the fabric of society, for who knows what to do or in what direction to go if there is no way to separate truth from falsehood? The Kim regime is built on lies: leaders lie to their followers and followers lie to their leaders. If the truth is ever revealed, the Kim regime will collapse. [20]

The moral tone in the above is unmistakable. Their rhetoric carries the air of the premonition of divine punitive intervention. But, after all, what exactly are the lies? Can a lie in one society not be deemed so in another? How about, for example, all the information spin about weapons of mass destruction (WMDs) that we were fed by the current U.S. administration and intelligence? That information was true to some, but an outright lie for many. What Oh and Hassig appear to be completely oblivious to is their own almost innocently naïve self-authorization to declare other nations false or arrogant. Does this type of self-righteousness reflect a long history of U.S. intervention, through which democratically elected foreign governments have been overthrown not once, but many times, using CIA operatives and military intervention? Is this degree of self-confidence about being "good" as opposed to "evil" the result of long-held U.S. proprietorship of the role of the world's policeman, now accorded the sole power to dispense justice following the end of the Cold War? Following Aidan Foster-Carter's suggestion, Oh and Hassig propose that we use North Korea's history as a reference point when assessing its present and future.[21] The same technique should perhaps be deployed when approaching works such as the one by Oh and Hassig: the solid tradition of armed intervention in other nation's affairs by the United States has contributed to the creation of the kind of logic displayed by Oh and Hassig; that is to say, a facile envisioning of an end or evaporation of another nation-state, paralleled by a lack of self-critical reflection on the history and ideology of their own country.

4. In This Book

This book is intended to be an intervention aimed at deepening our understanding of North Korea from multiple directions, involving internal analyses of its society as well as interpretations of the current international environment as it relates to North Korea. We use multiple windows through which to look at North Korea, including history, literature, filmmaking, human rights advocacy, and international relations, in order to see beyond what I call rhetorical excesses related to security and enmity.

In chapter 1, "North Korea and the Birth Pangs of a New Northeast Asian Order," Gavan McCormack gives a comprehensive synthesis of recent events responsible for North Korea's demonization by the United States and Japan. McCormack questions how it is that a regime that has largely refrained from doing harm to other nations should be regarded as a rogue state and punished by another regime that has a history of invading, interfering with, and attacking others on multiple occasions. This is a valid question. For, ever since the launch of the endless U.S. global war against terror, the world has come to starkly deem some regimes as evil, regardless of what they have or have not done, conferring disproportionate power on certain others that have basically self-righteously appointed themselves as the world's supreme arbiters of justice. Such a view itself preemptively precludes the possibility of dialogue with North Korea, McCormack warns.

Chapter 2, "Socialism, Sovereignty, and the North Korean Exception" by Charles K. Armstrong, shows how fiercely North Korea has tried to safeguard its sovereignty in an increasingly hostile international environment. Armstrong's analysis of North Korea's internal structure and international standing relies on Giorgio Agamben and Carl Schmitt's notion of the sovereign as an exception, and he offers many original insights as to how we must understand North Korea's adamant defense of its sovereignty in what it perceives to be a hostile environment in the context of a continuing war.

The discussion of the sovereign opened up in Armstrong's chapter is further explored by myself in chapter 3, "Biopolitics or the Logic of Sovereign Love—Love's Whereabouts in North Korea." Here, I inquire into North Korea's internal social structure and relations using the concept of love and the sovereign as embodied in literary texts and novels written from the 1960s through the 1980s. Inspired both by Georges Bataille and Giorgio Agamben, I explore the way in which North Korean individuals are connected (solely) to the leader. My focus is not so much on the leader himself or his personal attributes but on the positionality of the leader as an exceptional being: he belongs in society only as an exceptional being. I attempt here a preliminary rethinking of totalitarianism, its culture, and the selves under it, in the context of North Korea.

In chapter 4, "The Split Screen: Sin Sang-ok in North Korea," Steven Chung explores film and filmmaking in North Korea by a famed movie director, Sin Sang-ok, an alleged defector/abductee from South Korea, and his wife, Choe Eun-heui, a classical South Korean movie superstar. Allegedly kidnapped by North Korean agents, Sin and Choe produced a number of important films in Pyongyang. Chung gives the reader a unique opportunity to look at North Korea through a cinematic window by tracing the couple's footprints through the period prior to their entry to North Korea, for the duration of their stay there, and after their exit. This chapter focuses on Kim Jong Il's reign in particular, as his fondness for cinematic art seems to have been instrumental in bringing about Sin's and Choe's entry to the North.

No volume on North Korea would be complete without a substantial account related to South Korea. In chapter 5, "The Politics of Unification and Neoliberal Democracy: Economic Cooperation and North Korean Human Rights," Hyun Ok Park explores the historical interplay between North Korea's internal problems and their external ramifications. She explores South Korea's role as a recipient of migrants and refugees during a period when it has made a radical turn toward civilian government as well as toward a neoliberal market political economy and civil society. Park's accounts display particularly acute foresight in that they closely capture the direction the Korean peninsula is taking in the broader context of contemporaneous regional transformation in northeastern Asia.

In chapter 6, "Refugees, Abductees, 'Returnees': Human Rights in Japan–North Korea Relations," Tessa Morris-Suzuki directly addresses human rights issues related to North Korea. The global community is concerned about suspected gross human rights violations in North Korea, both with regard to its so-called illegal migrants (across the Chinese border) and the "defectors" who have made safe exits from North Korea and have been resettled in South Korea. While the way in which these so-called defectors are treated in the South is also a concern, suffering from ongoing surveillance, a lack of freedom, and the resulting feelings of hopelessness, alienation, and self-hatred, the fate of the North Koreans, who risk their lives crossing the national border, is of more concern due to the conspicuous absence of information in this area. For this reason, this chapter by Morris-Suzuki makes a valuable contribution toward our understanding of North Korea.

Morris-Suzuki looks in particular at the trajectory of irregular or erratic human flows between North Korea and Japan—first, the post–Korean War "repatriation" of Koreans from Japan to North Korea on a large scale from 1959 until the 1980s, then the practice of return migration, secretive and on a much smaller scale, from North Korea to Japan, and also a more recent incident in which a North Korean family reached Japan in a small boat. Morris-Suzuki brings it home that the so-called North Korean problem is in fact an East Asian problem that includes Japan and South Korea. Her chapter also shows that the way in which human rights (as a universal concept) is appropriated by diverse groups in Japan is acutely revealing of very particularistic political stances. Indeed, diverse border crossings—Japan to North Korea and then back to Japan, North Korea to China and then to South Korea, North Korea to Japan and then to South Korea—offer a metonym of uncertainty and instability that shrouds the human flows connecting the Korean peninsula, parts of mainland China, and the Japanese archipelago: every border crossing involves a serious risk to personal safety and human lives.

Reflecting the divisive positions held by commentators, scholars, and researchers on North Korea, academic discourse on this topic in the West is conspicuously lacking in examples of collaborative effort. This book hopes to fill that void, and it presents a comprehensive volume on North Korea on the basis of a candid exchange of views held by scholars and writers of diverse backgrounds, reflecting various forms of disciplinary training and writing positions. As such, this volume does not pretend to present a unified view: some chapters even contradict each other, but these disagreements are meaningful in themselves in that they embody the multiple possibilities when approaching and attempting to understand North Korea.

Many contributors to this book have visited North Korea, written about it, and been engaged with it in many different ways—as researchers, as long-term observers, and as concerned individuals. Many have stood on both sides of Panmunjeom, visited both Pyongyang and Seoul, talked and interacted with both North Koreans and South Koreans. This volume, therefore, is also an expression of the contributors' concern about the basic safety and well-being of North Koreans and the Korean peninsula as a whole, rather than being a reflection of certain partisan affiliations. In light especially of the ending of the eight-year term of George W. Bush's presidency, the United States and the world are facing a new phase in dealing with North Korea. The inclusion of ideas offered in this book in future policy formation and the further understanding of North Korea will, I hope, result in enabling new, mutually engaging relations with North Korea. I hope also that the reader will recognize the efforts made here to move away from the currently dominant security discourse and one-sided moral characterizations related to North Korea toward a deeper understanding of this nation as a society of human beings.

Notes

1. For example, see David Kang's chapters in Victor Cha and David Kang, *Nuclear North Korea: A Debate on Engagement Strategies* (New York: Columbia University Press, 2003). Unlike Cha, whose chapters are rough and mostly polemic in tone, Kang attempts to approach the topic of North Korea with rigor, but his efforts are often thwarted due to a lack of information, a problem that he admits candidly and frequently.

2. A plethora of books on North Korea has appeared in recent years, including Bruce Cumings, *North Korea, Another Country* (New York: New Press, 2004); Kang Chol-Hwan, *The Aquariums of Pyongyang: Ten Years in a North Korean Gulag* (New York: Basic Books, 2002); Bertil Lintner, *Great Leader, Dear Leader: Demystifying North Korea under the Kim Clan* (Chiang Mai, Thailand: Silkworm Books, 2005); Michael Harrold, *Comrades and Strangers: Behind the Closed Doors of North Korea* (Chichester, UK: Wiley, 2005); Bradley Martin, *Under the Loving Care of the Fatherly Leader: North Korea and the Kim Dynasty* (New York: St. Martin's / Thomas Dunne, 2004); and Andrei Lankov, *North of the DMZ: Essays on Daily Life in North Korea* (New York: McFarland, 2007), among many others.

3. See chapters 1 and 2 of my *Japan and National Anthropology: A Critique* (London: Routledge, 2004), where I discuss the role of anthropologists, especially Ruth Benedict, who is to this day one of the most highly regarded U.S. anthropologists of Japan.

4. Hazel Smith, *Hungry for Peace: International Security, Humanitarian Assistance, and Social Change in North Korea* (Washington, D.C.: United States Institute of Peace Press, 2005), 24.

5. See, for example, Stephan Haggard and Marcus Noland, *Famine in North Korea: Markets, Aid, and Reform* (New York: Columbia University Press, 2007).

6. Bruce Cumings, *The Origins of the Korean War*, vol. 1, *Liberation and the Emergence of Separate Regimes, 1945–1947* (Princeton, N.J.: Princeton University Press, 1981); and Cumings, *The Origins of the Korean War*, vol. 2, *The Roaring of the Cataract, 1947–1950* (Princeton, N.J.: Princeton University Press, 1990). As for recent works on the Korean War, see, for example, Edward Marolda, ed., *The US Navy and the Korean War* (Washington, D.C.: U.S. Naval Institute Press, 2007); T. R. Fehrenbach, *This Kind of War: The Classic Korean War History* (Washington, D.C.: Potomac Books, 2001); Bill McWilliams, *On Hallowed Ground: The Last Battle for Pork Chop Hill* (Washington, D.C.: U.S. Naval Institute Press, 2003); Richard Peters and Xiaobing Li, *Voices from the Korean War: Personal Stories of American, Korean and Chinese Soldiers* (Lexington: University Press of Kentucky, 2005); David Halberstam, *The Coldest Winter: America and the Korean War* (New York: Hyperion, 2007).

7. As early as 1946, at least one author wondered why officers stationed in Korea had been given no cultural training or preparation, as opposed to those stationed in Japan. See M. Fainsod, "Military Government and the Occupation of Japan," in *Japan's Prospect*, ed. D. G. Haring (Cambridge, Mass.: Harvard University Press, 1946), 302.

8. See, for example, Katharine Moon, *Sex Among Allies* (New York: Columbia University Press, 1997).

9. See chapter 1 of my *Japan and National Anthropology*. Studies of culture at a distance became a one-time popular endeavor among Columbia University–affiliated anthropologists under the leadership of Margaret Mead. In the face of the postwar debacle related to fieldwork, where researchers were either cut off by the iron curtain or by independence movements of diverse peoples that used to be referred to as "primitives" and offered fieldwork sites for Western anthropologists, Mead and others theorized on a new methodology for anthropology that did not necessarily make fieldwork mandatory. See Margaret Mead and Rhoda Metreaux, *The Study of Culture at a Distance* (Oxford: Berghahn Books, 2000).

10. Bruce Cumings, *The Origins of the Korean War*, 2 vols.; Charles Armstrong, *The North Korean Revolution, 1945–1950* (Ithaca, N.Y.: Cornell University Press, 2004); Wada Haruki, *Kinnissei to manshū kōnichi sensō* [Kim Il Sung and the Anti-Japanese War in Manchuria] (Tokyo: Heibonsha, 1992); and Hyun Ok Park, *Two Dreams in One Bed: Empire, Social Life, and the Origins of the North Korean Revolution in Manchuria* (Durham, N.C.: Duke University Press, 2005).

11. Cumings, *The Origins of the Korean War*, vol. 1.

12. Kongdan Oh and Ralph Hassig, *North Korea through the Looking Glass* (Washington, D.C.: Brookings Institution Press, 2000), 2, 1. The term "rogue" was to appear later in a book title as *Rogue Regime: Kim Jong Il and the Looming Threat of North Korea*, by Jasper Becker (New York: Oxford University Press, 2006).

13. Oh and Hassig, *Looking Glass*, 10.

14. Doug Struck and Steven Mufson, "North Korea's Kim Sheds Image of 'Madman,'" *Washington Post*, October 26, 2001, A-1, quoted in Bruce Cumings, *North Korea: Another Country* (New York: New Press, 2004), 47.

15. "The President's State of the Union Address," January 29, 2002, at www.white -house.gov/news/releases/2002/01/print/20020129-11.html (accessed on October 25, 2007). In fact, many world powers that possess nuclear weapons programs are impoverished, and a large proportion of their populations may be starving. See, for example, India.

16. Oh and Hassig, *Looking Glass,* 92.

17. Oh and Hassig, *Looking Glass,* 92–93.

18. "White House Under Fire Over Cheney Shooting," *MSNBC,* February 13, 2006, at www.msnbc.msn.com/id/11312757/ (accessed on October 26, 2007); "Hunter Shot by Cheney Has Minor Heart Attack," *CNN.com,* February 15, 2006, at www.cnn .com/2006/POLITICS/02/14/cheney/index.html (accessed on October 26, 2007).

19. See Ed Pilkington, "Bush's Golf Claim Angers Veterans," *The Guardian,* May 15, 2008, at www.guardian.co.uk/world/2008/may/15/georgebush.usa (accessed on May 18, 2008). See also *The Daily Show with Jon Stewart,* video, May 15, 2008, at www .thedailyshow.com/video/index.jhtml?videoId=168642&title=golf-war (accessed on May 18, 2008).

20. Oh and Hassig, *Looking Glass,* 186–87.

21. Aidan Foster-Carter, "Regime Dynamics in North Korea: A European Perspective," in *Understanding Regime Dynamics in North Korea,* Chung-in Moon, ed. (Seoul: Yonsei University Press, 1998), 113–39. Quoted in Oh and Hassig, *Looking Glass,* 193.

1

North Korea and the Birth Pangs of a New Northeast Asian Order

Gavan McCormack

I N FEBRUARY 2007, agreement was reached at the six-party talks in Beijing on the parameters for resolution of the North Korean nuclear issue. The frame was one of comprehensive settlement of one of the long-unresolved legacies of the twentieth century and the prospect it opened was for a new, diplomatic, military, political, and economic order.

In this chapter I ask why the settlement has taken so long to be reached, consider the major obstacles to its implementation, and assess its prospects. I argue that to understand the "North Korea problem," close attention has to be paid to the "America problem" and the "Japan problem." I suggest that, while North Korean strategic objectives have been consistent through the decade and a half of crisis, the United States and Japan have vacillated, torn between conservative, neoconservative, and reactionary forces on the one hand and "realists" on the other. The U.S. strategic shift of February 2007 heralds the dawn of a twenty-first-century Northeast Asian order; whether that dawn is to prove a true or false one remains unclear.

1. The Problem

In the summer and autumn of 2006, as the UN Security Council twice denounced North Korea and imposed sanctions on it with seemingly global unanimity, who would have guessed that within one year the prospects for reconciliation could have advanced as they did in the twelve months that followed?

The deal was reached at the Beijing six-party talks in February: North Korea was to shut down and seal its Yongbyon reactor as a first step toward permanent "disablement," while the other parties were to grant it immediate energy aid, with more to come when North Korea presented its detailed inventory of nuclear weapons and facilities to be dismantled. At the same time, the United States and Japan were to open talks with North Korea aimed at normalizing relations, while the United States was to "begin the process" of removing the designation of North Korea as a state sponsor of terrorism and "advance the process" of terminating the application to it of the Trading with the Enemy Act. Five working groups were set up to address the questions of peninsula denuclearization, normalization of Democratic People's Republic of Korea (DPRK)–U.S. relations, normalization of DPRK-Japan relations, economy and energy cooperation, and Northeast Asian peace and security.[1] The Beijing parties promised to "take positive steps to increase mutual trust" and the directly related parties to "negotiate a permanent peace regime on the Korean peninsula."

Shortly after the agreement, U.S. deputy secretary of state Negroponte visited the capitals of the region to explain President Bush's desire for a permanent peace regime on the peninsula,[2] and U.S. ambassador Vershbow spoke of the prospect of a treaty to end the Korean War and of improving relations between his country and North Korea by the spring of 2008.[3] A second South-North Korean summit was held in October 2007 and it was clear that plans were proceeding in Seoul for a massive "Marshall Plan"–scale program of South-North economic cooperation, with an estimated cost over the coming decade of $126 billion.[4] Trains crossed between South and North for the first time in fifty-seven years in May 2007 (albeit only on a trial run),[5] and the international university (funded by South and North Korea, China, and the United States), Pyongyang University of Science and Technology, opened in Pyongyang in September 2007.[6] The capitalist enclave of the Kaeseong Industrial Complex modestly thrives, with sixty-six South Korean light manufacturing companies operating within it already and another two hundred signed up to lease land for further stages in its expansion.[7] Both government and opposition parties in Seoul plan cooperation on the premises of eventual unification, and Seoul's National Defense Institute is even drawing up plans for a stage-by-stage unification of the armed forces of South and North.[8] Perhaps even more than these grand plans, it is the small, everyday things that bespeak the new era, such as the North Korean under-seventeen football squad conducting its training camp on Cheju Island.

As of autumn 2007, North Korea was committed to providing the inventory of its nuclear facilities and dismantling them by year's end, while the United States was looking positively at the removal of the designation "terror-supporting state" and the lifting of the "trading with the enemy" sanctions. The former Korean War combatants (the United States, China, and South Korea) have agreed that, provided North Korea dismantles its nuclear weapons program as promised by December 2007, they would enter upon negotiations to convert the existing armistice into a peace treaty,[9] and Japan has said it is ready for serious and sincere negotiations that will cover both the "unfortunate past" (of colonialism) and the North Korean abductions of the more recent times.[10]

The tectonic plates under East Asia are shifting. North Korea has been the enemy of the United States for longer than any state in history, including George III's England, Stalin's Soviet Union, Mao's China, Ho Chi Minh's Vietnam, and Castro's Cuba, and none of these cases involved a personal sentiment to match the "loathing" of the kind that George W. Bush has expressed for the North Korean leader as "evil," or the ferocity of the vice president's statement: "You do not negotiate with evil, you defeat it." For all of this to be resolved, and resolved peacefully, would be truly historic.

Peace and cooperation begin to seem possible in East Asia, radiating out from the very peninsula that was in the twentieth century one of the most violently contested and militarized spots on earth. Japanese colonialism, the division of Korea and its consequent civil and international war, the long isolation of North Korea and its confrontation with the United States and with South Korea, and the bitter hostility between it and Japan—all these things suddenly seem to be negotiable.[11] The historical significance of 2007 will be huge if even a significant part of this promise is fulfilled.

2. The "North Korea Problem" and the "U.S. Problem"

The very term "the North Korea nuclear problem," as framed by American policymakers, begs a major question. It assumes that it is North Korea that is irrational, aggressive, nuclear-obsessed, and dangerous, and the United States that is rational, globally responsible, and reacting to North Korean excesses. To thus shrink the frame of the problem is to ignore the matrix of a century's history—colonialism, division, half a century of Korean War, Cold War, as well as nuclear proliferation and intimidation.[12] Using this frame of reference, the United States assumes that what it describes as "the North Korean nuclear weapons program" can be dealt with while ignoring the unfinished issues of the Korean War and the Cold War, and even of Japanese imperialism.

What this formulation of the "North Korea problem" ignores is something that I have referred to as the "U.S. problem," the United States' aggressive, militarist hegemonism and contempt for international law.[13] Although North

Korea is widely regarded as an "outlaw state" and held in contempt by much of the world, it has not in the past fifty years launched any aggressive war, overthrown any democratically elected government, threatened any neighbor with nuclear weapons, torn up any treaty, or attempted to justify the practices of torture and assassination. Its 2006 missile and nuclear weapons tests were both provocative and unwise, but neither breached any law, and both were carried out under extreme provocation. The North Korean state plainly runs roughshod over the rights of its citizens, but the extremely abnormal circumstances under which it has existed since the founding of the state in 1948, facing the concentrated efforts of the global superpower to isolate, impoverish, and overthrow it, have not been of its choosing. Frozen out of major global institutions and subject to financial and economic sanctions,[14] denounced in fundamentalist terms as "evil" (and beyond redemption), North Korea could scarcely be anything but suspicious and fearful. Suspicion and fear, on the part of a state as well as of an individual, are likely to be expressed in belligerence.

In particular, North Korea has faced the threat of nuclear annihilation for more than half a century. If anything is calculated to drive a people mad, and to generate in it an obsession with unity and survival, the threat of nuclear weapons must be such an experience. North Korea's demand for relief from nuclear intimidation was unquestionably just and yet was ignored by the global community, until, eventually, as we know, it took the matter into its own hands. Being a small country, however, and one without diplomatic allies, the world's great and middle-sized powers criticized it while turning a blind eye to the injustice of the system from which it suffered. While the world's fingers were pointed at North Korea, its eyes were, by and large, averted from the suffering and denial of human rights suffered by the U.S. prisoners at Abu Ghraib or Guantanamo, or the citizens of many countries whom the CIA in recent years has ferried secretly around the world, delivering them to torturers in a global gulag beyond the reach of any law, not to mention from the United States flouting its obligations under the Non-Proliferation Treaty to dismantle its arsenal.

It is sometimes said that the Cold War ended in 1989 (or even that history itself ended) with the victory of the "free world," especially the United States, but in East Asia it ended rather with the defeat of "free world"–supported "national security state" regimes at the hands of the democratic resistance, or "people power," in the Philippines with the overthrow of the Marcos regime in 1986, in Korea with the overthrow of the Chun Doo Hwan regime in 1987, and in Indonesia with the overthrow of Suharto in 1998. These were only partial and incomplete victories, but were nevertheless the precondition for the advance of democracy and human rights. In Korea, it was the people's victory of 1987, preceding the end of the Cold War, that made possible the new historical era that slowly replaces it, especially the prospect of a post-division system Korea.

Bush and North Korea, 2002–2005

George W. Bush came to power charging North Korea with a secret, highly enriched uranium (HEU)–based, second-track nuclear weapons program in breach of the Agreed Framework of 1994 and denouncing North Korea as part of the "axis of evil." Pronouncing the regime "evil," the administration refused to talk to it; consider any form of security guarantee or any phased, step-by-step, reciprocal mode of settlement; or make any reference to the principles of the 1994 Framework. It maintained that there was nothing to be discussed but North Korea's unilateral submission, or CVID (complete, verifiable, irreversible dismantling of its nuclear weapons and materials).

Without attempting to resume the full record of the Bush administration's policy toward North Korea, let me address here primarily two aspects that are important as the root of the crisis in relations with North Korea: (1) from 2002 to 2005, the highly enriched uranium, or HEU, program; and (2) from 2005 to 2007, counterfeiting, especially of hundred-dollar notes. Like the allegations of Iraqi weapons of mass destruction, both were essentially intelligence beat-ups. Inflated to suit a policy of intimidation and regime change, they were just as easily deflated when circumstances changed.

Over the following years, many commentators accepted Washington's story about the HEU deception, but the remarkable fact is that other parties to the Beijing talks remained unconvinced, even after a special U.S. mission with "evidence" was sent around East Asian capitals in 2004. The South Korean unification minister told the National Assembly in Seoul in late February 2007 that there was "no information to show that North Korea had a HEU program."[15] Only years later, when the origins of the crisis had been half-forgotten, was the intelligence about HEU, initially rated "high," downgraded to "mid"-level,[16] and significant "data gaps," as they were delicately described, identified. The thin and ambiguous intelligence of November 2002 was that the North had begun "constructing a centrifuge facility" that could be operational by mid-decade. This information was blown up to the assertion that North Korea had a fully fledged program capable of completion by 2003 and producing enough HEU for up to six nukes a year.[17] The State Department's Christopher Hill in 2007 put it this way: a weapons program would have required "a lot more equipment than we know that they have actually purchased," and "production techniques that we're not sure whether they have mastered," as well as aluminum tubes that might have gone "somewhere else."[18] The intelligence thus manipulated (or "fixed" in the words of the Downing Street Memo)[19] to suit the political agenda of 2002, they (the Bush administration) "trashed the framework" (in Robert Gallucci's words).[20] Although most of the world joined the United States in blaming North Korea and denouncing it for deception, once the exaggerated U.S. claims were discounted, North Korea responded, admitting at the bilateral meeting in Geneva that it had indeed imported some aluminum materials; the issue seemed no longer difficult to resolve.

The HEU issue was only resolved gradually, in a general context of U.S. retreat under mounting, eventually decisive diplomatic pressure. Unable to impose its will in Beijing and unable to rely on the support of any of its partner countries save Japan, in September 2005, having exhausted all possibilities of delay and being fearful of becoming what Jack Pritchard, formerly the State Department's top North Korea expert, described as "a minority of one . . . isolated from the mainstream of its four other allies and friends,"[21] and facing an ultimatum from the Chinese chair of the conference to sign or else bear responsibility for their breakdown,[22] the United States accepted an agreement, one that was multisided but contained essentially the same provisions as those of the Clinton-era framework—a graduated, step-by-step process leading to North Korean denuclearization in exchange for diplomatic and economic normalization. In other words, the United States bowed to the will of the Beijing majority. Thus ended phase one of the Bush North Korea policy.

Bush and North Korea, 2005–2007

However, the "vacillation" and "inconsistency" of U.S. diplomacy,[23] and its inability to "resolve the feuds within its own ranks"[24] were incorrigible. From the day following the September 2005 Beijing agreement, the U.S. government launched financial sanctions designed to bring the Pyongyang regime down. Refusing North Korean overtures for discussion, it denigrated the North Korean regime as a criminal state. Without resort to military force, it set out to cut North Korea off from the world economically and financially, in yet another effort to bring about regime change.

The allegations of counterfeiting, money laundering, and drug dealing were central. Under Section 311 of the Patriot Act (2001), the U.S. Treasury is empowered to declare any bank in the world "a primary money-laundering concern," thereby in effect depriving it of the right to do business, without right of appeal or right to know the reason. A tiny bank, Banco Delta Asia (BDA)—the fourth-smallest (employing only 150 people)[25] of twenty-seven banks in the Chinese special administrative region and gambling mecca of Macao—was accused of dealing in counterfeit, North Korean–made, hundred-dollar notes. From that allegation, banks around the world were put under pressure to refuse any dealings with BDA or North Korea. Failure to comply risked loss of access to the U.S. market. At issue on the surface were suspect deposits of some twenty-odd million dollars, but underlying this incident was the question of North Korea's right to engage in any economic transactions of any kind beyond its borders. The United States was intent on closing down not just the tiny BDA but North Korea itself.[26] David Asher, the architect of the policy and senior adviser on North Korea matters to the Bush administration, spoke proudly of his success in delivering a "catastrophic blow" or "a direct blow at the fundaments of the North Korean system." He was describing a policy of strangulation, not regulation.[27]

The world was told, and almost universally believed, that North Korea, a country long frozen out of all high-technology markets, whose thirty-year-old printing presses were apparently unable even to produce its own currency, could nevertheless perform feats of genius in the production of perfect hundred-dollar notes. So good are these counterfeit "supernotes" that the Swiss federal criminal police recently described them as actually superior to the originals. Whoever it was that had such mastery of materials and technology, and the capacity presumably to flood world markets with billions of these super dollars, produced only twenty-two million of them over almost two decades.[28] Despite the enormous effort and cost, they produced these high-quality art works in "quantities less than it would cost to acquire the sophisticated machinery needed to make them."[29] While the U.S. Treasury introduced nineteen different and highly sophisticated refinements in an attempt to outwit the counterfeiters, every one of them was promptly matched. Someone, in other words, was playing a strange game of technological one-upmanship, goading the experts of the U.S. Treasury for no apparent reason other than the inherent satisfaction. Could Kim Jong Il really command a scientific establishment of such astonishing genius, and might he also, perhaps, possess a delicate and hitherto unsuspected sense of humor?

But, if not North Korea, then, who? Before blame for the "supernotes" was sheeted home to the North Koreans, it had been attributed at one time or another to the Iranians, the Syrians, and even the East Germans. However, the German specialist on banknotes, Klaus Bender, makes the pregnant comment that, apart from the U.S. Treasury itself, the printing machines, ink, and other technological refinements were most likely accessible only to the CIA.[30]

While North Korea was reviled as a criminal state and singled out for global punishment for putting twenty-odd million dollars of these "super hundreds" into circulation, the much larger sum of thirty-eight million counterfeit "ordinary" dollars was seized during the same period in Columbia,[31] and in the single year of 2004–2005 the Israel Discount Bank of New York processed a staggering $35.4 billion for "originators and beneficiaries that exhibited characteristics and patterns commonly associated with money-laundering" (as a

Treasury official put it).[32] Yet in neither case were global sanctions imposed, or the Patriot Act invoked. The *Wall Street Journal* in July 2007 revealed another case, of a Saudi bank suspected by U.S. authorities of financing terrorism but protected by the political consideration of U.S.-Saudi friendship and supposed cooperation in the "War on Terror."[33] Despite the international furor over North Korea as a criminal, counterfeiting state, when three agencies of the U.S. government (Treasury, Federal Reserve, and Secret Service) in 2006 reported jointly on "US currency holdings and counterfeit activity abroad," neither the DPRK nor Macao was even mentioned.

The BDA had been guilty of some infringements in 1994, and possibly 1998, involving the trivial sum of a quarter million dollars in counterfeit currency.[34] When U.S. legal and accounting firms in due course investigated, they did indeed find evidence of lax bookkeeping, but of criminal misconduct, none. North Korea's frozen funds were returned under an agreement on July 3, 2007. The BDA matter, having wrecked the September 2005 agreement, was thus quietly resolved, leaving only the bank's much-aggrieved owner to pursue his case against the U.S. Treasury in the courts. In Article 311 of the Patriot Act, however, the U.S. government had created a powerful financial weapon. While set aside for the time being against North Korea, the administration began to exploit the possibilities thus opened against Iranian, Syrian, and Russian companies and banks.[35]

Bush and North Korea, 2007

By 2007, the Bush administration's policy shift from "regime change" to negotiated settlement amounted to a 180-degree reversal. The CVID formula of 2003 had morphed by 2007 into something like its opposite: partial, prolonged, unverifiable (any agreement would have to rely, fundamentally, on trust), and reversible (since the experience of producing and testing nuclear weapons could not be expunged). Allegations of North Korean crime that rested on the evidence of defectors and intelligence agencies persisted,[36] but the more carefully and critically the evidence was analyzed, the less convincing it became.[37]

As for the drug charge, while it was included on the list of accusations by the State Department in 2003, in 2007 North Korea was simply deleted from the list of offending countries (twenty in all) without explanation;[38] whether because the original U.S. intelligence had again been flawed or because North Korea had reformed is impossible to know. The generic denunciation of North Korea as "evil" or as a "soprano state" was simply dropped.

Having faced down U.S. denunciation, abuse, and threat, having pressed ahead with missile and nuclear tests and ignored the UN Security Council's two unanimous resolutions of condemnation and its ensuing sanctions, in other words, having stuck to its guns, both metaphorically and literally, North Korea in 2007 appears to be on the brink of accomplishing its long-term objectives—security, an end to sanctions, and normalization of relations with both the United States and Japan. If so, the much derided and friendless country might be about to pull off one of the greatest diplomatic coups of modern history, converting its 1953 stalemate truce with the United States into something tantamount to a victory.

But, facing such a historic victory, could it actually bring itself to give up the nuclear card, for which it had paid such a price and which it had already celebrated publicly as a historic event and guarantee of security? Kim Myong Kil, North Korea's deputy ambassador to the UN, spoke vividly of such a process as akin to "castrating a bull,"[39] and in truth the analogy could be formulated even more forcefully: the North Korean bull being asked to castrate itself. It is impossible to dismiss the skepticism of John Bolton, who writes, "Kim Jong Il's regime will not voluntarily give up its nuclear weapons program."[40] Despite that bleak assessment, however, the point of the Beijing agreement was to construct a framework of trust and cooperation in which other "assurances" of security would become unnecessary. Under such conditions, voluntary denuclearization just might be possible.

It is true that in the short-term Kim Jong Il stands to be "rewarded" by the kind of settlement underway, but the fact is that the greatest beneficiaries are likely to be the long-suffering people of North Korea. War, moreover, periodically given serious consideration by the United States, would have brought unimaginable disaster, not only to the people of North Korea but also to the entire region. Where "pressure and sanctions," as South Korea's former unification minister commented, "tend to reinforce the regime rather than weaken it,"[41] normalization is going to require the leaders of North Korea's "guerrilla state,"[42] whose legitimacy has long been rooted in their ability to hold powerful and threatening enemies at bay, to respond to the demands of their people for improved living conditions and greater freedoms.

3. The "North Korea Problem" and the "Japan Problem"

As for Japan, dependence on the United States and hostility to North Korea have been fundamental to national policy for over half a century, and a new and deeper level of subjection to U.S. regional and global purposes was negotiated in 2005–2006.[43] The sudden, February 2007 policy reversal on North Korea under George W. Bush therefore constituted a "Bush shock" that commentators in Japan likened to the "Nixon shock" over China three and a half decades ago. If the North Korean nuclear issue is now to be resolved, and relations on all sides with North Korea normalized, Japan will be shaken to its foundations. It will have to rethink its post–Cold War diplomatic posture, especially its relationship with China. If peace treaties (U.S.–North Korea, Japan–North Korea) and normalization on all sides were to be negotiated, U.S. forces would serve no further function in South Korea and Japan (except to contain China, and that case would have to be argued for the populations to accept it) and so might in due course be withdrawn (or sent elsewhere). That would indeed signify a new era.

James Kelly (former U.S. assistant secretary of state) said in Beijing in late April 2007 that Japanese politicians faced a "hard choice" over priorities.[44] Former deputy secretary of state Richard Armitage suggested that North Korea "might remain in possession of a certain amount of nuclear weapons even as the [Korean] peninsula comes slowly together for some sort of unification," and that the United States might have to "sit down" with Japan to explain it.[45] If so, nobody in Japan's government was ready for such a "sitting down." While the five other "six-party" countries now sought to resolve the nuclear problem and address the legacies of history by implementing the February agreement, in Japan (as of September 2007) Abe, who owed his rise to political power in Japan above all to his ability to concentrate national anti–North Korea sentiment over the issue of abductions of Japanese citizens in the 1970s and 1980s,[46] took the unique position that abduction concerns were paramount. According to Abe, the abductions, not nuclear weapons, and still less the resolution of the military and diplomatic divisions of the Korean War and after, constituted "the most important problem our country faces" (sic).[47]

Japan's giving priority to the abductions and its determination to stick to sanctions and remain aloof from the six-party process until satisfied left it on a limb in the context of the Beijing agreement, even as the Abe government's revisionist and denialist approach to history and its clumsy attempts to evade responsibility for the wartime "Comfort Women" system alienated its closest allies in Washington.[48] Though there were obvious lacunae in the North Korean explanations, Pyongyang had apologized for the abductions and returned to Japan the five it said were the sole survivors and the ashes of those who had died. The international scientific community, through the journal *Nature*, had expressed sharp criticisms of the unscientific grounding of the Japanese government's position.[49] With Bush's policy shift in Beijing, Japan's North Korea "containment policy," as the *Asahi shimbun* described it on February 15, "falls apart."[50]

Japan was isolated at Beijing because it allowed domestic political considerations to prevail over international ones in framing the North Korean abductions of 1977 to 1982 as a greater problem than nuclear weapons and as a unique North Korean crime against Japan rather than as a universal one of human rights. In any universal human rights frame, Japan itself would become the greatest twentieth-century perpetrator of abductions, and Koreans, North and South, the greatest victims. No amount of global diplomatic effort under Koizumi and Abe could overcome the problem caused by exclusive focus on Japan's own victims and the denial of its own abduction responsibility. The Japanese government's plea of concern for its abducted citizens was also not consistent with its studied neglect of the rights of its citizens abandoned in China, Sakhalin, and elsewhere since the end of the Second World War; its continuing coldness toward those fleeing from political persecution and seeking refuge in Japan; or its cruel policies of the 1950s and 1960s designed to get rid of as many Koreans as possible (with North Korean complicity), recently documented by Tessa Morris-Suzuki.[51]

A rift slowly opened between Washington and Tokyo during 2007. Previously unimaginable rumbles of criticism of the Bush administration began to be heard from Tokyo.[52] The ministers of Defense and of Foreign Affairs, no less, referred to Iraq as a "mistaken" war, without justification, pursued in "childish" manner, and to the United States as being too "high-handed" in Okinawa. Protesting that it would not be party to any aid to North Korea until the abduction issue was settled, and therefore refusing to shoulder any financial responsibility, the Japanese government was reduced to pleading with the Bush administration to not take steps required under the Beijing agreement such as lifting the terror support label from North Korea. In the sharpest comment of all, the head of Japan's Liberal Democratic Party (LDP) Policy Council, Ishihara Nobuteru, denounced U.S.–North Korea policy as "appalling" (*hidoi*) and declared it would be no bad thing for Japan to abandon the six-party talks.[53] That way, however, lay absolute and potentially catastrophic isolation. Perhaps the worst Japanese fear was that the United States might be in the process of a large-scale shift in its Asia policy, with China gradually coming to replace Japan as its strategic partner. That really would be a Japanese nightmare.

4. Conclusion—A New Deal for East Asia

The reasons for the U.S. reversal can only be surmised, but probably include North Korea's missile and nuclear tests, the Republican defeat in the mid-term U.S. elections, the deepening catastrophe in Iraq, and perhaps, too, in some unquantifiable measure, the success of North Korean overtures of friendship.[54] But, was the U.S. shift strategic and long-term, or tactical, and, if the latter, might it be reversed again in the near future?

As peace begins to seem possible on the Korean peninsula, the Beijing parties head toward a multipolar and post-U.S. hegemonic order in Northeast Asia, with the six-party conference format likely to be institutionalized in due course as a body for addressing common problems of security, environment, food, and energy—the precursor of a future regional community. North Korean nuclear weapons and its distorted, rights-denying, family-cult-centered polity are indeed serious problems, but they are best seen as symptomatic, parts of larger, primary problems, not capable of resolution in isolation.

Looking back at the years of the George W. Bush presidency, especially since September 11, 2001, it is clear that fundamentalism has been a key element—both of Islam (although scarcely a major consideration in Northeast Asia) and of the United States, where assumptions of a simple moral order pitting good against evil and god against the devil, and a readiness to destroy the world in order to save it, are deeply rooted in the society, and where under George W. Bush in particular a neoconservative group, extremists even by conventional U.S. standards, was able to seize power and manipulate the state (and the world) in disastrous and antidemocratic ways. In due course, the failure of the war in the Middle East, the exhaustion of the armed forces, the revolt of the electorate, and the rout of the Republican Party in the mid-term elections combined to shift the balance back in a pragmatic direction, but the underlying, quasi-religious mentality remained strong.[55]

The larger issues that constitute the frame within which the North Korean problem has taken shape, and which will somehow have to be addressed as part of its resolution, include

1. The refusal of their legal and treaty obligations for nuclear disarmament by the global superpowers and the insistence on the part of the United States on the prerogative of nuclear threat.
2. The persistence in the United States of fundamentalism, unilateralism, and militarism, even as its hegemonic position has been seriously weakened by the catastrophe in the Middle East.
3. The persistence in Japan, too, of a kind of fundamentalism, in the form of neonationalism, that is, the combination of deepening subjection to the United States with exaggerated stress on the symbols of nation, denial of war guilt and responsibility, and insistence on national beauty.
4. The reluctance of both the United States and Japan (even as the Bush administration scrambles to solve this problem in its remaining span of office) to move beyond the institutions of the Cold War and adjust to the emerging new Northeast Asian order.
5. The obsequious position adopted by America's allies. The uncritical, unconditional support pledged by Britain's Blair, Australia's Howard,

and Japan's Koizumi (later Abe) undoubtedly helped make war on Iraq possible and protracted, and helped prolong and intensify the North Korean crisis.[56]

Between the crisis of 2006 and the promise of 2007, the frame of the "North Korea problem," and of East Asian diplomacy shifted radically, East Asian Confucian realism and humanism displacing Western neoconservative fundamentalism. Yet the balance of forces remains fragile. Whether North Korea and the United States on the one hand, and North Korea and Japan on the other, can build trust in sufficient measure to outweigh the accumulated half-century (and in the Japanese case a full century) of hostility remains to be seen.

If there is a North Korean "lesson" relevant to global crisis points in this record of North Korea in its confrontation with, and looming triumph over, George W. Bush, however, it might be the paradoxical one that it pays to have nuclear weapons and negotiate from a position of strength (unlike Saddam Hussein, or the present leadership of Iran), and that it helps to have no oil (at least no significant and verified deposits), no quarrel with Israel, few Arabs or Muslims, and no involvement (despite the rhetorical excesses of the Bush administration) in any "axis of evil." Undoubtedly, too, it pays to have neighbors like North Korea's, who have ruled out any resort to force against it.

Despite the apparent progress of 2007, the commitment of the Bush administration to carry forward the radical (Condoleeza) Rice-(Christopher) Hill agenda remains uncertain. Has the president really signed off to normalize relations with one he loathes as much as Kim Jong Il? And even if he has, has he the time left in his lame-duck phase to carry it through? Many within the Bush regime will resist meeting U.S. obligations to lift the terrorist label and end sanctions, let alone "trust" and relate normally to a regime it has hated passionately. As for North Korea, Kim Jong Il will have to deploy all his power and prestige to enforce his commitment to submit the inventory of his nuclear weapons, materials, and facilities; abandon the 50 kilos of plutonium the United States estimates it holds;[57] and then dismantle its works. Can he really reverse fifty, or even eighty, years of guerrilla state mobilization, and persuade his military to accept the goal of becoming the Libya, rather than the Pakistan of East Asia? As for South Korea, although it faced presidential elections late in 2007, it seemed likely that there would be continuity of basic policy toward the North—irrespective of the outcome. It was the conservative candidate, Lee Myung Bak, who promised to take steps to double the per capita national income of the North. For Japan, however, North Korea is the concentrated expression of multiple security, diplomatic, and even identity dilemmas. Facing isolation unless it "makes a substantial course correction in its North Korean policy"[58] as the Beijing parties head toward a new, multipolar and post-U.S. hegemonic order in Northeast Asia, North Korea constitutes for Japan a crucial test.

All of these countries stand at a crossroads. The vigorous support of the civil societies of them all, and of the world, will be necessary to ensure that the governments concerned do not backtrack and that the promise of February 2007, the best chance the region has ever had to set the troublesome twentieth century behind it and advance the twenty-first-century agenda of regional peace, cooperation, and prosperity, is borne out in the months ahead.

Notes

"North Korea and the Birth Pangs of a New Northeast Asian Order" originally appeared in *The Asia-Pacific Journal: Japan Focus*, japanfocus.org. This is a revised version of the original article.

1. "Initial Actions for the Implementation of the Joint Statement," Joint Statement from the Third Session of the Fifth Round of the Six-Party Talks, *Nautilus Institute, Special Report*, February 13, 2007. See detailed discussion in Charles L. Pritchard, *Failed Diplomacy: The Tragic Story of How North Korea Got the Bomb* (Washington, D.C.: Brookings Institution Press, 2007), 159.

2. "Dokyumento—Gekidō no nanboku chōsen" [Document—Tumultuous North and South Koreas], *Sekai* (June 2007), 263–70, at 269.

3. "Heiwa kyōtei 9 gatsu made ni" [Peace Agreement by September], *Asahi shimbun*, May 11, 2007.

4. Limb Jae-un, "Think Tank Assigns 116 Trillion Won Tab for South-North Deals," *Joongang ilbo*, October 17, 2007.

5. Unification Minister of South Korea Lee Jae Joung spoke of "reconnecting the severed bloodlines of the Korean nation."

6. See en.wikipedia.org/wiki/Pyongyang_University_of_Science_and_Technology.

7. "Sanbutsu wa tōitsu? Gaika?" [Would the Result be Reunification or Foreign Currency?], *Asahi shimbun*, June 15, 2007; Dick K. Nanto and Mark E. Manyin, "The Kaesong North-South Korean Industrial Complex," *CRS Report for Congress*, July 19, 2007.

8. "Dokyumento—Gekidō no nanboku chōsen" [Document—Tumultuous North and South Koreas], *Sekai* (September 2007), 302–9, at 308.

9. George W. Bush at APEC summit in Sydney, September 2007, was explicit on this when pressed by President Roh Moo-Hyun. (And see "New Era of Peace Is Coming on the Korean Peninsula," *The Hankyoreh*, September 8, 2007.)

10. Reports of the September 2007 six-party working group sessions between the United States and North Korea in Geneva and between Japan and North Korea in Ulan Bator.

11. Paik Nak-chung, "Twenty Years after June 1987: Where Are We Now, and Where Do We Go from Here?" Keynote speech to International Symposium on Democracy

and Peace-Building in Korea and the Choice of 2007, Los Angeles, May 12, 2007, at japanfocus.org/products/details/2440.

12. Gavan McCormack, *Target North Korea: Pushing North Korea to the Brink of Nuclear Catastrophe* (New York: Nation Books, 2004).

13. Gavan McCormack, "Criminal States: Soprano vs. Baritone—North Korea and the United States," *Korea Observer* 37, no. 3 (Autumn 2006): 487–511, and (in Korean) as chapter 1 of *Beomjoegukga: Bukhan geurigo miguk* [Criminal State: North Korea and the U.S.] (Seoul: Icarus, 2006), 15–40.

14. For a compendium of all U.S. sanctions against North Korea prepared by the Atlantic Council, see "U.S.-North Korean Relations: An Analytic Compendium of U.S. Policies, Laws and Regulations," April 13, 2007.

15. "Kita chōsen uran nōshuku hontō" [North Korea's Uranium Enrichment Is True], *Asahi shimbun*, February 26, 2007.

16. David E. Sanger and William J. Broad, "U.S. Had Doubts on North Korean Uranium Drive," *New York Times*, March 1, 2007.

17. See David Albright, "North Korea's Alleged Large-Scale Enrichment Plant: Yet Another Questionable Extrapolation Based on Aluminum Tubes," Institute for Science and International Security, February 23, 2007.

18. "U.S. Acknowledges Gaps on N. Korea Nuclear Program," *Reuters*, February 22, 2007.

19. *The Sunday Times*, May 1, 2005. See Mark Danner, "The Secret Way to War: The Downing Street Memo and the Iraq War's Buried History," *New York Review of Books* 52, no. 10 (June 9, 2005).

20. Robert Gallucci (chief negotiator of the 1994 agreement), quoted in Richard J. Bernstein, "How Not to Deal with North Korea," *New York Review of Books* 54, no. 3 (March 1, 2007), at www.nybooks.com/articles/19923.

21. Charles L. (Jack) Pritchard, "Six Party Talks Update: False Start or a Case for Optimism," Conference on The Changing Korean Peninsula and the Future of East Asia, sponsored by the Brookings Institution and *Joongang ilbo*, December 1, 2005.

22. Funabashi Yoichi, *Za peninshura kueschon* [The Peninsula Question] (Tokyo: Asahi shimbunsha, 2006), 610. See also Joseph Kahn and David E. Sanger, "U.S.-Korean Deal on Arms Leaves Key Points Open," *New York Times*, September 20, 2005.

23. C. Kenneth Quinones, "The United States and North Korea: Observations of an Intermediary," lecture to U.S.-Korea Institute at Johns Hopkins University School of Advanced International Studies, November 2, 2006, at www.uskoreainstitute.org/events/Fall06/quinones. Audio link available.

24. Tom Lantos, from January 2007 chair of the House International Relations Committee, quoted in Selig Harrison, "A humbled administration rethinks North Korea and Iraq," *The Hankyoreh*, November 28, 2006.

25. Tim Johnson, "Macao Tycoon Wants His Bank Back," *McClatchy Newspapers*, Washington Bureau, July 6, 2007.

26. David Asher, senior adviser on North Korea matters to the Bush administration, interviewed in Takase Hitoshi, "Kin shōjitsu o furueagareseta otoko" [A Man Who Terrified Kim Jong Il], *Bungei shunju*, October 2006, 214–21, at 216.

27. David Asher interview.

28. U.S. Treasury figure of October 2006; and see Gavan McCormack, *Client State: Japan in the American Embrace* (London: Verso, 2007), 110.

29. Kevin G. Hall, "Swiss Authorities Question U.S. Counterfeiting Charges Against North Korea," *McClatchy Newspapers*, May 22, 2007.

30. Klaus Bender, "The Mystery of the 'Supernotes': Washington Accuses North Korea of Counterfeiting Dollar Bills on a Huge Scale, the Evidence Militates against It," *Frankfurter Allgemeine Zeitung*, January 7, 2007. See also Bender's *Moneymakers: The Secret World of Banknote Printing* (Weinheim, Germany: Wiley-VCH, 2006).

31. "North Korea: Illicit Activity Funding the Regime," U.S. Senate Committee on Homeland Security and Governmental Affairs, April 25, 2006, at hsgac.senate.gov/public/index.cfm?FuseAction=Hearings.Detail&HearingID=07ae22d5-17cd-44d3-b7ed-e7c201cf7ff0.

32. McCormack, *Client State*, 110.

33. Glenn R. Simpson, "US Tracks Saudi Bank Favored by Extremists," *Wall Street Journal*, July 26, 2007.

34. See part two of John McGlynn, "North Korean Criminality Examined," "Financial Sanctions and North Korea under the Patriot Act's Catch 22," *Japan Focus*, June 2007.

35. Paul Bracken, "Financial warfare," Foreign Policy Research Institute, E-Notes, September 2007, at www.fpri.org/enotes/200709.bracken.financialwarfare.html.

36. For two recent pieces in this genre, see Sheena Chestnut, "Illicit Activity and Proliferation: North Korean Smuggling Networks," *International Security* 32, no. 1 (Summer 2007): 80–111; and Bill Powell and Adam Zagoria, "North Korea: The Sopranos State," *Time*, July 12, 2007.

37. See the three-part analysis by John McGlynn, "North Korean Criminality Examined: The U.S. Case," *Japan Focus*, May–July 2007.

38. Christy McCampbell, Deputy Assistant Secretary for International Narcotics and Law Enforcement Affairs, "Briefing on Release of Annual Report on the Major Illicit Drug Producing Countries for FY 2008" (Washington, D.C.: International Narcotics and Law Enforcement Affairs, September 17, 2007).

39. Ryu Jae Hoon, "Rocky Road Ahead, and Not a Lot of Time, for NK Denuclearization," *The Hankyoreh*, July 9, 2007.

40. John Bolton, "Pyongyang Pussyfooting," *Wall Street Journal*, July 3, 2007.

41. "Kim Jong Il and the Prospects for Korean Unification," U.S.-Korea Institute, Johns Hopkins University, School of Advanced International Studies, November 28, 2006.

42. Japanese historian Wada Haruki's term, in his various writings on the modern history of North Korea.

43. This matter is addressed in detail in my *Client State*.

44. "Keri moto beikokumu jikanho rachi 'Nihon wa kibishii ketsudan mo'" [According to the Former Assistant Secretary of State Kelly, Japan Should Also Consider a Harsh Measure Regarding the Abductions], *Asahi shimbun*, April 29, 2007.

45. "North Korea may still be nuclear in 2020," *The Hankyoreh*, February 18, 2007.

46. For detailed analysis, see Gavan McCormack and Wada Haruki, "Forever Stepping Back: The Strange Record of 15 Years of Negotiation between Japan and North

Korea," in *The Future of U.S.-Korean Relations: The Imbalance of Power*, ed. John Feffer, (London and New York: Routledge, 2006), 81–100.

47. Abe, on June 16, 2007, quoted in "Shushō no doshi uttae tesaguri" [Prime Minister: In Tough Search of Comrades], *Asahi shimbun*, June 28, 2007.

48. See my "Reshaping the Japanese State: the Koizumi and Abe Agenda," in the forthcoming Routledge volume edited by Glenn D. Hook and Hiroko Takeda.

49. David Cyranoski, "DNA Is Burning Issue as Japan and Korea Clash over Kidnaps," *Nature* No. 453, Feb. 3, 2005, 445.

50. Naohito Maeda and Nanae Kurashige, "With US Shift, Abe's N. Korea Containment Policy Falls apart," *Asahi shimbun*, February 15, 2007.

51. Tessa Morris-Suzuki, *Exodus to North Korea: Shadows from Japan's Cold War* (Lanham, Md.: Rowman & Littlefield, 2007).

52. For a brief account, see "Criticism of Iraq War," editorial, *Asahi shimbun*, February 8, 2007.

53. Speaking on TV Asahi on September 16, quoted in "Rokusha kyōgi ridatsu mo" [Withdrawal from Six-Party Talks Possible], *Asahi shimbun*, September 16, 2007.

54. North Korea seems eager to become an American friend. Vice Foreign Minister Kim Gye Gwan in New York in March 2007 suggested the United States think of using North Korea as a kind of buffer to contain China. A similar point was made to visiting New Mexico governor Bill Richardson on his April visit to Pyongyang. (Quoted in "Bei to no kyori kankoku hyōryū" [South Korea Maintaining Distance from the U.S.], *Asahi shimbun*, March 16, 2007.)

55. On this controversial point, see the writing of James Carroll, whose views are captured in "Tomdispatch Interview—James Carroll, American Fundamentalisms," *TomDispatch.com*, September 17, 2007, at www.tomdispatch.com/post/174837/tomdispatch_interview_james_carroll_american_fundamentalisms.

56. All of theses state might learn from South Korea. Both South Korea's current president, Roh Moo Hyun, and his predecessor Kim Dae Jung, have been noted for plain-talking to their opposite number in Washington.

57. Christopher Hill, quoted in Brian Lee, "No Peace with Plutonium, Hill Says," *Joongang ilbo*, October 17, 2007.

58. Gerald L. Curtis, "The US in East Asia: Not Architecture, but Action," *Global Asia* 5, no. 2 (Fall 2007): 43–51, at 51.

2

Socialism, Sovereignty, and the North Korean Exception

Charles K. Armstrong

Sovereign is he who decides on the exception.

—Carl Schmitt[1]

1. North Korea, a State of Exception

PERHAPS NO MODERN STATE has more forcefully and consistently defended its right to national sovereignty and self-determination than has the Democratic People's Republic of Korea (DPRK). This emphasis on national independence has long been embodied in the term *juche* (often, but inadequately, translated as "self-reliance"), and its derivative terms *juche sasang* (*"juche* ideology"), *jucheseong* (*"juche*-ness," or the state of independence), and so on.[2] These slogans became prominent in North Korean official discourse in the late 1960s, although Kim Il Sung had referred to the term *juche*—without much emphasis or fanfare—as early as December 1955.[3] But North Korea's hypersensitivity to perceived threats to its sovereignty has roots going back to the very beginning of the regime, arising out of the DPRK's history as one of the first post–World War II nations to emerge from a struggle against colonialism, its adaptation of Soviet-Stalinist "Socialism in one country" of the 1940s, and its fifty-seven-year-long military mobilization against the South Korea and the United States. Anticolonialism, indigenized Stalinism, and siege mentality are thus the foundations of North Korea's desire for "ultrasovereignty."

Given this background, it should not come as a surprise that North Korea has been fiercely protective of its independence and sovereignty in the post–Cold War period. After its main superpower patron the Soviet Union had disappeared China had chosen to recognize South Korea, the DPRK faced a hostile and confrontational United States amidst international isolation and domestic economic collapse. Under these circumstances, it should also have been perfectly predictable that North Korea in the 1990s refused to compromise its political system and was extremely wary of dealing with the outside world. In fact, what is remarkable is the degree to which North Korea in the past decade has been able to accommodate itself to its erstwhile enemies, the United States, South Korea, and Japan, and now seems on the verge of both serious economic reform and a change in its international position. Denuclearization, normalization of relations with the United States and Japan, and an accelerated economic integration with South Korea appear far closer now than they did just one year ago. Does this mean that North Korea is changing its own approach to the question of sovereignty, both internally and in relation to the outside world? Is North Korea no longer a "*juche* state"? This paper seeks to explore this question through a historical overview of North Korea's articulation of state sovereignty, as directed both inwardly—appearing in part as North Korea's despotic or "totalitarian" characteristics—and outwardly—in its relations to the regional and global international systems. We begin with a brief discussion of sovereignty in modern political theory and, in particular, the concept of the "state of exception" (*Ausnahmezustand*) analyzed by the German legal scholar Carl Schmitt in the Weimar period and more recently by the Italian philosopher Giorgio Agamben.

The sovereign state, as Hobbes was one of the first to articulate, rests upon the successful linking of the solitary person to the national collective, the submission of the free individual to the authority of the state.[4] Sovereignty emerged in the modern period as a key characteristic of the international system, which is defined as a system of equally sovereign states.[5] The sovereign state, of course, requires a sovereign, and in a postmonarchical age the sovereign has usually been defined as "the people" represented by a leadership chosen (though not necessarily in a formally democratic process) by the people. But from the birth of the modern republican state in the late eighteenth century—beginning, in fact, from the emergency decrees of the French Constituent Assembly in July 1791—modern states have suspended their "normal" political processes in self-described states of exception.[6] Carl Schmitt, writing on the cusp of the Nazi takeover of Germany (a regime he would gain much notoriety for supporting), was greatly concerned with the need for the leader to apply emergency measures to restore order in a period of severe economic or political disturbance. Such measures he referred to as "states of exception," and the exception, for Schmitt, brought the nature of sovereignty into bold relief. Schmitt in fact defined the sovereign as "he who decides on the exception."[7]

The problem was that interwar Europe seemed to be facing a continuous emergency; as Walter Benjamin wrote in 1942, partly in response to Schmitt, "the state of exception . . . has become the rule."[8] The Nazi and Stalinist regimes that emerged out of this period were regimes of "permanent exception," concentrating power in the hands of despots. North Korea as well was born in a state of emergency, with roots precisely in this period (specifically, in Japanese colonial militarism and Stalinism) and has existed in one ever since. Sovereignty for the DPRK is absolute both outwardly and inwardly: outwardly, North Korea has generally refused external intervention into its internal affairs; inwardly, the rule of the sovereign has been utterly unquestionable.

Such modern historical conditions that have shaped the DPRK are in turn built upon and intertwine with earlier, specifically East Asian ideas of individual and national subjectivity. In the late nineteenth and early twentieth centuries, China, Japan, Korea, and Vietnam shared a common, Chinese-character vocabulary of neologisms dealing with such concepts as "self," "individual," and "nation."[9] Meiji Japan was the first East Asian state to promote the idea of "national essence," or *kokutai*, the nation as a collective self (personified in Japan by the emperor), subsuming the individual within. The idea of *kokutai* reached an apotheosis of sorts in the quasi-Fascist ideology of the wartime 1930s and early 1940s. It was this corporatist notion, in its colonial form, that provided the context and focus of resistance for the Koreans of Kim Il Sung's generation who became the first leaders of the DPRK.

In effect, North Korea inverted the signs but maintained the form of Japanese wartime corporatism, with its god-like leader, indivisible mass, and sacred national purpose, linked together in an organic whole.[10] The "*che*" in *juche* is the "*tai*" in *kokutai*—essence, body. *Juche* literally means "to rule the body" or "master the essence," and *jucheseong* or the "state of *juche*" is identical to the Japanese term *shutaisei*, which means "subjectivity" in a literary or philosophical sense, a favored term among Japanese Marxists and other leftist intellectuals in the post–World War II period.[11]

This "*che*" is also the first character in the word "*chemyeon*"—dignity or "face," as in "to lose face." *Juche* is sovereignty as individual dignity, and its loss is shame in a very personal, Confucian sense. There is also a certain religious aspect to the way *juche* is used in North Korea, with the elevation of the nation, the leader, and the party to a state of immortality and transcendence. Although other mass-mobilizing dictatorships, and even more mundane nationalisms, have a certain religious tinge as well, the worshipful fervor of North Korean official ideology is immediately striking to most outside observers.[12] If, as Carl Schmitt argued, "all significant concepts of the modern theory of the state are secularized theological concepts,"[13] North Korea's articulation of *juche* as a quasi-theological concept linked to the quasi-divine personage of Kim Il Sung inverts this process, turning the secular theory of state sovereignty back into theology. Kim, in short, embodies the sovereign—both during his rule and now even in death, as we will explore below.

2. A Genealogy of North Korean Sovereignty

The "Guerilla Band State"

Several overlapping strata of historical experience have shaped North Korean sovereignty. To begin with, North Korea's approach to national sovereignty, and indeed its representation of its own national identity, are strongly linked to experiences of founding leader Kim Il Sung and his cohort in the struggle against Japanese colonialism in the 1930s and early 1940s. The reliance on this experience as the foundation myth of and metaphor for the DPRK creates what Wada Haruki has called a "Guerilla Band State."[14] The characteristics that Wada outlines include a tightly knit ruling group, with the supreme leader at its core, formed out of a shared guerilla experience; deep suspicion of outsiders beyond the group, and of foreigners in general; a determination to protect the group/nation in the face of overwhelmingly more powerful outside forces; and a reliance on subterfuge, deception, and other "weapons of the weak." Although Kim and his group were not unequivocally at the apex of the North Korean power system until the 1960s, from that point onward the guerilla experiences of that group became the touchstone of the North Korean state. Only with the physical demise of the Manchurian guerilla group in the 1990s did this emphasis begin to decline, but it still remains an important pillar of North Korean state identity.

Stalinism

The DPRK was founded under a Soviet occupation in the late 1940s when Stalin was at the height of his international power and reputation. Although it is clear in retrospect that Kim was not merely a Soviet puppet, and even at the beginning he appealed often to Korean patriotism and Korea's "complete independence,"[15] the influence of the Stalinist system on the formation of the DPRK is unmistakable. But what Kim took from Stalinism was not the idea of incorporation in a Moscow-dominated international division of labor, which the Soviets tried to impose on North Korea—especially in the Khrushchev period—but the political and economic model of Stalin's USSR along with the idea of "Socialism in one country."[16] In other words, North Korea adopted what it found useful from Stalinism—political centralization (including the "cult of personality"), rapid industrialization, and autarkic development—without simply copying the USSR wholesale or giving more than lip service to "Socialist internationalism." Stalinism added another layer to North Korea's national identity, but probably a less important layer than the guerilla band nationalism that preceded it and the family regime dynamics that developed later.

War Mobilization Regime

No visitor to North Korea even today can escape the feeling that the DPRK is a country at war. The war that began in June 1950 appears in the DPRK media as if it had just begun yesterday, and in fact the Korean War has officially never ended, despite the 1953 armistice. The sense of imminent and mortal threat from the United States, heightened at the time of the Iraq invasion in 2003, has never gone away since the Korean War began. On the one hand, what Selig Harrison has called North Korea's "permanent siege mentality" has helped bond the society together and solidify the unchallenged rule of Kim Il Sung and Kim Jong Il.[17] On the other hand, the American security threat is no mere fiction from Pyongyang's perspective. No other country in the world has faced the threat of nuclear annihilation by the United States for nearly sixty years, as has North Korea; no country has been for so long the explicit target of American attack. It is the condition of war, more than any other single factor, that justifies North Korea's permanent state of emergency.

Anti-Imperialism and "Third-Worldism"

In the 1960s and 1970s North Korea presented itself as a model of postcolonial nation-building, and this idea had more than a few subscribers in the Third World itself. North Korea could argue that it had been founded by antiimperialist fighters, built up an impressive industrial economy, and successfully resisted (albeit with considerable Chinese assistance) the military might of the United States in the Korean War. With no foreign troops on its soil after the withdrawal of the Chinese People's Volunteers in 1958, North Korea looked particularly good in contrast to the South, heavily dependent on U.S. economic assistance and host to tens of thousands of American troops. Externally, the DPRK propaganda line was consistently in favor of anticolonial nationalism and independence throughout the Third World. Kim Il Sung regularly pointed to "U.S. imperialism" as the main enemy of the Third-World peoples, and advocated *juche* as the very embodiment of anti-imperialism. The DPRK portrayed the North Koreans' struggle against the United States and South Korea as identical with the struggle of Third-World peoples for independence, and completely compatible with "proletarian internationalism": "We should unite closely with the peoples of all the socialist countries; we should actively support the Asian, African and Latin American peoples struggling to throw off the imperialist yoke, and strengthen solidarity with them."[18]

This revolutionary spirit was very much in sync with a good many movements for Third-World solidarity in the age of decolonization. When Kim Il Sung visited Indonesia for the tenth anniversary of the Bandung Conference on Afro-Asian Solidarity in 1965 (he had not participated in the original conference in 1955), he articulated *juche* publicly for the first time: "Juche in ideology, independence in politics self-sustenance in the economy and self-defense in national defense—this is the stand our Party has consistently adhered to."[19] It was an idea resonant with a period of global decolonization, and although that time may have long since passed, anti-imperialism and Third-World solidarity still informs North Korean foreign relations today, at least rhetorically—as witnessed, for example, in Supreme People's Assembly president Kim Yong Nam's speech at the 2006 Non-Aligned Movement meeting in Havana.[20]

The Family State and "Military First-ism"

North Korean sovereignty has survived intact the death of its first and most important sovereign. On the third anniversary of Kim Il Sung's death in July 1997, while the North Korean famine was at its peak, a massive obelisk was erected in the center of Pyongyang engraved with the words, "The Great Leader Comrade Kim Il Sung Lives Forever in our Hearts." The slogan was replicated in plaques over the doors of public buildings throughout the capital. In October that year the son of the Great Leader, Kim Jong Il, was elevated to General Secretary of the Korean Workers' Party, the first official title designating him the successor to his father. The body of the Great Leader was thus doubled between the physical body on display in Keumsusan palace and the spirit that "lives forever," expressed in the body of Kim Il Sung thought that, according to the North Korean slogan, can never die. The immortalization of the Great Leader is strikingly resonant with the nature of medieval European kingship described by Ernst Kantorowicz in his classic study *The King's Two Bodies*. Kantorowicz explains that in Christian political theology the king had two legal bodies: the corporeal and mortal body, and the political and immortal body.[21] Analogous to the mystical body of Christ, the latter body was eternal: *le roi ne meurt jamais* ("the king never dies").[22]

In a similar manner, the immortalization of the elder Kim was reinforced at the Tenth Supreme People's Assembly meeting in September 1998 when, contrary to the expectations of most North Korea watchers, Kim Jong Il was not made president in place of his father. Rather, the younger Kim was named head of an enhanced National Defense Committee, and his deceased father was declared in the revised constitution "the eternal State President."[23] As if to further reinforce the Christ-like role of Kim Il Sung's life, the official North Korean calendar was re-dated to start from the year of Kim Il Sung's birth (1912) and dubbed the "Juche Calendar." Time itself was officially divided into "Before Kim" and "After Kim."

The successful passage of power from father to son has established North Korea as the first Socialist family state.[24] At the same time, North Korea has become explicitly a military-led regime under the slogan *seongun cheongch'i* ("military-first politics"). Even the term *seongun sasang* ("military-first ideology") has emerged in North Korean media over the last few years, apparently superseding *juche* ideology, the latter used much less frequently now than in the past.[25] Along with the rise of military ideology has come an overt emphasis on Korean ethnic nationalism (*minjokchueui*, or *minjok cheiljueui*, literally "nation-first-ism"). Some analysts have argued that North Korea is no longer Socialist in any meaningful sense, if indeed it ever was.[26] But what military first-ism and ethnic nationalism seem to suggest is that even the veneer of Marxist-Leninist Socialism has now been removed, and North Korea is revealed in its true nature as a highly nationalistic, militarized, and defensive state that places sovereignty above all other ideological and economic concerns.

3. The Post–Post Cold War: North Korea with/against the World

Since the end of the 1990s, after the consolidation of Kim Jong Il's power and the solidification of the military in control of the machinery of state, North Korea has gone forward both with internal economic reform and a cautious reconnection with the outside world. The Pyongyang summit meeting between Kim Jong Il and Kim Dae Jung in June 2000 was an important symbol of the latter, the economic reforms beginning in the summer of 2002 were the most dramatic development to date of the former. But for North Korea, the key both to improving its economic conditions and its relationship with the outside world was to establish a new, less hostile relationship with the United States. Between the first inter-Korean summit of June 2000 and the second summit of October 2007, North-South relations were on a gradual upward path, while the American relationship with North Korea went on a roller-coaster ride from bilateral engagement under Clinton, to confrontation under Bush, to multilateral engagement, to a crisis over North Korean missile and nuclear weapons tests, and finally to a new set of diplomatic agreements. North-South relations were inextricably tied to the United States: for South Korea, the United States was its most important ally; for North Korea, an improved relationship with the United States was seen as the key to improving its economy and ensuring its security.

While North Korea went forward with its internal reform, its engagement with the South went quietly forward as well, primarily in the economic area. But the improvement of ties with the United States, which Pyongyang had pursued in close connection to its policy toward the South, and which had built considerable momentum in the Clinton administration, ground almost to a halt with the beginning of the Bush presidency in 2001. The reverse-course in America's North Korea policy under Bush, and the second nuclear crisis that erupted in late 2002, revealed a profound disconnect between U.S. and South Korean policy toward North Korea. Not until early 2007 were the two allies fully in sync in a policy of engagement toward the North (although the United States studiously avoided the word "engagement," much like North Korea had earlier avoided the word "reform"). The DPRK responded harshly to George W. Bush's condemnation of North Korea as part of the "axis of evil" along with Iran and Iraq in the president's State of the Union address in January 2002. A Foreign Ministry spokesman called the Bush speech "little short of declaring war against the DPRK" and accused the U.S. administration of "political immaturity and moral leprosy."[27] In contrast to the condemnation of terrorism and de facto sympathy for the United States right after September 11, the DPRK spokesman suggested that the United States had only itself to blame: "Herein lie answers to questions as to why the modern terrorism is focused on the U.S. alone and why it has become serious while Bush is in office."[28] North-South relations were dampened considerably by the Bush administration's statements. It took a visit to Pyongyang by Kim Dae Jung's special envoy Lim Dong Won in early April to get inter-Korean dialogue restarted. On April 28, Pyongyang agreed to resume reunion meetings of separated family members and to move forward with high-level contacts and economic cooperation. On August 11–14 the first ministerial-level North-South meetings in nearly a year took place in Seoul. At the same time, the two sides marked the fifty-seventh anniversary of liberation from Japanese colonial rule on August 15 with an unprecedented joint celebration, including the visit of more than one hundred North Korean delegates to Seoul.

Washington-Pyongyang relations also showed signs of thaw in late July and early August 2002, when Secretary of State Colin Powell met briefly with North Korea's foreign minister at an ASEAN meeting in Brunei, and the Bush administration sent Jack L. Pritchard as its first official envoy to the DPRK. Pritchard, who had met with Pyongyang's ambassador to the United Nations several weeks earlier in New York, went to North Korea in early August for the ceremony marking the start of construction on the first light-water nuclear reactor to be built by KEDO, the U.S.–South Korean–Japanese consortium formed under the auspices of the 1994 Agreed Framework. And on the DPRK-Japan side, Prime Minister Koizumi's unprecedented summit meeting with Kim Jong Il in Pyongyang in September, where Kim made his extraordinary admission that North Korea had abducted over a dozen Japanese citizens in the 1970s and 1980s, seemed at first to open up a new era in Japan–North Korea relations and start the two countries on the road to normalization. It turned out, however, that the Japanese media and public response to these revelations would illicit such feelings of hostility toward North Korea that normal relations appeared to be farther away than ever in subsequent months.

The belated and tentative moves toward restarting U.S.-DPRK dialogue in late summer and early fall 2002 were dramatically derailed by the "Kelly revelations" of October. On October 16, the U.S. State Department announced that, some eleven days earlier, Assistant Secretary of State James A. Kelly had confronted his counterparts in Pyongyang with evidence that North Korea had "a program to enrich uranium for nuclear weapons, in violation of the Agreed Framework and other agreements." According to U.S. accounts (North Korea later denied the accusation), the DPRK officials acknowledged the existence of this program and declared the Agreed Framework "nullified."[29] But North Korea insisted that the United States was to blame for the failure of the Agreed Framework, and offered to enter a new set of talks to resolve the crisis. The United States repeatedly refused to negotiate with North Korea before Pyongyang ceased all of its nuclear-related activities, and in November Washington suspended deliveries of fuel oil to North Korea, required under the Agreed Framework. This was followed by a rapidly escalating set of moves on the part of North Korea toward restarting its plutonium program, frozen by the 1994 Agreement: Pyongyang announced its intention to reopen its nuclear power plant at Yongbyon, expelled International Atomic Energy Agency (IAEA) inspectors at the end of December 2002, announced its withdrawal from the Nuclear Proliferation Treaty (NPT) in January 2003, and began to remove spent nuclear fuel rods from storage in February—the latter an act that had brought the United States and North Korea to the brink of war in 1994.

While the crisis in U.S.-DPRK relations deepened in 2003, North-South relations continued to move forward. Indeed, a distinctive aspect of the 2002–2003 crisis was the common ground Pyongyang could find with the Seoul government in criticizing the American approach to Korea. This was the reverse of the 1993–1994 crisis, in which the South Korean government of Kim Young Sam deeply feared U.S.-DPRK "collusion" at the expense of South Korea's national interest. This is not to say that Seoul-Pyongyang relations became cordial or that Seoul suddenly broke its ties with Washington; Seoul decried North Korea's development of nuclear weapons, for example, and Pyongyang attacked the Roh Moo Hyun government for agreeing to send

South Korean troops to Iraq. Roh visited Washington in May, and he and President Bush tried to put a unified face on their policy toward North Korea; Pyongyang condemned the Roh-Bush joint statement as an act which goes against the basic spirit of the June 15 North-South Declaration. But various agreements and meetings between the ROK and DPRK went ahead despite the new nuclear crisis, including a seven-point agreement on inter-Korean economic relations, signed by the representatives of North and South Korea in Pyongyang in late May. The two sides agreed on the establishment of a special Industrial Complex in the North Korean city of Gaesong, reconnection of east and west coast railway lines, and other joint projects. The agreement was presented positively and in detail in the DPRK media, although it was uncertain whether much could come of it until the conflict between Pyongyang and Washington was resolved.

In April 2003 North Korean, American, and Chinese officials met in Beijing to discuss a way out of the impasse. North Korea dropped hints of developing its own nuclear deterrent. The United States, while stating it did not intend to attack the DPRK, acted as if coercion and pressure alone would resolve the problem—by North Korea either giving in to American demands or collapsing. Finally, however, the six parties of North and South Korea, China, Russia, Japan, and the United States agreed to hold talks on the issue. The six-party process had begun, setting off a new cycle of "crisis diplomacy."

In September 2004, the DPRK announced its unwillingness to proceed to a fourth round of talks. At a speech at the UN General Assembly by DPRK vice foreign minister Choe Su-hon. The main reason North Korea could not participate in further talks, Choe said, was the "hostile policy" of the United States, especially its insistence on complete, verifiable, irreversible dismantling of nuclear weapons (CVID) and its real intention of overthrowing the North Korean regime. In light of this, "the DPRK is left with no other option but to possess a nuclear deterrent."[30] At a press conference following the speech, Choe clarified the point that North Korea had already reprocessed the 8,000 spent fuel rods from the Yongbyon plant and "weaponized" the material. Nevertheless, Choe said, North Korea would still be willing to dismantle its nuclear program if the United States abandoned its hostile policy and normalized relations with the DPRK. In other words, North Korea was still playing the same game of brinksmanship from the early 1990s. In effect, North Korea was revealing its hand, claiming to actually possess nuclear weapons rather than leaving the issue ambiguous. The next step would have to be a North Korean underground nuclear test. North Korea did in fact return for a fourth round of talks, which established a rather vague agreement for Korean denuclearization on September 19, 2005. A fifth round ended in November after the United States announced it would freeze North Korean bank assets in

Macau, at the Banco Delta Asia (BDA), due to suspicion that North Korea was using the bank to launder money for illicit purposes. The North Korea missile launches of July 2006 were probably, in part, a response to this American action.[31] Finally came the nuclear test of October 9.

The effects of these North Korean provocations on North-South relations were less than one might have expected, despite South Korea's agreement to UN Security Council Resolution 1695 in response to the July missile test, and the much more strongly worded Resolution 1718, following the October nuclear weapon test. For example, South Korea agreed with the sanctions called for in the latter resolution, but later indicated that it would not intercept North Korean cargo ships to enforce the sanctions, as the United States had requested.[32] Nor would South Korea's projects in Keumgang Mountain tourism and the Kaeseong Industrial Complex be discontinued. The Roh government was widely criticized domestically for its lack of concrete response to the North Korean nuclear test, despite its initial criticism of the North Korean action. For Seoul, engagement with the North and maintaining "peace and prosperity" on the Korean peninsula was seen as more important than resolving the nuclear issue; in a very short time, South Korea's policy toward the North was essentially back to business as usual.[33] The leverage that economic interaction had supposedly given the South over the North failed to deter North Korea from actions universally condemned by the international community, including the UN Security Council. In the end, even the United States appeared to back down from its condemnation, offering a set of incentives for North Korea to return to the six-party talks.[34] Once again, the world had pulled back from the brink over North Korea.

North Korea did return to the talks, and the result was the agreement of February 13, 2007, which called for the DPRK to shut down and abandon its Yongbyon reactor, invite back IAEA inspectors, and fully reveal the extent of its nuclear program. In exchange, the United States and Japan would move toward normalization of ties with the DPRK, and they and other countries would offer energy and humanitarian assistance to North Korea.[35] The agreement, greeted as a major breakthrough in the nuclear crisis by all parties concerned, hit its first roadblock the following month when North Korea was unable to retrieve its $25 million frozen in Macao's BDA. Pyongyang refused to go forward with its part of the February 13 Agreement until the funds were released, and the sixty-day deadline for shutting down the Yongbyon plant on April 13 came and went. Eventually, with some assistance from Russia and Hill's personal visit to Pyongyang in June, the BDA funds were released. North Korea followed by shutting down its reactor in July, and the six parties proceeded to a sixth round of talks in Beijing from September 27 to 30, just days before the second inter-Korean summit. The result of the sixth round of six-party talks was a joint statement, released by the Chinese Foreign Ministry on October 3, which added more substance to the framework established in the February 13 agreement.[36] This time, North Korea promised that it would shut down its nuclear facilities in Yongbyon and "provide a complete and correct declaration of all its nuclear programs in accordance with the February 13 agreement" by the end of 2007. Furthermore, Pyongyang reaffirmed its promise not to transfer nuclear materials, technology, or know-how. The United States and Japan, for their part, reaffirmed their commitments to move toward normalization of relations with the DPRK; furthermore, North Korea would receive the equivalent of up to one million tons of heavy fuel oil—twice as much as in the 1994 Agreed Framework—in an arrangement to be worked out by a Working Group on Economy and Energy Cooperation. Less than a year after Pyongyang's nuclear test, the mood around the North Korean nuclear test had changed from visions of the apocalypse to hopes for peace and economic cooperation.

This cooperative spirit was doubly reinforced by the concurrent Second Inter-Korean Summit. At the time the six-party agreement was being finalized, Roh Moo Hyun met Kim Jong Il in Pyongyang between October 2 and 4. The summit had originally been scheduled for late August, but North Korea had requested a postponement due to severe flooding in the North that summer. The resulting eight-point agreement signed on October 4, more detailed and specific than the June 2000 agreement, outlined a wide range of cooperative activities. Prior to and during the summit, Roh had emphasized economic cooperation, which was embodied in Article 5 of the agreement; among other things, the two sides agreed to create a second special economic zone in the area of Haeju. But perhaps the most interesting section—from the perspective of the other countries in the six-party process—was Article 4, which recognized "the need to end the current armistice regime and build a permanent peace regime." For this, "the leaders of the three or four parties directly concerned" would "convene on the Peninsula and declare an end to the war."[37]

For North Korea, the six-party agreement and the second Pyongyang Declaration must have appeared as clear foreign policy successes. North Korea's primary adversaries arguably conceded more than Pyongyang. North Korea agreed to disable its Yongbyon nuclear facilities and declare its nuclear programs, but in exchange it received promises of aid and movement toward normalization from both the United States and Japan. The United States in particular, after years of tough talk and name-calling, made an almost complete reversal in its policy and entered into an agreement with North Korea strikingly similar to the 1994 Agreed Framework that the Bush administration once loathed. As far as the South was concerned, inter-Korean economic "cooperation" would mean, for the foreseeable future, South Korean aid to and investment in the North. And, for perhaps the first time, there seemed to be a real prospect for a new peace regime on the Korean Peninsula. All of this is premised on the continued existence of North Korea more or less in its present form. "Regime change" is not in the cards for anyone. Against great odds, the DPRK has managed to preserve its sovereignty and convince the world that it is not likely to disappear any time soon.

But it is not only North Korea that has existed in a state of exception. Since September 11, 2001, the president of the United States has claimed significantly increased powers in an open-ended "global war on terror." As Agamben has pointed out, this corresponds very closely to Carl Schmitt's *Ausnahmezustand*.[38] But the contemporary American case may be more dangerous than an "ordinary" state of exception. Schmitt believed that conflicts between nations were endemic, and that an "enemy" was both normal and necessary for the sovereign state. But he feared the global consequences of a state justifying its actions on the basis of universal principles, turning the enemy into "an outlaw of humanity." Under the guise of ridding humanity once and for all of evil, "a war waged to protect or expand economic power must, with the aid of propaganda, turn into a crusade and into the last war of humanity."[39] The first George W. Bush administration seemed determined to carry out such a crusade, and remove such inconvenient states as Iraq, Iran, and North Korea from the face of the earth. In the last few years the United States has been greatly chastened in these ambitions. Perhaps the normalization of relations between North Korea and the United States can help to extricate both from their states of exceptions, and return us to a more normal condition of conflictual—and even cooperative—politics.

Notes

1. Carl Schmitt, *Political Theology: Four Chapters on the Concept of Sovereignty*, trans. and intro. by George Schwab (Chicago: University of Chicago Press, 2005 [1934]), 5.

2. For one typically immodest expression of the *juche* idea as national sovereignty, see "A Brilliant Example of the Building of a Sovereign State," *Immortal Juche Idea* (Pyongyang, NK: Foreign Languages Publishing House, 1979), 162–82.

3. Brian Myers points out that both foreign scholars and the DPRK itself have greatly exaggerated Kim's 1955 "Juche Speech" as a watershed in North Korean political development. See Myers, "The Watershed That Wasn't: Re-evaluating Kim Il Sung's 'Juche Speech' of 1955," *Acta Koreana* 9, no. 1 (January 2006): 89–115.

4. R. B. J. Walker, "Foreword," in *Sovereignty and Subjectivity*, Jenny Edkins, Nalini Persram, and Veronique Pin-Fat, eds. (Boulder, Colo.: Lynne Rienner, 1999), xiii.

5. Jens Bartelson, *A Genealogy of Sovereignty* (Cambridge: Cambridge University Press, 1995), 186–236.

6. Giorgio Agamben, *State of Exception,* trans. Kevin Attell (Chicago: University of Chicago Press, 2005), 4.

7. Schmitt, *Political Theology,* 5–8.

8. Cited in Agamben, *State of Exception,* 6.

9. David G. Marr, "Concepts of 'Individual' and 'Self' in Twentieth-Century Vietnam," *Modern Asian Studies* 34, no. 4 (2000): 769–96. See also Lydia Liu, *Translingual Practice: Literature, National Culture, and Translated Modernity—China, 1900–1937* (Stanford, Calif.: Stanford University Press, 1995).

10. Bruce Cumings, "Corporatism in North Korea," *Journal of Korean Studies* 4 (1982–1983), 269–94.

11. J. Victor Koschmann, *Revolution and Subjectivity in Postwar Japan* (Chicago: University of Chicago Press, 1996). It may be that the Japanese intellectuals' use of the term *shutaisei* in the 1940s and 1950s directly influenced the development of North Korean *juche* ideology, as there was a fair amount of intellectual exchange between Japan and North Korea at that time, but the use of *juche sasang* appears to be more resonant with the wartime mobilization of the 1930s.

12. Han S. Park, *North Korea: The Politics of Unconventional Wisdom* (Boulder, Colo.: Lynne Rienner, 2002).

13. Schmitt, *Political Theology,* 36.

14. Wada Haruki, *Kin nichisei to manshū kōnichi sensō* [Kim Il Sung and the Anti-Japanese War in Manchuria] (Tokyo: Heibonsha, 1992).

15. Bruce Cumings, *The Origins of the Korean War,* vol. 2, *The Roaring of the Cataract, 1947–1950* (Princeton, N.J.: Princeton University Press, 1990), 312.

16. Balazs Szalontai, *Kim Il Sung in the Khrushchev Era: Soviet-DPRK Relations and the Roots of North Korean Despotism, 1953–1964* (Stanford, Calif.: Stanford University Press, 2005).

17. Selig S. Harrison, *Korean Endgame: A Strategy for Reunification and U.S. Disengagement* (Princeton, N.J.: Princeton University Press, 2002), 8.

18. Kim Il Sung, *On the Juche Idea* (New York: The Guardian, 1980), 262.

19. Kim Il Sung, "On Socialist Construction in the Democratic People's Republic of Korea and the South Korean Revolution," *Selected Works* (Pyongyang, NK: Foreign Languages Publishing House, 1971), 230.

20. "Kim Yong Nam Calls for NAM's Increased Role," Korean Central News Agency, September 19, 2006, at www.kcna.co.jp/item/2006/200609/news09/19.htm.

21. Ernst Kantorowicz, *The King's Two Bodies: A Study in Mediaeval Political Theology* (Princeton, N.J.: Princeton University Press, 1959).

22. Cited in Giorgio Agamben, *Homo Sacer: Sovereign Power and Bare Life,* tran. Daniel Heelr-Roazen (Stanford, Calif.: Stanford University Press, 1998), 92.

23. Stephen W. Linton, "Life After Death in North Korea," in *Korea Briefing: Toward Reunification,* David R. McCann, ed., (Armonk, N.Y.: M. E. Sharpe, 1997), 83–85.

24. Charles K. Armstrong, "Familism, Socialism, and Political Religion in North Korea," *Totalitarian Movements and Political Religion* 6, no. 3 (December 2005), 383–94.

25. "Seongun sasangeun uri sidae jajuwieopeui pilseung pulpaeeui kicniida" [Military-First Ideology Is an Ever-Victorious, Invincible Banner for Our Era's Cause of Independence], *Rodong sinmun,* March 21, 2003, 1.

26. Ruediger Frank, "The End of Socialism and a Wedding Gift for the Groom? The True Meaning of the Military First Policy," Nautilus Institute DPRK Briefing Book, December 11, 2003, at www.nautilus.org/DPRKBriefingBook/transition /Ruediger_Socialism.html.

27. "Spokesman for DPRK Foreign Ministry Slams Bush's Accusations," Korean Central News Agency, January 31, 2002, at www.kcna.co.jp/index-e.htm.

28. "Spokesman for DPRK Foreign Ministry Slams Bush's Accusations," Korean Central News Agency.

29. James Kelly, "Ensuring a Korean Peninsula Free of Nuclear Weapons, Remarks to the Research Conference—North Korea: Toward a New International Engagement Framework," February 13, 2004, at www.nautilus.org/DPRKBriefingBook/multilateral Talks/Kelly_NKChanceforRedemption.html.

30. Cited in CanKor Virtual ThinkNet on Korean Peace and Security, No. 181, October 1, 2004, at www.cankor.ligi.ubc.ca/index.html.

31. Leon V. Sigal, "What North Korea's Missile Test Means," Nautilus Institute Policy Forum Online 06-62A, July 27th, 2006, at www.nautilus.org/fora/security/0662Sigal. html.

32. Norimitsu Onishi, "South Korea Won't Intercept Cargo Ships From the North," *New York Times*, November 14, 2006.

33. International Crisis Group, "North Korea's Nuclear Test: The Fallout," *Asia Briefing*, no. 56 (November 13, 2006): 8.

34. See Nautilus Institute, NAPSNet Daily Report, December 6, 2006, at www .nautilus.org/napsnet/dr/2006/dec/ndr06dec06.html#item1.

35. See www.state.gov/r/pa/prs/ps/2007/february/80479.htm.

36. For the full text of the agreement, see www.chinaconsulatesf.org/eng/xw/ t369084.htm.

37. "Declaration on the Advancement of South-North Korean Relations, Peace and Prosperity," at www.korea.net/news/news/newsView.asp?serial_no=20071004023. The ambiguous phrase "three or four parties" appears to reflect the fact that South Korea is not a signatory to the armistice, which was signed by representatives from China, North Korea, and the United States (representing the United Nations).

38. Agamben, *State of Exception*, 22.

39. Carl Schmitt, *The Concept of the Political*, trans. and intro. George Schwab (Chicago: University of Chicago Press, 1996 [1932]), 79.

3

Biopolitics or the Logic of Sovereign Love—Love's Whereabouts in North Korea

Sonia Ryang

H OW DOES A NORTH KOREAN find worth in another human being?

Without this act of investment, a society would collapse. To find another individual worth noticing, helping, and caring for, worthy of protection or education, or worthy of minimal respect would be an imperative force for any society to be viable.

Let us call this, heuristically, "love"—as in Simone Weil's words: "Among human beings, only the existence of those we love is fully recognized. Belief in the existence of other human beings as such is love."[1]

In any society, love thus defined creates engagement, interaction, and relationship among humans. In the United States, we assume that love is available or flows among the population in diverse, uncircumscribed, and (mostly) unprescribed directions. Although this does not cancel out the hierarchy of love, we assume here that we tend to be both recipients and givers of love, mostly at the same time.

In this chapter, I explore love's whereabouts in North Korea. In order to do this, I shall make a conceptual detour by using the notion of the sovereign, reaching the endpoint of biopolitics, or the logic of sovereign love in North Korea. In this way, I would like to touch upon the question of totalitarianism, though only in a preliminary way.[2]

1. Preliminary Note (I)

In order to develop my contention, I wish to draw attention to the work of Giorgio Agamben and Georges Bataille, who both discuss the notion of the sovereign, albeit it in slightly different ways, yet touching upon a crucial key to understanding love in North Korea. I shall refer to these two thinkers' notions in a synthesized and embedded manner below.[3]

Topology

Agamben, following Carl Schmitt, declares that the sovereign is one that decides and, most definitively, the one that decides on his exception. He becomes the law by exempting himself from law. The shape of his existence manifests most clearly in an emergency, such as the state of exception under martial law: He is the one who declares martial law, to which everyone must submit, while he is accorded exceptional power and remains above this order. Thus, national emergencies such as wars enable the sovereign exception to emerge unambiguously and be accepted unproblematically. In this scheme, he is simultaneously the law and above the law. He decides on everything, including his own exception from his decisions.

Morphology

Bataille's exploration of the sovereign emphasizes his capacity to pursue consumption for the sake of consumption, pleasure for the sake of pleasure. He does not produce and does not consume as a reward of production. He does not love others—does not find worth in others—and loves only himself. He is not bound by necessity. He lives in excess. He lives for the sake of living, not for the sake of achieving a set of goals. His life itself is the end, not a means.

Paradox

In Greek terms, *bios* (life) is politically and socially meaningful life; *zoē* (life) is life that any living being can claim, life that is bare and simple. The sovereign, therefore, has a life whose *bios* completely overlaps with *zoē*. His life is most politicized (through his mere existence), and his life is most bare (again, through mere existence). Thus, he could be an entity that is either alive or dead, it being irrelevant whether or not he has "human" life. The only thing that matters is that he exists, topologically and morphologically.

2. Preliminary Note (II)

According to North Korean rhetoric, it is the people or *inmin* who possess sovereignty or *jukweon*. However, from the above exercise it can be seen that the form of existence that has all the attributes of the sovereign in North Korea is the Leader or *suryeong*. Whether it has to be the now deceased Kim Il Sung or his son, current Leader Kim Jong Il, matters less. It is the Leader's *position* and *form* that decide who the sovereign is. An exploration of the unique characteristics of the North Korean sovereign is in order.

The Loving Leader

Pace Bataille, the North Korean sovereign is loving. He is presupposed to love the *inmin* endlessly and, hence, the mechanism of "returning" his love is secured. This is the key to understanding how human worth in North Korea is perceived among its population.

Self and Leader

The concepts of self and the individual are crucial in North Korea, unlike what is usually assumed to be the case in a totalitarian society. Not as elements of a collective or group, but individuals as individuals are each responsible for their own moral-ideological purity, discipline, and perfection. This includes bodily perfection (see below). Thus, often, even one's own family members are irrelevant. The most valued and exclusive human connection in North Korean society is that between individuals (each isolated and in separation from the other) and the sovereign Leader.

Paradox

Thus, individuals acquire the status of sovereign being by way of connecting with the sovereign Leader. In this sense, paradoxically, *inmin* are indeed sovereign, but only via their fusion with the sovereign Leader. In North Korea, living (and dying) for Him becomes the highest and most noble goal in life. This must not be understood as a one-sided devotion or sacrifice on the part of the population. As proposed by Charles Lindholm in his study of charisma, this connection with the sovereign is preconditioned by the self-elevation on the part of the followers by way of being one with Him.[4]

3. Political Life as Sovereign Love's Creation

Jeongchijeok saengmyeong or political life, argued North Korea's literary theorists in the 1980s, is the most decisive factor distinguishing new human beings fit to live in the age of *juche* from all other forms of human existence. *Juche* is shorthand for the philosophy of Kim Il Sung. Denoting master (*ju*) and body (*che*), the idea of *juche* insists on self-determination and self-reliance (see below). "The age of Juche is fundamentally distinguished from all historical ages that preceded it. It posits the historical task of having to clarify the precise directions and methodology of constructing, creating, and developing a literary art that is compatible with the demands of the new age. . . ."[5]

In this age of *juche*, a new type of human being is created. "The new human model that fits our time is that of the communistic human of the Juche type. The Juche type communistic human [*juchehyeong eui kongsanjueuijeok ingan*] is a passionate revolutionary and authentic communist that possesses the purest and cleanest loyalty and sincerity toward the *suryeong* and the party."[6] It is important to remember that in the 1980s, North Korean rhetoric used the term *tang* or the party to refer to the Leader's son, Kim Jong Il. Occasionally, it referred to him as *hugyeja* or the successor, but more often, it utilized the expressions *tang, uri tang,* or *tang jungang:* the party, our party, or the party center.

For this new type of human, the utmost meaning is found in the context of political life.

> Humans are social beings and therefore, for them, *jajuseong* (self-mastery) is life. . . . That a human being strives to realize his self-mastery corresponds to . . . enhancing one's political life. For humans, whose life is self-mastery, political and social life is more important than bio-physical life. If a human does not have socially and politically meaningful life [i.e. *bios*], he has no true life. . . .[7]

So, how does one obtain such a "political life"? The answer is: "Endless loyalty toward the Great *suryeong* is the most fundamental quality of a communist [of our age]. Only when one is loyal to the *suryeong* does one gain political life [*jeongchijeok saengmyeong*]."[8]

One gains it by being endlessly loyal (loving) toward the *suryeong,* while only the *suryeong* can provide this to one—a tautologous self-propagation.

> Humans' bio-physical life is given to them by their parents, but their political life is given by the *suryeong* and nurtured by the party. Just as bio-physical life is unthinkable without parents, we cannot speak of human political life away from the bosom of the party and the *suryeong.* The political life that our *inmin* possess today is the most valuable political life that is given by the Great *suryeong* and nurtured by the glorious party.[9]

But, then, the existence that embodies the most valuable form of life for humans, political life, is the Leader, the sovereign, the *suryeong.* "The *suryeong* is the heart of the revolution and the brain of the *inmin.* . . . The *suryeong* is the utmost embodiment of the interests of the party, the revolution, the working class, and the *inmin*, and his ideas are the collective will of the party, the working class, and the *inmin*."[10] Note here that the *suryeong* is in each individual's heart and brain, yet at the same time, he leads them the entire population. Likewise,

> The *suryeong* is the possessor of the most noble humanity and the embodiment of the most benevolent nature. Because of this, the *suryeong* receives the *inmin*'s endless respect and reverence, its absolute trust and support. . . . Our respected and beloved *suryeong*, Comrade Kim Il Sung, embodies the greatest human qualities, equipped with the warmest love and majestic revolutionary camaraderie for the *inmin*, the biggest heart and capacity to tolerate and accept [anyone], endless modesty and the most simple grace. Our respected and beloved *suryeong* has attained the most noble [form of] communistic human love that no other human has ever attained. . . .[11]

Does this mean that the creator is swallowed and internalized by its creations, as if to say that the creator is conceived by the creation? Note, again, the inherently tautologous, circular nature of the connection between the *suryeong* and each individual member of the *inmin*.

Most interestingly, the sovereign's love is said to have already been in existence solely due to the autochthonous nature of sovereign love; that is to say, the sovereign already possesses the capacity for love toward the *inmin*. It is the *inmin* that need to learn to love the sovereign in return for this preemptively declared love by the sovereign for them. Thus, although a tautologous logic, in fact, a one-sided demand of love for the sovereign is constantly made of the *inmin*. We may recognize here the morphology of the sovereign: the sovereign lives in excess (an excess of love siphoned up from the *inmin*); the sovereign does not produce but consumes (consumes the love of the *inmin*); the sovereign exists for the sake of existence, plays for the sake of play, lives for the sake of living; the sovereign makes himself the exception purely by being, existing.

4. Love's Perpetual Triangle

Love in North Korean literature is always achieved via the lovers' devotion for the *suryeong*. They recognize each other's human worth by measuring and examining the depth, breadth, and, above all, authenticity of the loyalty shown to the sovereign Leader. Without this quality, no one in North Korea is worthy of love or even deserves to live. Every novel, regardless of its motif, background, theme, or assortment of protagonist, has the *suryeong* at its core (or what North Korean literary theory calls *chongja* or the seed of the story).

Because of the way the sovereign is loved by the population as the absolute object of adoration, yet also due to the party's demand for the production of *sahoejueui sasiljueui munhak* or Socialist realist literature, North Korean writers face an extraordinary task in having to depict personal relationships between individuals in parallel with (or, in reality, in subordination to) the sovereign-self connection. Love in North Korean literature is perpetually ridden with triangular contradictions, but such triangles link two individuals on the basis of the loyalty each demonstrates for the sovereign. They love each other because the other loves the *suryeong*.

Here, I draw illustrations from a North Korean novel, *Yonggwangro neun sumsuinda* or "The ironworks furnace is breathing" by Yun Se-Jung.[12] North Korean novels are filled with examples of war stories, labor/construction stories, and farm/production stories. Intellectual protagonists and college life, for example, may be depicted, but mainly in subordination to *hyeonjang* or the field, and such contexts never provide the scene for the climax of a story. In other words, all important events, including Kim Il Sung's direct guidance, happen at sites of construction or production or on the battlefield. *Yonggwangro* is an example of a story located at a site of construction.

Set in the mid-1950s, it is a story of ironworkers facing the arduous task of having to reconstruct the main furnace, which was destroyed in U.S. air raids during the Korean War. Typical for a North Korean story, technical difficulties are overcome by the concerted hard labor of the workers, party supervisors, and technicians, and the story reaches its climax with the scene of a gigantic furnace being erected amidst the fanfare and passionate cheering of the heroic working class. Along the way, complex human relations are depicted.

The story revolves around the main protagonists, who are all male: Sang-Beom, the chief technician; Il-Byeok, the head manager; and Taek-Su, the party supervisor. A subcategory under these three includes another group of male workers of lower rank who nevertheless play an enthusiastic role in overcoming difficulties whenever the team faces a problem. Then, there are a couple of reactionaries, one an alleged *kancheop*, or spy, sent by the *migugnom*, or American wretches, and the other an opportunist that joined him. Finally, there are a few women, including Hak-Sil, who lost her husband during the war and later marries Sang-Beom, who also lost his wife and baby during the war; Yeong-Ae, a young, hardworking girl who plays a key role in revealing the reactionaries' subversive plot; and *halmeoni*, or the Grandmother, Sang-Beom's mother, who functions as an element to make the story appear more realistic, as she speaks old-fashioned Korean, for example. Women unanimously occupy comparatively minor roles in the novel.

The First Connection

Human relations between the lead male workers are depicted as very important. They are in constant interaction with each other, relentlessly critical, yet overwhelmingly generous and warm-hearted toward each other, and even after many confrontations and disagreements, ultimately cooperative and mutually respectful. They admire each other's strengths and respect each other's intellectual and other capacities. But, above all, they express their utmost mutual respect and deep friendship when they renew their pledges to be eternally loyal to the Great Leader. On the other hand, when they notice that any of them are lacking in courage or weak in their determination to do their best in demonstrating their loyalty to the Leader, they tolerate not even a hint of compromise or impurity. Upon receiving genuinely supportive criticism from their comrades, they candidly admit their weaknesses and shortcomings and go through the most honest and thorough self-criticism in order to rejoin the rank of the committed revolutionaries. Let us now look at one such scene.

It was late at night. Sang-Beom knocked on the door of the ironworks party committee office . . .

"Comrade Sang-Beom, long time since I saw you last . . . How are things?"

The [committee] chairman warmly welcomed Sang-Beom with a smile. The chairman had already been briefed about today's technical meeting [at the works, in which Sang-Beom had fiercely confronted Il-Byeok, the manager], but he kept quiet about it and let Sang-Beom in.

"Comrade Chairman, I have something that I need to talk about with you."

The chairman sensed something serious in Sang-Beom's expression and asked, "What is it?"

"It's a little difficult to tell you this, but I'd like to request to be sent to the factory. I'm unable to continue my technical duties any more. I don't think I have the capacity for them."

Sang-Beom had been supervised by this chairman since the end of the war and, therefore, he felt close enough to him to bring this up directly.

"So, who should be in charge of building the furnace, then?"

The chairman spoke unexpectedly coldly. Sang-Beom hesitated, but said, "I can make a better contribution to building the furnace by working in the factory. My current responsibilities are beyond my capability. It is painful."

The chairman smiled in his mind [and said],

"I am not disregarding your intention . . ."

The chairman adjusted the way he sat in the chair, and continued, "I have a request . . . You are a person who works for the party . . . you are here because the party trusts you. You will receive greater responsibilities in the future. The manager also is someone who is trying to fulfill his duty. Why couldn't you work with him?"

Sang-Beom lost his words and kept quiet.

"What do you think? Comrade Sang-Beom, do you understand what I'm saying?"

Sang-Beom inhaled a deep breath and continued his silence . . .

[The chairman said to Sang-Beom]

"I'd like to tell you something that I've been wanting to tell you lately. You are definitely compromising your quality as a member of the party. You must first understand that. You are now trying to abandon the duty that you owe to the party and that's why I'm thinking you are losing your focus on the party. If it were an order from the party, one must not hesitate in jumping into fire or water. You are trying to run away from difficulties. Think about the invincible will and revolutionary spirit of the [anti-Japanese guerrilla] fighters, who were endlessly loyal to the Great Leader Comrade Kim Il Sung. Our revolutionary tradition is teaching us [that we need to be like them]. If one were armed with the genuine working class spirit, one would never retreat from the revolutionary front, even if one were to be knocked down [by difficulties]. So, do you want to retire from the revolution?"

Sang-Beom was made to feel deep [emotions] by these words, and lowered his head. He first wondered about whom the chairman was saying these things. And then, when he realized that it was actually himself that the chairman was criticizing, he became alert.

"Comrade Chairman, that's a little too . . ."

Sang-Beom could not conclude his sentence.

"You think these words are too harsh? But, I'm forced to say these to you. Your spiritual state is making me say these words!"

Sang-Beom lowered his head again.

"I'm sorry, Comrade Chairman. Please forgive me."

"What are you asking forgiveness for from me?"

"I shall never say the things that I have just said to you ever again."

Sang-Beom looked very sad. The chairman stood up.

"Please, sit down. Let's talk a bit more. Here, take a cigarette."

The chairman took out his cigarette case and lit one for himself, offering another to Sang-Beom.

"I fully understand that you have not been able to develop a good friendship with the other cadre members at work . . . You have become an oil drop in a puddle . . . How come? It is of course admirable that one should be critical of errors and miscalculations. But, it is more important not to be isolated from the rest of the party members. I'm not saying that you must forget about principles and just follow whatever others say. I'm telling you how important it is to live and work in a close and integrated fashion with other members of the party cadre and at the same time take initiative, just like a model core member and master of [your own work place]. We face difficulties all the time. But it is the core members that have to face these difficulties more willingly [than others]. Comrade Sang-Beom, do you understand my words?"

Sang-Beom somehow felt that something that had been blocking his vision had been suddenly removed, and felt fresh.

(That's right. I have not attained the best quality as a member of the party.)

He murmured in his mind.

"Comrade Chairman, I do understand [your words]. I've just realized so many things. I shall strive to improve my quality as a member of the party."

Sang-Beom was excited and his voice was trembling. The party chairman smiled to himself and accepted Sang-Beom's renewed determination.

Sang-Beom left the chairman's office and headed for his office. He felt as if he had acquired a set of wings. He was happy.

(Ah, I've been a limited person. I have not realized how I should live as a member of the party. The chairman is right. I must become a genuine master of our new society and a core member of the party cadre. I have lived without these realizations. Why did I not understand that the manager also is trying to do his best? Why did I not have a bigger heart?)

As he walked, Sang-Beom repeated these questions. . . .[13]

Let us now reflect on this scene briefly. Sang-Beom has not been able to befriend his comrades, and it is alluded that he has been too rigid and pedantically principled as, according to the comrade chairman, he has become "a drop of oil" in a puddle of committed cadres, prioritizing the criticism of others when they made errors rather than trying to get along with them. And the chairman declares that it is because he lacks the qualities of a good party member. Obviously, the impossibility and irreconcilable nature of the chairman's vague and intangible criticism does not deter Sang-Beom. Far from it. He is made to realize many of his shortcomings by the chairman's words, and is overwhelmed by this moving realization, his voice trembling with emotion. The chairman's mention of the importance of the qualities of a good member of the party makes him so happy that he feels as if he has acquired a pair of wings. And he blames himself for not having had a big enough heart to overlook others' errors, and realizing that it is more important to get along with other members of the cadre rank.

The Second Connection

Compared to this noble form of male bond, which reminds us somewhat of inter-polis interactions between patricians, romance between males and females is belittled and treated as a secondary or tertiary issue. More importantly, romance should only develop if it is between two individuals, both of whom are equally loyal toward the Leader. No private feelings must be prioritized over *suryeongnim kke deurineun tahameomneun heummo eui jeong gwa chungseongsim*, or endless reverence, adoration, and longing for, and loyalty toward, the Leader. Romantic feelings between men and women are subordinate to these most noble feelings toward the Leader. The worth of another individual is recognized only when the other person is shown to be as loyal toward the Leader as oneself—with a strong sexist bias, as will be shown.

Some background is necessary: Sang-Beom and Hak-Sil used to be close when they were young, but no concrete relationship developed, and they each met someone else and married. During the Korean War, Hak-Sil's husband and Sang-Beom's wife and baby were killed. Sang-Beom has one daughter, Bang-Seon (aged about eight or nine), from this marriage. Sang-Beom's mother has been worried about her son and granddaughter, and one day suggests that Sang-Beom should consider marrying Hak-Sil. In the story, Sang-Beom and Hak-Sil have been depicted as developing some kind of awkwardness toward each other, but there is no hint of erotic tension. The writer is, it appears, deliberately unclear about their romance, or has decided to leave it up to the reader's assumptions. There is no use of the standard North Korean word for love, *sarang,* in relation to Sang-Beom and Hak-Sil in the novel (but it appears elsewhere: see below). Toward the end of the novel, Sang-Beom decides to marry Hak-Sil, almost out of the blue. But it takes the form of a confession he makes not to Hak-Sil, but to her older brother, Byeong-Hun.

[Sang-Beom and Byeong-Hun are walking together.]
    "Comrade Byeong-Hun!"
    ". . . ."
    "Some time ago, you suggested that I get re-married. I think I should, too."
    ". . . ."
    "Since I'm not married, Comrade Hak-Sil seems to be agonizing. I feel strongly so."
    "Comrade Sang-Beom, honestly, I've been pained by that, too . . . It is already in the past, but at that time [i.e., when Sang-Beom and Hak-Sil were young and developed a closeness between them], if I had guided Hak-Sil more carefully, Hak-Sil would have been happier. I feel so about you, as well."
    "I could not make myself clear toward Hak-Sil at that time and I feel responsibility for that."
    ". . . ."
    "Comrade Byeong-Hun, some time ago, my mother told me about Comrade Hak-Sil. Mother has been thinking about this [possibility?] very carefully, it seems. I'm also concerned about Bang-Seon [his daughter: earlier in the novel, it has been depicted that Hak-Sil has been paying special attention to and taking care of Bang-Seon whenever she can]. I trust Comrade Hak-Sil will be able to make a family."
    Byeong-Hun's heart was overwhelmed at Sang-Beom's words, which were filled with good will, but he could not find an answer. He carried on walking, in shock.
    "Comrade Byeong-Hun, please forgive my shortcomings. I could not help confessing my mind to you tonight."
    "Comrade Sang-Beom, I thank you! Please raise Hak-Sil as your revolutionary comrade."
    "Let's go . . . there must be people waiting for you."
    Sang-Beom stepped forward. The two men climbed down the slope. In front of them, the lights of the residential district shone, as if smiling.[14]

Where do we find love in this exchange? Not between Hak-Sil and Sang-Beom, who are about to get married, but between Sang-Beom and Comrade Byeong-Hun, both of whom feel "responsible" for raising Hak-Sil as a revolutionary comrade in their journey toward perfecting their endless love for the Great Leader. Hak-Sil appears as a minor or imperfect human being, who requires male guidance or, more precisely, parenting, in order to become a true revolutionary loyal to the Leader. Sang-Beom's decision to marry Hak-Sil is seen as an act of fulfilling duty and responsibility. Hak-Sil's potential to improve her quality as a revolutionary is seen in the prospect of her being able to start a family. Important factors here include Sang-Beom's mother's intentions and his own concern for Bang-Seon; therefore, his decision to marry Hak-Sil is justified as an act performed in the service of others and not one aimed at responding to his own feelings or personal concerns. Thus, marriage here falls within the larger tenet of Sang-Beom's public spirit, his striving to become a more loyal follower of the Great Leader, his struggle to repay His great love.

The Leader Connection

Let us now look at the scene in which Kim Il Sung pays a surprise visit to the ironworks. This depiction is based on the standard story told in North Korea about Kim's January 1957 visit to the Hwanghae Iron Works in southwestern North Korea. According to this formula, he emphasizes the necessity of one additional furnace in North Korea at that time—only the Kangseon Steel Works had one—and encourages workers to join in the "battle" to build North Korea's own furnace. Hwanghae Iron Works was a frequent recipient of Kim's "on-the-spot" guidance after the end of the Korean War. In one of North Korea's official publications, which is prophetically entitled *The Path of Great Love*, we find:

> Two days after the armistice [of the Korean War], the great leader went out to the Hwanghae Iron Works [which was] overgrown with weeds to provide orientation on the rehabilitation and construction of the works. He provided the workers with strength, a fighting spirit and confidence by saying: "You've got to build a bigger open hearth on the spot where there was a small one, demolished by the Yankee devils, and erect brick buildings on the sites of the straw-thatched huts to show the Yankees what the Koreans are made of in this reconstruction as well."[15]

Obviously, the writer of *Yonggwangro*, Yun Se-Jung, is not allowed to deviate from the canonized version of Kim's visits, but he supplements his story with a description of the feelings and emotions of the protagonists, in addition to fictional details enhancing virtuous aspects of Kim's personality. Interestingly, this fictional enhancement captures the reality quite precisely here, as will be argued below. It is also interesting to see that, in the 1970s, writers were still allowed to quote Kim Il Sung's words as if he had actually spoken them, even though these words were in fact the product of the writer's imagination. Later, such endeavors became impossible, and Kim Il Sung stopped appearing in North Korean novels.

. . . .

"Long Live!"

"Long Live Comrade Kim Il Sung!"

Workers welcomed the *suryeongnim* with thunderous applause and cheers of joy. The Great Leader hailed [them] in response and came to a stop at a place near the furnace. He kindly and warmly grasped the hands of each worker there.

Sang-Beom bowed to the Great Leader with utmost respect.

"*Suryeongnim!* . . ."

He was overwhelmed and lost his voice. The Great Leader understood this and tightly held Sang-Beom's hands.

"You are working here! [Sang-Beom is supposed to have met Kim before.] How have you been?"

"Yes, I'm . . ."

Sang-Beom was simply too moved and his vision became clouded [with tears]. Today is only the third day of January and is the first working day. The Great Leader postponed hundreds of other matters that he needed to attend to and came over here to meet our workers. . . . How can we possibly compare such enormous trust and love (*sarang*) to anything [else] in the whole wide world?!

. . . .

The Great Leader looked at the faces of the workers. Everyone was wearing work outfits filthy with grease, mechanical oil, and dust. But, everyone looked grave and focused.

"Here, Let's sit down and talk."

Thus spoke the Great Leader. He took a seat on a cut tree trunk that had been placed nearby. His aides and the party cadres were very embarrassed [since they did not have a decent chair to offer him]. One officer brought out a wooden chair. But the Great Leader pushed it aside and told everyone to sit down.

Everyone was deeply moved and tried to swallow their tears of joy in the face of such generosity by the benevolent and loving Great Leader. Sang-Beom wiped the corners of his eyes with his left hand. The Great Leader then took his right hand and pulled him closer to Himself, so he would take a seat.

"Come on, sit here."

Sang-Beom tried very hard to resist his desire to embrace the Great Leader and took a seat beside him.

. . . .

"As you comrades know very well, today we have only one furnace. I cannot feel safe. If there is any accident, the Republic [North Korea] would have to give up iron . . .

. . . .

"We need iron in order to quickly develop our economy. Without iron, we cannot build the cities, the countryside, or the railroads . . . Without resolving the iron problem, we cannot resolve the *euisikju* [clothes, food, and housing] problems of the *inmin*."

. . . .

"Our party put forward the slogan of 'maximizing economization and production,' since it believes in the power of the working people, the power of people like you, comrades. How can we push on farther and faster with the construction of the furnace? Let me hear your opinions."

. . . .

Workers and technicians frankly stated their opinions, amidst [feelings of] honor, glory, and an overwhelming sense of joy and excitement. Their spirits flared with passion and courage, thanks to the Great Leader who prioritized the opinions of workers.

. . . .

The Great Leader asked Old Man To-Yun, who was sitting behind Sang-Beom. "How is your health?"

Old Man To-Yun stood up and said, "I can still work as hard as young people."

"That's great. But you cannot deceive me, can you? As I told you when we met during the war, you must not stretch yourself too thinly . . . ."

"Oh no, I still can work as much . . ."

"So you are saying I'm too mean." The Great Leader smiled most kindly and asked again, "Do you still live with your son?"

"Our oldest lives separately."

"The oldest daughter must have gotten married."

"Yes, she did."

"Please, take care of yourself. And we must mechanize [the production process: does the writer imply a connection between mechanization and lessening the burden of the workers? The connection is not clear] . . ."

The workers and technicians looked up, raising faces full of conviction and determination . . .

"Great Leader! We would build the furnace all by ourselves even if the sky were to fall down on us!" Sang-Beom said in tearful voice.

"Everything depends on your determination. I trust you!"

The Great Leader spoke very warmly, placing his hand on Sang-Beom's shoulder.

. . . .

Sang-Beom drowned in warm tears. He felt his heart warm up seeing the Great Leader who is the Father of us all, most benevolent and loving, and who loves workers deeply, as if each one of them were precious gold.

(*Suryeongnim!* Please do not be concerned about us! Just like we defeated the American wretches, we will build our furnace at any cost.) Sang-Beom renewed his solemn pledge in his mind.[16]

The difference between the depiction of this human connection and the rest is that the Great Leader appears as all-sagacious and all-loving, and appears only once; that is, one and only one time, irreplaceable and unable to be replicated. His kindness, holiness, wisdom, courage, beauty, virtue, and so forth play a baptizing role in the story. Thus, after this "on-the-spot guidance" or *hyeonjichido*, workers at the ironworks vigorously propel their mission toward success. Yet, as can be seen, the Great Leader is not depicted as aloof or otherworldly. He is friendly and has an amazing memory, remembering details related to the family situation of a worker, for example. He is caring in a down-to-earth manner, sitting on the dirt and casually holding workers' hands. In the face of this almighty, magical, and absolute goodness, everyone is mesmerized and falls in love (again) with him.

Unlike a knee-jerk depiction of a romance that leads to marriage between Sang-Beom and Hak-Sil, this scene is filled with invocations of eroticism and infatuated love. Sang-Beom resists the urge to embrace the Great Leader, and instead sits next to him with his heart pounding—like a shy, elated lover. Speechlessness and tears of joy are standard symptoms displayed by individuals in infatuated states.[17] Physical exaltation and emotional elation underpin the reactions of workers when the Great Leader is sighted. These belong to the realm of romantic love. The object of love, Kim Il Sung, is everyone's lover—he loves everyone and cares about everyone. Bataille's connection between the sovereign and eroticism works perfectly here. The sovereign can be the only object of erotic desire.[18] This scene also reminds us strongly of Charles Lindholm's theories, which approximate romantic desire with the mechanism of adoration for a charismatic leader by his followers.[19]

Critic's View

The official North Korean literary supplement sums up *Yonggwangro* as follows:

> The novel *Yonggwangro neun sumsuinda* artistically depicts the extraordinarily sagacious guidance of our Great Leader, who led workers and our working class toward miracles and innovations, through the story of the heroic battle of the working class of Hwanghae Iron Works, who built the main furnace in less than one year in difficult conditions where everything was in short supply.
>
> The ideological concept underpinning the entire novel is the belief that we can achieve any miracle, overcome all imaginable difficulties, and continue making revolutionary advances despite any predicaments we may encounter if we maintain our burning loyalty toward the Great Leader and exemplify the revolutionary spirit of self-reliance and endless struggle. . . .

In this novel, the great love of the benevolent fatherly Leader provides a source of endless power. His love encourages the protagonists to become invincible in battle and carry out heroic acts of bravery. . . .

In the character of [Sang-Beom], at the core is his endlessly pure and burning devotion for the Great Leader. He lives and works with only one thought [in mind]—that of trying to alleviate the worries of the fatherly Great Leader who said that iron was the key to the national economy.[20]

The supplement touches upon Sang-Beom and Hak-Sil only as follows:

Sang-Beom is depicted as heroic and courageous, as he excels in the creative struggle to achieve greater productivity. Also, through his interactions with his aged mother, whom he treats with respect and care, . . . and his relationship with Hak-Sil, revolutionary quality of Sang-Beom's comradely love (*hyeongmyeongjeok tongjiae*) and his moral purity (*todeokjeok sungyeolseong*) are captured.[21]

Although this is a fictional story, it nevertheless offers a model relationship that readers may strive to replicate in their real-life interactions. This take on Sang-Beom's love for the Leader is highly relevant in thinking about the self in North Korea.

5. Totalitarianism and Self

The type of sovereign prevailing in North Korea was probably able to emerge as a consequence of the extended period of martial law-like order in place there since the Korean War ceasefire. The unfinished war has, since 1950, created a permanent state of national emergency, allowing for an extraordinary form of human habitation. Under the rubric of the emergency, anyone who is deemed a traitor or enemy of the state can face arbitrary forms of retribution. Expiation is possible only through submission, not by providing contrary evidence or through self-justification. Conversely, the rhetoric of the national emergency almost necessitates an exceptional center such as the almighty *suryeong*, so that manpower may be utilized to maximum effect.

The recent CNN television production on North Korea, "Undercover in the Secret State" (first aired on November 13, 2005), showed public executions, a glimpse into concentration camps, examples of street crime, a poster declaring that Kim Il Sung was assassinated by his son Kim Jong Il due to the former's inclination toward pursuing an open-door policy toward the outside world, and so on. The scenes aired were not wholly surprising, and may even have been predictable. It is in a way expected that a totalitarian society such as North Korea would have public executions of traitors and domestic enemies—George

Orwell has already shown this, albeit in a fictional way. The most chilling imagery was not that which depicted such extraordinary events, but rather, that
which showed what we might call mundane or everyday reality.

One piece of footage captured a scene of a brief encounter between a young
female transportation officer and two middle-aged women passengers on a
train. When the officer checked their paperwork—no North Korean citizen
is allowed to travel from one town to the other without the written permission of the authorities—the women's permits turned out not to be in order.
The officer hysterically ordered them off the train. Realizing that the women
were dragging their feet, despite her repeated shrill orders, the officer began
pulling at their bags, which were perhaps filled with food they had purchased
from other towns for their families to eat or to be traded for goods that their
families needed in order to survive. The women, who were exhausted and
whose faces were tanned and emaciated, held on to their bags, covering their
faces with one hand, quietly sobbing, and murmured submissively, asking the
officer why she was treating them in this way. The officer began hitting the
women on their heads, while the women submitted without protest.[22]

This footage showed that the personal safety of North Korean individuals depends not on the rule of law but on the temperament of the officers,
administrators, and other uniformed representatives of authority. Their well-
being is left at the mercy of the officers' mood on that particular day and at
that particular moment. This precarious lawlessness in the name of the law
is precisely what Agamben calls the logic of the concentration camp, where
power is invested arbitrarily in the person of the representative of uniformed
officialdom, just as under martial law or in a state of emergency.[23]

The form of social institution that is most closely associated with the camp
is, needless to say, totalitarianism. According to Agamben, war is also the key
to understanding modern totalitarianism. In his words,

> modern totalitarianism can be defined as the establishment, by means of the
> state of exception, of a legal civil war that allows for the physical elimination
> not only of political adversaries but of entire categories of citizens who for some
> reason cannot be integrated into the political system. Since then, the voluntary
> creation of a permanent state of emergency (though perhaps not declared in
> the technical sense) has become one of the essential practices of contemporary
> states, including so-called democratic ones.[24]

What is unique about totalitarian society and its concentration camps is
that, in a fashion that goes against utilitarian principles, superfluous human
beings or undesirable elements are not put to work or made to produce materials for the society, but incarcerated, apparently with no obvious purpose
other than to be dominated and subjugated by the authorities.

We are aware that institutions such as concentration camps may well exist in North Korea.[25] But what I am trying to discuss here is that seemingly less drastic, less violent (or, at least, indirectly violent) forms of subjugation are more prevalent, more the norm and, hence, more effective in North Korea— or perhaps in any other totalitarian society.

Moreover, scholars appear to be far from reaching agreement on the nature and mechanisms of totalitarianism. The totalitarian economy, it has been said, presupposes that which the modern capitalist economy would regard as irrational and cost-ineffective (hence, such a catch-all phrase as "the End of Economic Man").[26] At the same time, when faced with the news that the Soviet government has exiled a poet to Siberia on the basis that he has been leading a parasitic form of life and has failed to contribute to society through useful labor, we are in effect being told that the totalitarian society presupposes maximum utility.[27] In some ironic way, therefore, we are not well equipped with a unifying set of conceptual and empirical tools with which to think about the social system known as totalitarianism.

Furthermore, as Slavoj Žižek remarks, if one of the clearest signs of totalitarianism is a lack of access to others' (and public) knowledge about oneself, North Korea does not quite fit, since its selves are more than willing to disclose themselves in relation to their introspective appraisals of the purity of their thoughts and acts toward the Leader.[28]

In a neoliberal economy, the quality of an individual's retirement depends upon their skill in managing their own retirement funds, not the funds in the state's centralized pension fund. In a similar way, under totalitarianism, the individual's ability to prove their loyalty to the leadership becomes a deciding factor in determining their relative well-being, at times even dictating whether they live or die. Here, the individual is alone and solely responsible for his or her own conduct. Back-to-back with the family-oriented and pseudo-kinship terminology that the North Korean state utilizes, especially in its references to the nation's Father (Kim Jong Il) and Grandfather (Kim Il Sung), individuals are not even in a position to trust their own family members. This is because when one commits a crime in the eyes of the authorities, the entire family is sent into exile—just as in the premodern Korean penal code. Thus, in this totalitarian society, the self and others exist in a random mixture of insecure connection and disconnection. The only certainty exists in the direct connection between the self and the Great Leader through the channel of loyalty toward Him.

The following words by Hannah Arendt capture well the isolation of the self in North Korea:

> The disturbing factor in the success of totalitarianism is rather the true selflessness of its adherents: it may be understandable that a Nazi or Bolshevik will not

be shaken in his conviction by crimes against people who do not belong to the movement or are even hostile to it; but the amazing fact is that neither is he likely to waiver when the monster begins to devour its own children and not even if he becomes a victim of persecution himself, if he is framed and condemned, if he is purged from the party and sent to a forced-labor or a concentration camp. On the contrary, to the wonder of the whole civilized world, he may even be willing to help in his own prosecution and frame his own death sentence if only his status as a member of the movement is not touched.[29]

I would add to this that in North Korea, the keyword that holds sway over every person's commitment to the revolution is love—love for the Leader or what I call sovereign love (see below). Judgment is made as to whether the self is good or evil based on this criterion: how deeply and how truthfully one loves the Leader. Here, one is held solely responsible for one's ideological purity. Any shortcomings are blamed on one's moral weakness—other people, or exogenous factors such as bad upbringing, material lack, or health problems, for example, should not be taken into consideration.

An institution that facilitates self-inquisition is the routine self-criticism/ group-criticism meeting or *pipan gwa chagipipan*. Individuals are typically made to write self-examination papers, referred to as *chonghwamun*. When writing such a paper, one first needs to be able to assess oneself in relation to criteria such as degree of loyalty and commitment toward the leadership, love of country, level of participation in teamwork, success in fulfilling given tasks, capacity for hard work, level of dedication, and so on. One then proceeds to critically recount aspects where one's efforts have been insufficient, where one has not made sufficient preparations, or where one has not made sufficient improvement since the previous criticism session. One is also expected to note the directions in which one has become distracted and the reasons why, what kind of bad influences one has been unconsciously receiving, in which area of work (i.e., department) one needs to try harder, and so on. The key here is to consistently and strenuously maintain that one's loyalty to the leadership and love for the country, party, and the masses are intact, while admitting that one has failed to be sufficiently vigilant in relation to one's speech, conduct, or personal weaknesses. It is imperative for one to present one's self-criticism in an immaculate order, this becoming a genre in itself. This is because, in some ways, it is more important to be able to criticize oneself in public in a proper and coherent manner according to the established format than to actually do the job well. In fact, if one deviates from the formulaic language in one's self-review, by way of being too original, this itself becomes a liability, presenting itself as the target of a new round of group criticism.

As can be seen in the above excerpts from Yun's novel, *Yonggwangro*, that even when a seemingly absurd criticism is made, one is morally obligated to accept it and reflect upon it with sincerity and care. When Sang-Beom is criticized for being aloof and unapproachable, and for having become "a drop of oil" among the ranks of the loyal cadre, despite the obvious point that an unprincipled style of unit leadership would compromise the overall goal of Socialist construction, Sang-Beom is depicted as accepting it, first with a certain amount of personal agony, yet eventually as a grateful recipient of such criticism. It is important to note that this is not represented as simple, mindless adherence or obeisance. Sang-Beom tries to logically understand the criticism, and accepts it with emotional satisfaction and no resentment. The novel's role in presenting such acceptance of contradictory criticism is crucial. By giving language to Sang-Beom's internal journey toward acceptance of such criticism, the novel offers an exemplary mental process that can be applied in the daily lives of North Koreans.

There is one canonical criterion for a good *chonghwamun:* correct and extensive citation of the words of Kim Il Sung or Kim Jong Il. North Koreans memorize the writings of both leaders word for word, sentence by sentence, from *The Works of Kim Il Sung* or *The Works of Kim Jong Il.* The ability to learn either of the two Kims' words by heart and recite them is used to measure the degree of truthfulness of one's self-criticism, and is the best means of demonstrating the extent of one's commitment and sincerity toward the revolutionary and patriotic cause of North Korea. Conversely, if one were to misquote the Kims' sacred words, incurring awe and cosmic wrath, the consequences could be catastrophic (even life-threatening), since this would be seen as evidence of a lack of loyalty or, worse still, a claim of false loyalty toward the sovereign Leader.

In this way, in North Korea's leader-focused totalitarianism, self-reference becomes a life-and-death concern for citizens. This mechanism in turn maintains the accountability of each member of the population toward the leader as well as to their own individual consciences. But, as can be seen in the example where Sang-Beom convinces himself of the validity of the chairman's criticism and the correctness of his newly (re-)chosen path, this is done in such a way so as not to suppress the self, but rather enhance its ability to be reflexive. It is commonly imagined in the West that, under totalitarianism, no self can be a self and that the population merely submits to whatever the state (or the authorities) demand of it. However, the North Korea–style totalitarian society works on the basis of the autonomous isolation of the self from the rest of society, with each individual responsible for his or her monitoring his or her own conduct and degree of conduct and loyalty toward the Leader. In North Korea, the self and its actions (including self-enactment, self-criticism, reflection, self-analysis, and self-assessment) are crucial elements of the socioeconomic mechanism/process whereby society reproduces itself.[30] Thus, though in very different directions and with different effects, self-accountability is the key to understanding the workings of both North Korea–style totalitarianism and the variety of neoliberal audit culture found, for example, in advanced Western capitalism: both presuppose a disciplinary regime of incessant anti-heretical self-inquisition. Only that which is seen as heresy differs between these societies.

6. Biopolitics, or Love's Whereabouts

The British filmmakers Daniel Gordon and Nicholas Bonner have documented close to one year in the lives of two young, state-trained gymnasts in Pyongyang, North Korea. Pak Hyon Sun, thirteen at the time of filming, and Kim Song Yun, eleven, were selected by the government following a request by the filmmakers. The two young gymnasts, along with thousands of others aged from five or six up to their early thirties, practice mass game routines every day, year-round. They are highly accomplished young gymnasts who have been loftily rewarded already at their young ages. The families of both girls are given the privilege of living in a well-appointed apartment in Pyongyang with modern amenities, such as television sets, as a reward for their children's participation in the mass games. As the film goes on to show the actual mass games in which the two girls performed, the viewer is mesmerized by the flawless unity of hundreds and thousands of individuals, whose bodies look and move as one body. Bent, stretched, and spinning, the bodies of these men, women, and children turn the unthinkable into a visual reality. A perfectly synchronized, choreographic masterpiece challenging the limits of human bodily movement makes one forget that this is in fact an aggregation of thousands of different individual bodies.[31]

Anthropologists have long explored sociality, symbolic properties, and the cultural semantics of the body, away from or against the biomedical gaze.[32] In a society like North Korea, the body is always socially appropriated and never individually owned, yet, at the same time, the individual is held responsible for its maintenance, improvement, and transformation.

This is the logic that sustains the socialization of the body in North Korea. Individual bodies together form the social body. As such, it is not dissimilar to the prewar and wartime Japanese doctrine of the *kokutai*, or national body, where the corpus of the Emperor was supposed to be sustained by a fusion of the bodies of the population into one. The aesthetics of the *kokutai* culminated in eugenics, where healthy and strong bodies were seen as beautiful, in that they best served the Emperor.[33] In North Korea, there is a different twist. The economy of the North Korean social body does not presuppose eugenics as such, as it cannot afford to be selective due to the numerical limitations of the population. The aesthetics of the body, on the other hand, also manifest themselves in a different way to wartime Japan. Here, healthy and strong bodies are not promoted per se; instead, frequent and all-pervasive references are made to the image of the Leader.

Interestingly, this, too, is done in such a way as to make the sovereign Leader an exception. The two Kims have a rather atypical physique for North Korea: both appear rounder and fleshier in build than the average North Korean. But, upon closer observation, it becomes clear that the two Kims have different physiques. However, in the context of aesthetics, the difference between the two is minimized. Whenever they appear together in artistic imagery, if not in photographic representations, they appear approximately the same size, assume symmetrical poses, and have almost identically radiant smiles on their fair complexions, with white teeth, red lips, and baby-like pink cheeks. In reality, the son measures a foot shorter than the deceased father, and they have contrasting facial contours: while the father has a square jaw, masculine face, and straight hair, the son has a small jaw, feminine-looking face, and curly hair. In the aesthetic imagery of the Leader, however, these real-life differences are minimized and the similarities are accentuated. Together, they are differentiated from other members of the population, with their bony frames, tanned and dry faces, and tired, crusty skin. Whether the two Kims are truly as angelic as they are depicted in the imagery is beside the point. Rather, my point is to assert that North Korean aesthetics of the body are not about how beautiful (whatever the criteria of beauty may be) one's body is, but about how responsible one is in maximizing the gifts and overcoming the weakness of one's body, as demonstrated in the cases of Hyon Sun, Song Yon, and thousands of other gymnasts.

The fusion that individual bodies crave for with the body of the Leader is prominently depicted in Yun's *Yonggwangro* during the scene where Sang-Beom trembles like an infatuated adolescent, overwhelmed with the desire to embrace the Great Leader. The novelist then presents an emotional rhetorical question, "How can we possibly compare such enormous trust and love (*sarang*) to anything in the whole wide world?!" This type of love is related to the odd aftertaste that one experiences after watching the mass games in Pyongyang, at the end of which the thousands of participants reach an unmistakably orgasmic climax, their faces variously contorted in heightened, almost painful excitement and unspeakable joy.

In this regard, we must remember that even bodies in concentration camps are not desocialized—they are social in that their redundancy and superfluousness as forms of existence on the extreme margins of life's boundaries mark them out as objects for particularly extensive (if not effective) attempts at domination by the state.

Discursively, body-oriented rhetoric abounds in North Korea. From around the 1970s, Kim Il Sung's doctrine of *juche* came to dominate the nation's ideological discourse. Made up of two Chinese characters: *ju* (main or master) and *che* (body), *juche* ironically, or perhaps logically, means subject; that is to say, people are the subject of their own society as well as subjected to society. In itself, it is a rather innocuous doctrine, mainly due to its lack of intellectual sophistication and systematic and coherent internal structure. Nevertheless, seen hand-in-hand with the way the North Korean population is placed vis-à-vis its sovereign Great Leader, it begins to emerge as one of the most dreadfully lethal doctrines of totalitarianism. Under this catch-all phrase, the members of the population identify themselves closely with the Leader, and not simply that: they do so by identifying themselves as the originary point of self-subjection to the sovereign. One of the favorite banners of North Koreans reads: "Let us all become revolutionaries whose body has only *Juche*-type blood." The *corpus* of the population is at once individualized and collectivized—individuals are held responsible for making themselves into better and purer North Korean subjects by way of self-referential criticism and ideological cleansing; at the same time, they are expected to form one organic body in their march to attain the goals set out by the Great Leader. Another favorite North Korean saying is, predictably, *Widaehasin suryeongnim gwa chinaehaneun chidojatongjireul moksumeuro powuihaja*, or "Let us defend our Great Leader and Dear Leader with our own lives." Evidently, one's life is of lesser value than that of the sovereign Leader.

For North Korea's *inmin*, *bios* (socially meaningful life) is acquired by way of political submission. Here, life is not *zoē* (simple life), in that life is politicized. Life in North Korea is at its most bare and most politicized, yet submission here is something that is chosen: North Koreans carry out a sovereign act in renouncing sovereignty. Of course, one might think that this is a product of indoctrination, but it is notoriously difficult to determine in what way and by what kind of channel such an effect is secured. North Korea's *bios* is formed in such a way as to be extremely close to *zoē*, yet is inundated with political meaning (death being the most certain proof of political life). Life, therefore, is death, and death is life in North Korea.

National sovereignty, in this totalitarian structure, completely overlaps with the sovereign Leader, and the *corpus populi* with the body of the sovereign. In this society, life is extremely politicized and, paradoxically, supreme political life is achieved only through death. In one North Korean tale relating to the Korean War, we find Hero Li Su-Bok, who sacrificed himself in suicide bomber fashion in order to destroy a U.S. tank. His story appears in elementary school textbooks, children's stories, and songs. Such references can best be understood through the concept of *jeongchijeok saengmyeong*, or political life.

Despite his death or, rather, precisely because of his death, Hero Li acquired eternal political life—he is with us forever. The inversion of life and death, or the acquisition of life by way of death, is characteristic of North Korean totalitarian discourse.

In a cynical twist, this all makes sense—whereas birth is not a sovereign act, death is; whereas one cannot be born according to one's own will, one can clearly die by one's own choosing. As such, taking one's own life appears as a sovereign act. Yet, in North Korea's version of totalitarianism, even suicide in general has lost its sovereign attributes—only when one dies (willingly) for the Leader, one's death (suicide or not) is deemed an exercise of a (final) sovereign right.

This reminds us of Simone Weil's notion of God as absence. Let us read a brief excerpt from her work: "Creation is an act of love and it is perpetual. At each moment our existence is God's love for us. *But God can only love himself. His love for us is love for himself through us.* Thus, he who gives us our being loves in us the acceptance of not being."[34]

There is an almost uncanny resemblance between Weil's "God's love" and North Korea's sovereign love—the sovereign Leader loves only himself, but by loving himself, he loves us all.

The epitome of *jeongchijeok saengmyeong* is the way in which the late Kim Il Sung is referred to as immortal—having eternal life (*yeongsaengpulmyeol*) or being eternally with us (*yeongweonhi uriwa hamkke*). But if the death of Kim Il Sung (in 1994) was exceptional in being that of the sovereign, the way in which the supreme leadership has been succeeded by his son Kim Jong Il is less than banal. In my view, while nepotistic anomalies are less relevant in thinking about North Korean totalitarianism than other aspects of its society, such as the way the population is disciplined into a form of self-replicating, self-referential existence, they nevertheless lead to an enigmatic question about sovereignty or, more precisely, the exception of the sovereign. If, as Carl Schmitt stated, "Sovereign is he who decides on exception," Kim Jong Il is the exemplary of all: he *is* the law and, therefore, he is excepted from subjection to the rule of law.[35] At the same time, time and again, the North Korean population is told that the people are the masters of their own society. The rhetoric of self-mastery is repeated ad infinitum: when they play no part in decision making—such as when they participate in mandatory voting for the single candidate preselected by the state—they are told that all the decisions are theirs.

We are witnessing one of the most effective and efficient manifestations of biopolitics in modern history. As Agamben has written:

If there is a line in every modern state marking the point at which the decision on life becomes a decision on death [. . .] this line no longer appears today as a stable border dividing two clearly distinct zones.... [C]ertain events that are fundamental for the political history of modernity (such as the declaration of rights), as well as others that seem instead to represent an incomprehensible intrusion of biologico-scientific principles into the political order (such as [...] the contemporary debate on the normative determination of death criteria), acquire their true sense only if they are brought back to the common biopolitical (or thanatopolitical) context to which they belong. From this perspective, the camp—as the pure, absolute, and impassable biopolitical space (insofar as it is founded solely on the state of exception)—will appear as the hidden paradigm of the political space of modernity, whose metamorphoses and disguises we will have to learn to recognize.[36]

As archaic as it may appear to some, North Korea (and totalitarianism, for that matter) is a modern phenomenon just like the market economy or neo-liberalism. As far as the effects of biopolitics are concerned—where the life and death of the population are enmeshed within the process of state decision making, and where bare life and politicized life become almost indistinguishable—North Korea is not, therefore, bizarre or different.

7. Closing Note

How does a North Korean find worth in another human being? Through loving the Great Leader. The most important ground rule is that the lover to whom one makes physical, sexual, and erotic advances in public must be the sovereign Leader. The logic of the mass games (which to outsiders seem like a total waste of manpower and financial expense) resides here: these events offer festivities for total consumption of love by the sovereign and constitute the only context where the population becomes physically exhibitive and explosive at the same time. The orgasmic climax of the mass games, where all participants jump up and down chanting "long live," unable to control their emotions, can only be understood in this way.[37] When Sang-Beom resists embracing the Leader in public and, instead, takes a seat right next to him, he is behaving exactly like a man trying to hide his erection. The ecstasy of the ironworkers, smeared with uncontrollable outflows of bodily fluid—tears in this case—also falls within this genre of sovereign love. The fact that the sovereign Leader is the possessor of exceptional beauty (in the sense in which I argued above) in contradistinction from the rest of the population is all the more reason for adoration.

As I have stated above, without the initial investment by which love is invested by one human in another's very being, society cannot be sustained. The idea of the sovereign as embodied by the North Korean Leader defies our understanding of utilitarianism (and by extension, our understanding of totalitarianism as utilitarian), since it denotes a form of existence that does not offer anything in exchange for the devotion of others, a being that contributes in no productive or constructive way to the society. As such, this sovereign does not participate in the exchange of moral goods or material products. The only meaning of its existence is this existence in itself, and, therefore, it exists only through consumption—consumption of glory, luxury, and, above all, the devotion and love of others.

If love fails, can the end of the society be far behind? It remains to be seen how the whereabouts of love might be implicated in the specific and unique context of totalitarianism in North Korea.

Acknowledgments

I wish to thank Dr. Hoon Song of the University of Minnesota for reading this draft closely and commenting on it.

Notes

1. Simone Weil, *Gravity and Grace* (New York: Routledge, 1952), 64.
2. I am currently writing a book, tentatively entitled *Exploration in the Political: Ethnological Study of North Korea*, exploring the logic that moves North Korean society using North Korean literature created during the late 1960s through to the 1980s.
3. In the main, I am relying on Giorgio Agamben, *Homo Sacer: Sovereign Power and Bare Life* (Stanford, Calif.: Stanford University Press, 1995); Agamben, *Remnants of Auschwitz: The Witness and the Archive* (New York: Zone Books, 1999); Agamben, *State of Exception* (Chicago: University of Chicago Press, 2005); and Georges Bataille, *The Accursed Share*, vols. 2 and 3, *The History of Eroticism, Sovereignty* (New York: Zone Books, 1993).
4. Charles Lindholm, *Charisma* (Cambridge, Mass.: Blackwell, 1990).
5. Han Jung-Mo and Jeong Seong-Mu, *Juche eui munye riron yeongu* [A Study in Juche's Literary Art Theory] (Pyongyang, NK: Sahoekwahakchulpansa, 1983), 2. All translations in this chapter are mine.
6. Han and Jeong, *Juche eui munye riron yeongu*, 40.
7. Han and Jeong, *Juche eui munye riron yeongu*, 37.
8. Ryu Man and Kim Jeong-Ung, *Juche eui changjak riron yeongu* [A Study in Juche's Literary Creation Theory] (Pyongyang, NK: Sahoekwahakchulpansa, 1983), 57.
9. Ryu and Kim, *Juche eui changjak riron yeongu*, 58.
10. Han and Jeong, *Juche eui munye riron yeongu*, 79.
11. Han and Jeong, *Juche eui munye riron yeongu*, 86.
12. Yun Se-Jung, *Yonggwangro neun sumsuinda* [The Iron Works Furnace Is Breathing] (Pyongyang, NK: Munyechulpansa, 1974).

13. Yun, *Yonggwangro*, 32–35.

14. Yun, *Yonggwangro*, 395–96.

15. Foreign Languages Publishing House, *The Path of Great Love* (Pyongyang, NK: Foreign Languages Publishing House, 1977), 7.

16. Yun, *Yonggwangro*, 105–10.

17. For example, see Helen Fisher, *The Anatomy of Love: A Natural History of Mating, Marriage, and Why We Stray* (New York: Fawcett Columbine, 1992); and Dorothy Tennov, *Love and Limmerence: The Experience of Being in Love* (New York: Stein and Day, 1979), on infatuation.

18. Bataille, *The Accursed Share*, 197ff.

19. See Lindholm, *Charisma*.

20. Ryu Man et al., *Choseon hyeondae munhak jakpum haeseol* [Supplement to Modern Literary Works in Korea], vol. 1 (Pyongyang, NK: Kwahak paekkwasajeon chulpansa, 1987), 279–81.

21. Ryu Man et al., *Choseon hyeondae munhak jakpum haeseol*, 282.

22. "Video Shows Executions, Life Inside North Korea," *CNN.com*, November 14, 2005, at www.cnn.com/2005/WORLD/asiapcf/11/13/nkorea.hiddenvideo/index.html (accessed November 22, 2006).

23. Agamben, *Homo Sacer*, chap. 7; and Agamben, *Remnants of Auschwitz*.

24. Agamben, *State of Exception*, 2.

25. See Kang Chol-hwan, *The Aquariums of Pyongyang: Ten Years in a North Korean Gulag* (New York: Basic Books, 2002), for example.

26. During the 1930s, Peter Drucker wrote: "The most fundamental, though least publicized, feature of totalitarianism in Italy and Germany is the attempt to substitute noneconomic for economic satisfactions, rewards, and considerations as the basis for the rank, function, and position of the individual in industrial society" (*The End of Economic Man: The Origins of Totalitarianism* [New Brunswick, N.J.: Transaction Publishers, 1994], 129). Of course, this fits in well with the Soviet system. But one also wonders if it is so far removed from the so-called modern capitalist market economy, where nonmonetary rewards in the form of fame and prestige play an active role in providing incentives for workers to make greater efforts.

27. See Thomas Sasz, *Ideology and Insanity* (Syracuse, N.Y.: Syracuse University Press, 1991), 29–30.

28. Slavoj Žižek, "Happiness after September 11," in *Welcome to the Desert of the Real* (London: Verso, 2002), 63.

29. Hannah Arendt, *The Origins of Totalitarianism* (New York: Harcourt and Brace, 1974), 307.

30. See Sonia Ryang, "Critical Synthesis on North Korea as Embodied Ideology," *Social Epistemology* 6, no. 1 (1992): 3–12; and Ryang, "Technologies of the Self: Reading North Korean Novels from the 1980s," *Acta Koreana* 5, no. 1 (1992): 21–32.

31. Daniel Gordon, *A State of Mind*, DVD (2004).

32. See, for example, Margaret Lock and Nancy Sheper-Hughes, "The Mindful Body," *Medical Anthropology Quarterly* 1 (1987): 6–41, for one of the earliest interventions.

33. See, for example, Carol Gluck, *Japan's Modern Myth: Ideology in the Late Meiji Period* (Princeton, N.J.: Princeton University Press, 1985), on the *kokutai*.

34. Weil, *Gravity and Grace*, 32.

35. Carl Schmitt, *Political Theology: Four Chapters on the Concept of Sovereignty* (Chicago: University of Chicago Press, 1922).

36. Agamben, *Homo Sacer*, 122–23.

37. In my *Explorations in the Political*, I call this "an ongoing ritual state" by which time and space in North Korea are reconfigured to circle around endless celebration of the never-ending war, the ever-prospering nation, and the immortal leader.

4

The Split Screen:
Sin Sang-ok in North Korea

Steven Chung

1. Chungmuro, Pyongyang, Hollywood

Sin Sang-ok occupies a central position in the expansion of film as a commercially viable and socially integral art form in postcolonial-postwar Korea. Having trained in Tokyo and apprenticed in Harbin and Shanghai under colonial rule, and then abetted by the mechanically industrialist cultural policies of the Park Chung Hee regime (1961–1979), Sin built a studio that was singular in its technological advancement as well as in its star- and hit-making apparatuses. The largely young, newly urbanized population of the postwar period was hailed as an audience for an astounding output of diverse and accomplished films that both screened the lived realities of socioeconomic growth and vividly animated the modes of material desire, cultural nostalgia, and social fantasy that are inherent to capitalist modernization. While Sin's dominance ebbed in the 1970s under a fully realized authoritarian state, he returned spectacularly to the center of the Korean ideological theatre when he began an eight-year stint in North Korea in 1978. Before his return from North Korea in 1986, he established a massive studio through which he directed seven films, produced eleven others, and laid plans for a number of projects, most of which were eventually realized. According to his memoirs and the numerous interviews in which he recorded his experiences, not only were the films themselves wildly successful, but they also marked a profound shift in North Korean film arts. These claims are largely supported by the informal testimony of defectors, fledgling research into North Korean film cultures, and the scant remains of North Korean publishing on the episode.

This dramatic border crossing has defined Sin's public image, likely at home and certainly abroad, more vividly than the prolific filmmaking career that he forged in the preceding decades. The episode, however, remains enigmatic, captured amidst a series of competing discourses: the complex promotional and protective impulses of Sin's own testimonies, the "national interests" of state agencies and institutions, and the variously sensationalist or orientalist interests of domestic and international media and scholarship. Further, few outside of North Korea have seen all of these films, barred from public exhibition as they were in 1986.[1] This chapter does not, indeed cannot, aim at the truth of the episode; the record is incomplete and the issues too complex. Rather, it is guided by a specific set of questions: How can a mass cultural apparatus refined in the South function in the North? How might this inflect our understanding of the ostensibly opposed ideological structure of the two states? And does the episode prompt us to think any differently about the relationship between mass culture and ideology?

The real novelty of Sin's border crossing is not whether or how his filmmaking adapted to opposed ideological milieus; modern Korean history is permeated by narratives of political conversion and renunciation aligned with the radical shifts from colonial to Cold War to neoliberal statehood. Rather, the interest lies in how the same institutions, modes, and imperatives of film production could function as popular art forms across that ideological divide and how this comes to bear on the constitution of the divide itself within the cinema. There are clearly stories, and images, and figures that do not signify in the same way in the North and the South. Nevertheless, components of the filmmaking machinery—a carefully compartmentalized and highly organized studio production system, a vigorous marketing and sales structure for the promotion of stars and films—functioned in slightly altered but essentially parallel ways in the Republic of Korea (ROK) and Democratic People's Republic of Korea (DPRK) versions of Sin Films studios. Further, modes of affect and spectacle—and indeed an uncannily familiar melodramatic sensibility—are deployed to render a high degree of formal, if not political, continuity. And North Korea cinema under Sin Sang-ok proved surprisingly inclined to appropriate the technical consultation and stylistic formulae of various national cinemas (South Korea as well as the United States, Japan, and Hong Kong) and enthusiastic about participating in international film exhibition circuits. On the other hand, the disjuncture between North and South Korean filmmaking is located in sometimes unexpected spaces. For while the implicit goal of Sin's films might have been "to pave the road to totalitarianism" and "maintain class rule," they often did so via detours through the complexities of family and kinship, and the instability of cinematic extravagance and play. Sin Sang-ok's North Korea cinema both highlighted and troubled the border between Chungmuro and Pyongyang, inviting Hollywood into a liminal space it had not theretofore tread.

2. *Juche*, Spectacle, Affect

Despite the fact that the films themselves are rarely seen outside its borders, North Korean cinema is far from being an unknown entity.[2] This is due as much to the central importance of filmmaking to the sociopolitical life of the isolated state as it is to the centrality of the image and of spectacle to the apprehension of the state to foreign observers. The picture of North Korea, especially in the West, continues to be dominated by a neat dyad of the leader and the masses: the figure Kim Jong Il, portrayed as variously debauched or insane, against the hypnotic vision of the military procession, the orchestrated mass games, or the zealous performance of the child stars. Film figures crucially in the representation of this totalitarian nightmare, not only in the assumption of a monolithically propagandistic cinema, but also in the cinephilia for which Kim Jong Il's leadership and sanity is repeatedly mocked. Sin Sang-ok, of course, plays a vital role in this representation; his rumored abduction and enforced filmmaking accord vividly with the total coerciveness that is the hallmark of North Korean political life, and it was his recollection of Kim Jong Il's vast personal archives that confirmed the leader's film fanaticism.

The centrality of film to political and cultural life in North Korea is a fact, however, that exceeds its sensationalization in journalistic discourse. Thanks to volumes of official writing on film, records of a broad sampling of defectors, and incipient scholarly research, a clearer picture of the links between film and political administration and control has begun to emerge. Kim Il Sung, for instance, is credited with the creation of a number of "revolutionary operas" and plays and is listed as director for key cinematic works from the liberation period through to the 1970s. This crediting is absurd at the literal level; its rationality speaks more to the centrality of film than to the logic of production. Further, the one-thousand-won bill, presumably the most commonly traded currency, is stamped with images of the three classics of North Korean cinema, *Sea of Blood* [*Pibada*], *Flower Girl* [*Kkot paneun cheonyeo*], and *The Fate of a Self-Defense Corps Soldier* [*Han jawi daeweon ui unmyeong*]. And research has shown that as recently as the early 1990s, North Koreans were likely watching more films than any other people in the world, not only in theaters (with an average of thirteen visits per year), but on television (broadcast regularly on state television) and throughout the countryside (through the equivalent of the Soviet agit-trains), workplaces, and public spaces.[3]

This vitality of film and its saturation in everyday life is of course directly connected to its presumed ideological effect. Like the earliest Communist revolutionaries and Fascist demagogues in Russia, Germany, Italy, and China, the North Korean state quickly recognized the power of the cinematic apparatus to appeal to the widest possible demographic and therefore foster and help to sustain revolution. One of the central tenets of the seminal treatise *On the Art of the Cinema* [*Yeonghwa yesul ron*], attributed to Kim Jong Il, is that film in North Korea must advance a particular form, "*juche* realism."[4] Filmmaking should, according to Kim, project models through which to grasp the revolutionary nature of the present historical stage, understand *juche* or self-determination as the condition of that revolution, and recognize Kim Il Sung's leadership as both the manifestation and instrument of *juche*. Filmmakers must therefore fully master *juche* principles themselves and plant this seed (*joongja*) in all of their work. So while it shares with conventional Socialist realism the task of representing class contradiction, critics point out, North Korean film must also screen a reality—a "visual textbook"—in which self-determination is the only real solution to social problems.

But there is also a realm of complexity in North Korean filmmaking and film theory that is often ignored. This inhabits the seemingly redundant explications about film and the often absurd injunctions to specific formal practices of Kim Jong Il's writing on art and film. It also exists vividly, perhaps too obviously, in the films themselves, manifesting in an extreme magnification of both spectacle and affect, and in a particularly measured temporality. This second and crucially important element works in both the historical setting of the vast majority of the films as well as in their pacing and duration. Most of the feature films made until at least the end of the 1980s were confined to the narrow period between the mid-to-late 1920s and the end of the war in 1953. Not only the great canonical works, stretching from *My Hometown* [*Nae gohyang*] (1946) through *Sea of Blood* (1969) and *Star of Joseon* [*Joseon eui byeol*] (1980–1986), but even the more recent massive serials such as *Nation and Destiny* [*Minjok gwa unmyeong*] (1992–present) rarely move back beyond the March 1 movement or forward to anything like the present. In fact, the bulk of production investment has been made to replicate the late colonial, early liberation, and civil war periods: costumes, architectural fittings, and train claddings at the February 8 Film Studios were almost exclusively measured for those historical stages, and the sprawling Joseon Art Film Studios has one permanent set that is a faithful replica of a medium-sized town under Japanese colonial rule. The span is clearly the revolutionary time-space of the North Korean regime, after the shame of dependence on China and annexation to Japan and before the mundane but often violent processes of nation building. Filmmaking returns ceaselessly to this historical moment to mine it for new heroes and phases of radicalization or slightly reconfigured ways to tell the same revolutionary tales. But further, the narratives rarely move beyond the conditions of revolution or the process of radicalization. Rather, the films dwell continuously in the phases of darkness, suffering, and repression, only to end precisely at the moment of enlightenment, recognition, and release. It is a temporality that is more regressive than messianic, dwelling in pain more than in anticipation of redemption. Release of course does come, or is at least suggested, in the films, but the way to liberation is rarely projected, either because the free space is already too well known, or somehow for that reason unrepresentable. Here, too, the ideological imperative is clear: film art captures the conditions for and the process of grasping revolutionary relations, specifically the unceasing injustice of the landlord, the foreigner, the other, and the importance of self-actualization (whether in an act of vengeance, the agitation of a group or mob, or in the shining example of a leader). The release from that mode of suffering and the advance from the time-space of instruction is climactic but almost incidental; the real investment and pleasure in North Korean cinema exists in returning to the moment of humiliation, dwelling in injustice, and drowning in tears.

Seeing these sensationalized modes of representing suffering and dwelling in the moment of waiting presents no challenge to the ideological closures of North Korean film or political discourse. Whether the savior's entry is presented as an abrupt *deus ex machina* or whether the process or moment of enlightenment is implausible, the production of the film within the enclosures of *juche* realism renders whatever happens in the end literally a foregone conclusion. What matters, as official North Korean discourse repeatedly reminds us, is that the construction of the film will be good enough to move and instruct its audience. The lesson for critics outside of that enclosure, however, lies in the terms of consumption. For while North Korean film indeed presents itself as a monolithic ideological other to the institutional mode of capitalist filmmaking, it remains clear that both sides share a set of imperatives that condition their success, however differently that is defined. If the ideological must of necessity always contain some shred of the utopian to draw us into its trap, it might be equally important to consider that films, even in North Korea, require at least a shred of enjoyment (or at least the pleasure of masochism or victimization) to function as mass art. This is also the ground on which we can begin to understand Sin Sang-ok's translatability, indeed his fecundity, in North Korea. For, unless we are to assume some sort of ideological slippage or common ground between the North and South, or slip into speculation about the fluidity or emptiness of Sin's politics, it is important to identify the enablements of the traversal that lie specifically, perhaps exclusively, in the cinematic apparatus.

3. Sin Films North

While filmmaking and to a certain extent reception during the period of Sin Sang-ok's North Korea tenure is documented by a number of sources, the events of his departure and return, as well as the details of the eight years spent there, are only recorded by Sin himself. As a result, suspicion has long prevailed over his and his wife Choe Eun-hui's claims that they were abducted, forced to produce films, and managed to defect in a dramatic episode in Vienna. This was only bolstered by Sin's perhaps intentionally provocative claims sometime after his return that had he not been allowed to produce films in the South in the 1960s, he "would have gone North on [his] own two feet."[5] North Korean authorities for their part claim that Sin and Choe defected to the North voluntarily and that they embezzled millions when they sought amnesty in 1986.[6] The validity of their accounts is not the concern of this chapter. However, a summary of the episode told in their memoirs and interviews is necessary both to contextualize the films and to draw out their wider implications.

The latter half of the 1970s saw the demise of Sin Films amidst a string of box-office flops and a falling out of favor with the Park regime that left Sin un-usually vulnerable to a string of scandals, including a bribery count for which he was acquitted and later a censorship battle that his studios eventually lost. Lured to Hong Kong by the possibility of a new production deal, Choe disap-peared in January 1978. Following leads in his search for her from old partners in Hong Kong, Sin was taken in a bizarre series of events through Beijing to Pyongyang. While Choe was welcomed warmly in North Korea, accommo-dated in comfortable isolation at luxury villas, and eventually met Kim Jong Il (who praised her as the mother of Korean film), Sin was subjected to harsh treatment from the start and, owing to a series of failed escape attempts, spent the next five years in bleak internment camps subjected to re-education pro-grams. Released abruptly in 1983, Sin was reunited with Choe and met with Kim Jong Il at an elaborate reception. In a meeting that Sin managed to record, Kim espoused his views on cinema and explained why they had been "forcibly invited": he hoped that, backed by his resources and authority, they would take over filmmaking in North Korea and elevate to it international standards. Taking control of the existing February 8 and Joseon Art Film studios and reincarnating a North Korean Sin Films Studio, Sin and Choe collaborated on nearly twenty films over the next three years. The production scale was vast, requiring up to seven hundred staff that included technicians from Japan and Hong Kong, and filming on location around the country and in parts of Northeast China and Eastern Europe. Many of the films were screened at film festivals abroad; Choe Eun-hui won prizes for direction at the 1984 Karlovy

Vary Film Festival (for *The Secret Emissary*, which Sin directed but which he credited to Choe) and for acting at the 1985 Moscow Film Festival. Location shooting and negotiation for distribution afforded them relative freedom to travel and, in March 1986, on a trip to Vienna to source exhibition venues, they eluded their handlers, and requested amnesty at the U.S. Embassy. After a course of investigations within U.S. and South Korean diplomatic bureaus, the couple were released and found their way back to Seoul in June.

Upon their return to Korea, Sin and Choe were pressured to give a full account of their experiences both by parties suspicious about their claims of abduction and defection and by those curious to glean inside information from their unique double border crossing. They held press conferences and gave a series of public interviews, where their consciously glamorous posturing (Choe in her trademark oversized sunglasses and Sin decked out in his usual ascot) gave the lie to many about their harrowing experiences. Sin returned to filmmaking in 1990 with *Mayumi*, about the 1987 bombing of a Korean Airlines jet, which Sin claimed he was compelled to make to confirm his political identity and loyalty.[7] They also published a series of memoirs on the episode, which largely focused on recreating the events of their capture and escape, saving room for broad speculations about the fate of the North Korean regime.[8]

Most intriguing for the purposes of the present research is a long conversation (essentially a monologue) with Kim Jong Il, which Sin apparently taped with a machine bought in an officer's store and smuggled into the meeting. Here, the global visibility and prestige of North Korean cinema seems to be Kim Jong Il's central concern, the ideological effect on domestic audiences only secondary. He laments that where early North Korean filmmaking, produced by staff trained in the Soviet Union, was promising, subsequent work, with few exceptions, has been largely "embarrassing" and unworthy of the world stage. Kim dwells at length on his thwarted desire to host an international film festival, and while it is clear that he is concerned about what his people are watching, he couches his concern more in terms of the formal quality than the ideological content of the films:

> so despite what our people may want, there's a reason why we can't show foreign movies on television. Chinese and Soviet films, and even American films are really good. There are even good historical treatments, but because of that we can't really put it out there or else it will invite comparison, comparison with what we've got I mean. And because we've got these university educated types. With people at their level, at that level, if we're not careful things could turn nihilistic, so our propaganda department's got to be careful and that's why our television's so rigid and staging the same things days and night. . . . [9]

Kim's point (as poorly articulated as it is throughout the text) is that the native film industry must come to rival world filmmaking, both for the artistic and political (patriotic) satisfaction of that development in itself, as well as for the positive effects this would have on social order and the maintenance of *juche* ideals. Sin's task therefore, was not to make the best Socialist-*juche*-realist films, but rather to make quality films that would implicitly speak to the fact of self-realization.

By almost all reports, Sin's films instigated broad changes in the North Korean film industry, created a cultural sensation, and did penetrate the world market (if only in the Communist bloc). His memoirs call attention to his accomplishments repeatedly: establishing the first "private" film studio, fully crediting filmmaking staff for the first time (*The Secret Emissary* [*Dora oji aneun milsa*] 1984), filming the first screen kiss (*A Million Li Across the Rails* [*Cheol gil ttara cheonman li*] 1985), filming the first utterance of "love," and bringing about the first instance of ticket-scalping (*Oh My Love* [*Sarang, sarang nae sarang*] 1985). The work was also well received by Kim Jong Il, who was especially ecstatic about the international film festival prizes, as well as by Kim Il Sung, who praised *The Secret Emissary* as having the look of a European film, and *Record of an Escape* ([*Talchulgi*] 1984) for its dramatic power. A recent survey of one hundred defectors placed a number of Sin's films in the "Top Fifty" North Korean films—*Hong Gil-dong* (1986), for which Sin claimed development credit, was number one, while *Oh My Love*, placing twelfth, was fondly remembered for its scandalous scenes.[10] Another defector, writing anonymously in the online *Daily NK* on the occasion of Sin's death in 2005, wrote that Sin's new releases would cause such a commotion in Pyongyang that jobs in movie theaters became wildly popular.[11] Sin's works, the article reflected, were welcomed as "movies that were really like movies" and brought love and energy to an otherwise dry and sterile cinema.

Sin's North Korean films, then, had a significant mass cultural effect. Sin's studio altered modes of production, installed the master-apprentice studio system, shifted the horizon of expectations for film audiences, and opened North Korean filmmaking to a sort of cinematic internationalism or cosmopolitanism, as limited as that may have been. This certainly furnishes a way of thinking about Sin's translation from the South to the North. In effect, Sin crossed a border between two ideologically opposed but identically authoritarian developmentalist regimes. The state capitalism of the South, integrated within the world capitalist economy, early on facilitated, indeed demanded, cultural production that was fully articulated with (though continually forced to "match") Hollywood and the West. The centrally administered economy of the North, robust in its first few decades, was driven into increasing insularity by the continual withdrawal and liberalization of the Communist bloc, yielding cultural production that could no longer bear "comparison." Sin's hallmark technical rigor and sensitivity to sociopolitical zeitgeists allowed his filmmaking to become the most spectacular, though by no means singular, instance of peninsular border crossing. But further, as we have seen, this traversal is conditioned in less material and more enigmatic ways by the often overlooked codes of pre-Sin North Korean filmmaking. The particular forms of spectacle, affect, and temporality that governed iconic films like *Sea of Blood* and *Flower Girl* inhabit Sin's films in complex and diverse ways. While the episode certainly marks a sensational fracturing in Sin's life, it also signals continuity within the larger, cosmopolitan scope of his cinema.

4. Enlightenment Revised

Given the eclectic body of work Sin produced over three decades of filmmaking in South Korea, it comes as little surprise that his North Korean films are generically, stylistically, and thematically heterogeneous. As in his work throughout the 1960s, the films he produced under the auspices of North Korean Sin Films came out of a studio system with an explicit mandate to produce films with mass appeal. As sketched above, Sin directed seven films: an early modern historical epic (*The Secret Emissary*), two films based on colonial period "tendency" literary works (*Salt* [*Sogeum*], *Record of an Escape*), a classic enlightenment film (*Breakwater* [*Bangpaje*]),[12] a folktale rendered as musical (*Oh My Love*), a folktale rendered as fantasy (*Shimcheong-jeon*), and a folkloric monster film (*Pulgasari*). Films made under the Sin Films production label included a number of enlightenment films set in the colonial or early liberation periods (*A Road* [*Gil*], *A Million Li Along the Rails*, *Gwangju Calling* [*Gwangju neun bureunda*], *Endless Farewell* [*Heyeojeo eonje kkaji*]), war films (*Red Wings* [*Bulgeun nalgae*], *A Sinking* [*Gyeokchim*]), and a hagiographic sports film (*Run Joseon Run* [*Dallyora Joseona*]). And before his appearance in Vienna, Sin had also planned out two period pieces, the martial arts–inflected *Hong Gil-dong* and the multi-part historical epic *Im Kkeok-jeong*.

Salt, Record of an Escape, and *Breakwater* constitute the most coherent set of films and are most closely attuned to the *juche*-Socialist-realist standard. They are also most reminiscent formally and thematically of a remarkable series of melodramatic developmentalist films (*Until the End of This Life* [*I saenmyeong da hadorok*], 1960; *Evergreen* [*Sangnoksu*], 1961; *Rice* [*Ssal*], 1963) that Sin completed in the early 1960s and for which he won the sanction of the Park Chung Hee administration.[13] Sin Sang-ok, in fact, often referred to these films, especially *Record of an Escape*, with *Rice* and *Evergreen* in the same phrase, regarding them as his best work. The continuity is not at all surprising on the aesthetic level, given the primacy of realism in Korean film criticism (South and North), or on the political level, given the shared authoritarian developmentalism of the two states. A line of demarcation, though, can be drawn in terms of the peculiar temporality-affect structure sketched above. For where the South Korean films pushed relentlessly forward, dramatizing labor, progress, and overcoming, the North Korean films idle in suffering, returning again and again to moments of pain and humiliation. In a sense this stagnant temporality reflects the sensibility of the "proletarian" literary works they adapt. But given that the majority of the works of that school were forsaken and its leaders (Yi Gi-yeong, Han Seol-ya) purged by the North Korean regime in the 1960s (though they would make a return in the late 1980s), the structuring principle of these films is perhaps more complex.

Both *Escape*, adapted from Chae Seo-hae's seminal 1924 short story of the same title, and *Salt*, based on Kang Kyeong-ae's 1934 novel, are set in Kando, the eastern stretch of land north of the Tumen river that was an imaginative, if not quite political or economic, refuge of colonial period Korea. *Escape* follows the tragedies suffered by Seong-ryeol and his family, who, having been displaced by Japanese developers from their native soil, aim to stake out an existence in the new promised land. The film is a numbing catalogue of their difficulties as peasants, starting with their harassment by local bandits, following through to the death of their son, and culminating in a horrific scene that sees Seong-ryeol's mother mauled by the vicious dogs of a local businessman. The climax pictures the moment Seong-ryeol's forbearance is finally broken; in a long scene captured almost entirely in lurid slow motion photography, he picks up a crude axe and smashes the pharmacy that turned away his mother. *Escape*'s final image, however, is its most spectacular: to a voice-over explaining Seong-ryeol's abrupt conversion to Communism, the film ends with a bombastic shot of an exploding train, a terrorist culmination of repressed, humiliated energy.

The plight of the laboring poor is even more dismal in *Salt*. At the film's center are the losses suffered by the unnamed mother: her husband is killed by marauding bandits, her son flees to join a guerrilla band, and her children, denied treatment, succumb to an epidemic virus. The sharp irony of this last event is that her youngest son was in fact the offspring of rape (by a Chinese landlord), and that the mother, in the film's darkest scenes, had tried to abort and then to smother the child. Pushed to her limits, the mother attempts to hang herself, but is saved by her neighbor, who then suggests a venture that appeals to the mother's desire to escape everything: salt smuggling. The long final sequence mirrors that of *Escape* in its abruptness and spectacle. The mother, loaded with a sack of precious salt, treks over a precarious mountain trail with a band of weary smugglers. They are suddenly attacked by bandits, but who are in turn attacked themselves and run off by a band of Communist guerillas, who then announce to the smugglers that they will protect them as they protect all the suffering *inmin*. Gazing up at the fighters, the mother awakens dramatically to the fact that her husband had been a victim of colonial violence and that her son, rather than running off with hoodlums, had sacrificed his family for the *inmin* and become a hero. Leaving her commodity sack behind, she turns back to Kando, determined to find her son and true calling.

Both *Escape* and *Salt* bear the archetypal elements of North Korean Socialist realism. Chief among these is the broad polarization between the ruling-landed-wealthy classes and the laboring-peasant-poor people. The moral bankruptcy and malevolence of the upper classes is a dichotomy repeated throughout *Escape*: Seong-ryeol's wealthy cousin sells out to the Japanese; the Kando landowners exploit their desperate tenants; the doctors turn away Seong-ryeol's dying son; and the pharmacist refuses even palliative medication to the penniless family. *Salt* also inventories the cruelties of the landed classes, among them the landlord's sexual violence and the doctor's fatal refusal to administer basic medication to the children. This cruelty is balanced of course against the generosity and solidarity of the poor. In *Escape*, Seong-ryeol and his family are surrounded by a community that bands together to celebrate the birth of Seong-ryeol's son on one occasion and to mourn the death of his father on another. Toward the end of the film, after a long absence, the poor appear spontaneously to help Seong-ryeol carry his broken mother to the hospital and even accost the wealthy neighbor to live up to his responsibility for the attack. Peasants and poor neighbors appear sporadically throughout *Salt* as well, typified by the warm-hearted friend who lends the family salt, takes the mother in after her release from jail, cuts her down from her noose, and suggests the salt trade as a form of escape. Both films therefore cleanly, if somewhat inconsistently, set up the Manichean social structure to which the protagonists will eventually awaken.

Another crucial, perhaps uniquely highlighted, dimension of the North Korean Socialist realist world is the antagonism between foreigners (and their conspirators, lackeys, and sycophants) and the native *inmin*. In *Escape* these are the Japanese who buy up the land (the country farm as well as the forested hills) and the Chinese landlords and police who exploit their labor and harass them for bribes. *Salt*'s Kando is torn apart by ethnic conflict that victimizes innocent Koreans literally caught in the crossfire. The Chinese bandit groups steal from tenant farmers, and the Powi-dan, a local militia organized ostensibly to guard against the bandits, in fact mobilize only to protect Japanese colonial interests. The *inmin* are therefore doubly colonized, subject to the whimsies of the native ruling classes as well as the brutality of the foreign soldier and entrepreneur. The films take up the standard *juche*-realist model, anticipating a revolutionary awakening to the absolute restrictions of modern colonial society and its feudal social structures. Seong-ryeol and the mother, suffering a string of tragedies at the hands of the rich, move inexorably closer ("ripening") to proper class-consciousness, which will take the shape of guerilla warfare.

But if the films structure social relations in the archetypal, if exaggerated, Socialist-realist fashion, they ultimately come up short in carrying those arrangements through to their ideological conclusion. We can see this as a function of the ambiguous political orientation of the literary works from which they are adapted as much as of the mass cultural effect they were intended to achieve. For while Sin Sang-ok thought of Chae Seo-hae's story as "a point of origin" for Korean Communism,[14] the relationship between the earnest Korea Artista Proletaria Federatio (KAPF) literature and postwar North Korean ideology is at best problematic. For even those early literary critics such as Im Hwa who were enamored of Socialist thought tended to regard Chae's work as iterations of "vulgar Communism" and closer in spirit to anarchism.[15] Indeed, the majority of Chae's stories narrate a last-minute explosion of rage and are largely bereft of class analysis or any political organizing principles. Kang Kyeong-ae's ties to Communism are even more tenuous. While her writing contains some of the bleakest, most horrifying portraits of life under colonial rule, their radicalizing moments often only apply a lesson of basic human solidarity. It is no coincidence, however, that Sin chose these pieces as among his first projects in North Korea. Their political fluidity as well as their thematic proximity to the "enlightenment" films he produced in South Korea provided fertile ground for the compelling cinema he pledged to bring to North Korea. His experience rendering enlightenment as melodrama and spectacle, in other words, was easily translated in these ideologically ambiguous texts. But in some ways, his treatment of *Escape* and *Salt* highlights the tension between cinematic pleasure and political edification that is latent in model films like *Sea of Blood* and *Flower Girl*. For while the conclusions of these latter films are mitigated by the formalization of codes of waiting and longing (usually decorated with songs of waiting for a *gwi-in,* or "savior"), *Salt* and *Escape* tip the scale toward cinematic pleasure and in so doing aestheticize the process of suffering and maximize the suddenness, indeed artificiality, of Communist enlightenment.

On the one hand, the films are quieter and relatively less embellished than contemporaneous North Korean films, minimizing the use of music and going with longer shots and takes. Meticulous care was taken in *Salt* to recreate Kando's materiality, not only through detailed sets but also in the use of regional dialect. On the other hand, the films are produced as entertainment, and toward this end Sin employed a number of tools to magnify the spectacle.

The films make liberal use of the zoom, a technique Sin had exploited early on in his career for its (cost-effective) dramatic effect, zeroing in on pained faces and implements of suffering. Further, he also staged major spectacles, ranging from the awesome landscapes of the northern stretches of the peninsula, to mob scenes, to the celebrated train explosion (which Sin often referred to as the highlight of his career). And finally, and perhaps most significantly, he exploited Choe Eun-hui's stardom. For while there were certainly stars in North Korean filmmaking before Sin Films, none brought with them Choe's signifying power and depth. Her presence in *Salt*, held patiently, sometimes torturously, in the camera's frame, serves to narrow even further the affective and temporal focus on suffering. And Choe's performance is perhaps unprecedented in North Korean cinema in its naturalness and complexity, an indication not solely of her skill but also of how Choe mobilized acting practices (including the first use of regional dialect) uncommon in North Korean film, evoking the compelling force of a return to the suffering-woman roles she took on in South Korea in films like *Until the End of This Life* and *The Life of a Woman* [*Yeoja eui ilsaeng*] (1967).

The prolongation and magnification of suffering, then, is a part of the pleasure of conventional North Korean filmmaking that Sin appropriates for these films. But while this pleasure is ultimately transmuted into revolutionary enlightenment in classics like *Flower Girl*, it becomes subtly troubled and excessive in Sin's iteration. For while *Flower Girl*, however artificially, politicizes affect, *Salt* and *Escape* sensationalize it in the fashion of a big-budget studio picture. The effect is a greater absorption and even stagnation in the affect-spectacle itself, and a greater abstraction, though by no means departure, from the ideological lesson. Whether this was Sin's intention is unknowable and largely irrelevant. Rather, it is a clearer indication of the sometimes inarticulate lines of continuity and discontinuity between the propaganda and the developmentalist-policy film, both within and between North and South Korean film. Enlightenment narratives conjoin the ideological trajectories of the two developing states; the spectacle-affect of the enlightenment film meets but also exceeds the bounds of the ideological.

5. Love, the Remake

The porosity and excess of the ideological is also apparent in sometimes surprising ways in the other generic modes through which Sin Sang-ok produced films in North Korea. Sin revisited a number of works that he produced in South Korea as classic, (culturally) nationalist, and patriotic films, reconfiguring them in various ways for North Korean production. These included a return to the 1964 blockbuster air force picture *Red Muffler*, reimagined in 1985 as *Red Wings*, and, most famously, a revision of his 1961 *Seong Chunhyang* as the folk musical, *Oh My Love*. These returns, as have been suggested above, do not simply infuse the original works with the proper ideological content. While the North Korean "versions" certainly heighten the class conflicts that are latent in the film or literary originals, they also introduce more complex affective ties and mobilize cinematic pleasures that exceed easy ideological categorization.

The *Chunhyang* story has occupied a privileged position in the historiography of Korean film and a special place in the consideration of North Korean cinema in the South.[16] While it was formalized as a literary text sometime in the nineteenth century, its origins are likely as *pansori*, the folk oral dramatic form, and therein especially amenable to adaptation to modern theatrical and cinematic forms. Among the first feature film productions of the colonial period (1923), there have been at least sixteen film versions in one form or another. *Chunhyang* has therefore become a rich cultural-historical text, both in its latent presentation of problems of gender, class, and political ethics and in its enduring popularity and openness to adaptation and revision. There have also been at least three productions of the *Chunhyang* story in North Korea, Kim Ryeong-gyu's *Chunhyangjeon* (1959), Yu Weon-jun and Yun Ryeong-gyu's *Chunhyangjeon* (1980), and Sin Sang-ok's *Oh My Love*.[17] While other stories, such as *Hong Gil-dong-jeon* and *Simcheong-jeon*, have also been produced on both sides of the border, the latent social-class critique of the *Chunhyang* tale and therein its availability to North Korean propaganda has attracted the most critical attention. In her chapter comparing North and South Korean versions, Hyangjin Lee argues that ideological differences are manifested in the narrative revisions, concluding that the North Korean versions aim to "intensify class antagonism." In a more recent essay, Wang Sunnyeo structures her arguments in much the same fashion, though with a more sophisticated eye as to how the text is overdetermined by gender relations.[18]

Sin Sang-ok's particular inflection on the *Chunhyang* historiography in some ways typifies the arguments laid out by Lee and Wang, but in others exceeds the margins of their analysis. The points of convergence and departure in the films are not necessarily plotted along the more easily defined borders of political discourse. Both *Seong Chunhyang* and *Oh My Love* were exceedingly successful commercially. *Seong Chunhyang* was born of a rivalry between two leading director-producers (and lead actresses) and the incipient industrialization of the South Korean film industry. Its unprecedented success heralded the development of the Korean blockbuster and owed much more to its production scale (all-star cast, color cinemascope photography, expensive costume and set management) than its particular representation of feminine virtue. In terms of mass appeal, *Oh My Love* created an even more significant relative impact than its South Korean predecessor. A huge color cinemascope production that mobilized hundreds, if not thousands, of extras, *Oh My Love* seems to have been the first North Korean film to have generated surplus value: from ticket prices (the aforementioned scalping) and from lurid spectacle. Having debuted on television with *The Secret Emissary* and *Record of an Escape*, Sin had begun to build cultural capital by the time *Oh My Love* was released in theaters. The real sensation, however, was created by the film's title, the first explicit mention of "love" in any public artwork, and through word of the unprecedented explicitness of its depiction of sexual relationships. What Sin brought to both *Seong Chunhyang* and *Oh My Love* was more than an auteur's stamp or a particular cultural-critical voice; he also marshaled a production system and an enthusiasm for mass visibility that fit both sides of the peninsula in different though equally significant ways.

Oh My Love preserves *Seong Chunhyang's* narrative structure with little revision or embellishment. Chunhyang is the same virtuous daughter of a *yangban* father and *kisaeng* mother and equally subject to Mongryong's sexualizing gaze. When the latter abandons her to follow his father to Hanyang (Seoul), she rebukes him for his weakness and bemoans the injustice of the class system. She takes an equally strong stance with Byeon Hak-do, the corrupt and licentious new provincial governor, challenging his trespasses with her command of Confucian ethics. And when Mongryong returns to restore justice, she meets him with the same mix of joy and reproof. Critics have remarked with some surprise at how few concessions *Oh My Love* makes to "North Korean ideological forces," in contrast to an earlier North Korean production (Yu and Yun's 1980 *Chunhyangjeon*) that liberally reprogrammed the tale to read as a stark conflict between proletarian and bourgeois virtues (while preserving, in accord with North Korean social values, the patriarchal strictures of the original narrative). But, determined to discern the "cultural and ideological" difference of the North Korean text, Hyangjin Lee points out that there is an unresolved "competition between traditional and Socialist perspectives concurring in Chunhyang's actions [that] is clearly felt in the clashing images of the heroine as a *kisaeng* and simultaneously as the virtuous wife of a *yangban* man." Lee argues that this "oscillation" is a drawback that leads the film to "suffer from inconsistency in characterization and theme."[19]

But while this conflict between the alluring *kisaeng* and faithful *yangban* wife is certainly apparent in *Oh My Love*, its presence has less (if anything) to do with "Socialist perspectives" than with the contradiction endemic to the traditional perspective itself. One of the challenges of producing the *Chunhyang* tale in any sociopolitical context has been, primarily, in reconciling the spontaneous passion of the couple's "first night" with the enduring chastity of the rest of the narrative and, secondarily, the inconsistencies of a *yangban* social order that torments but can also liberate women. Contrary to Lee's assertions, these conflicts, especially the disagreement between Mongryong's departure and return, are sutured in *Oh My Love* not by resort to higher authority or the grafting of Socialist perspectives but rather by a turn to play. The real difference of Sin Sang-ok's northern rendition of the *Chunhyang* tale is its overwhelming entertainment value and spectacle, for *Oh My Love* is not solely a period melodrama but also a musical production made in the tradition, if not the spirit, of the story's *pansori* origins. The breakout into song and dance numbers was perhaps not entirely jarring in North Korea either generically or diegetically, given the close ties there between opera and film, but their effect is nonetheless striking. Perhaps the most notable sequence in the film is Chunhyang and Mongryong's performance of the title song "Love, Love, My Love" after they have consummated their "first night." The song is a lyrical modern duet and the dance is choreographed in a flowing ballet style (made up of classic *kisaeng* movements). Beginning in the small bedroom, the number breaks out (as walls slide away) to reveal a sprawling set hung with backdrops painted with traditional poetry and landscape renderings. The singing couple winds between a series of painted screens and finish their song under the bow of a painted tree. The sudden abstraction of the scene is striking, at once calling up a live theatrical performance and the dream sequences of filmic fairy tales.

The ultimate drawing power of the film, however, stemmed in all likelihood from the thrill of seduction and the celebration of love itself. Once Mongryong has secured Weolmae's consent, he wolfishly closes in on Chunhyang in the seclusion of her room. Smoothly undoing the sash on her *cheogori*, he gets as far as taking it off her shoulders, but, sensing her unease, he turns to the lamp and blows out the light. The next time we see the couple, they are lounging in the dimly lit space and before long they break into the aforementioned song. The "first night," then, is elliptical but daring, pushing the bounds of representation with the clear suggestion of disrobing and lust. It should be noted, however, that the seduction sequence is broken by comic snippets in which Bangja recites nonsense verse and doodles sketches of his beloved Hyangdan while covering for Mongryong (who should be studying). This incongruous cutting mitigates the shock of seeing the lovers, likely making it more palatable to censors; it has the effect, though, of rendering their relationship as play. Love takes on a lighter, more whimsical tone that balances against the darker thrill of seduction. This is continued in the following number where the song performed by Chunhyang and Mongryong merely testifies, with the fluffy repetitiousness of its pop-song-like lyrics, to the "truth" and "delight" of their love for each other. The question of Mongryong's sincerity (indeed dubious in any rendition of the tale) and Chunhyang's virtuousness is not resolved by the song but rather eschewed by it. And this is perhaps Sin Sang-ok's most radical intervention here: unburdening love and sex, if only for a moment, of its deeper and more serious sociopolitical attachments. The difference between Sin's South and North Korean *Chunhyang*s is certainly political; but complex manipulation of affect and spectacle—in other words, play—is suspended within that difference.

6. Extravagance, Play, and the Monstrous

In a number of other films, especially toward the end of his tenure under Kim Jong Il, Sin staged an even more radical departure from North Korean cinematic convention. This was, again, not screened as a resistance to or even a move away from mainstream political rhetoric; neither did the films diverge from his mandate to renovate the industry toward greater global visibility and esteem. In fact, with films like *Hong Gil-dong* and *Pulgasari*, Sin's work achieved a kind of apotheosis of both demands; in so doing, however, he demonstrated their tenuous viability but ultimate contradiction.

Sin brought a sort of extravagance to bear on future productions to diverse effect. His worldly and lavish production of *Hong Gil-dong*, completed under another director following Sin's exit from North Korea, but born of Sin's production company, is a striking example. Based on the Korean Robin Hood story in which the outcast son of a *yangban* official leads a band of virtuous mountain bandits that steals from rich travelers and feeds the poor, the film was ripe for North Korean production. The story's latent social critique is amplified in the film by inventing a subplot wherein Gil-dong, as a half-caste commoner, is forbidden to marry the daughter of a *yangban*, though they are madly in love. And the vague parallels to anticolonial guerrilla struggle are spelled out by inserting a Japanese invasion, which only Gil-dong can defend against, into the narrative. But the truly remarkable dimension of this film is its appropriation of Hong Kong martial arts film codes. For Gil-dong is not simply a skilled swordsman driven to banditry but a flying warrior trained from a young age by a bearded mountain hermit in mystical martial arts. *Hong Gil-dong*'s training and battle sequences are imbued with Hong Kong convention (the laughing master, the broken sword) and employ similar special effects (speeded-up film, wire work). Further, the Japanese invasion is led by a group of ninjas, contrasting the spectacular though honest fighting styles of Korea against the dark and devious arts of Japan. Sin Sang-ok called on martial arts film specialists in Hong Kong (choreographers, cinematographers) and had imagined *Hong Gil-dong* as the first Korean "kung fu" picture.

Though it was executed out of his control, the film struck a balance between class and *juche* discourse and went on to become one of the most popular in North Korean history.

But perhaps the richest of these later extravaganzas is *Pulgasari*, the tragicomic monster film Sin made just before his departure. *Pulgasari* is one of the only North Korean films to be seen outside the peninsula and has been the subject of a relatively large volume of criticism (mostly fan-based but some scholarly), though strangely it has not attracted much attention in South Korea. Referring to *Pulgasari* as the North Korean *Godzilla*, many critics point to the similarities between the Japanese ur-monster as well as to the fact that Satsuma Kenpachiro, one of many actors to don the Godzilla suit, was brought in to play the title character. The tendency therefore has been to view the film as an uncanny copy and to see North Korean political rhetoric faithfully reproduced within it. More nuanced readings have discerned a subtle critique of that rhetoric, citing the monster's insatiable hunger and its deleterious effects on the poor, and attribute that resistance to Sin Sang-ok's personal resistance to a regime from which he was preparing to escape. But while there are certainly measures of propaganda and censure in the film, it seems more productive to see those as grounded in the mechanisms of cinematic pleasure and populism at which Sin, even in the North, always aimed his work. If there are slippages in *Pulgasari*, they are not only the sly manipulations of the author but also the consequence of the contradictions of Sin's (and Kim Jong Il's) cinematic project.

Pulgasari is set sometime in a Koryo period torn by strife between the tyranny of the king and a peasant insurgency. An old blacksmith is ordered by the local governor to forge weapons for the king's army, but when he discovers that the iron he is given for his work has been plundered from the poor farmers of his village, he refuses and is promptly thrown in jail. In his cell, he is beaten to a pulp and deprived of food; however, when his young daughter, Ami, throws rice through the bars, he stubbornly refuses to eat while his village suffers. Instead, he moulds a tiny figurine out of the rice and, with his dying breath, imbues it with the redemptive spirit of the people. Ami later recovers the figurine and when she accidentally pricks herself with a sewing needle, the drop of blood brings the tiny monster to life. She and her brother, Takse, fawn over the adorable Pulgasari and marvel as he consumes the needle and any other metallic objects he can find. Pulgasari becomes the village's protector, terrorizing the governor's men into submission. When word of the monster's trespasses reaches the king, the imposing General Hwang is dispatched to quell the growing threat. He launches a series of attacks and schemes to destroy the monster and put down the rebellion; when the monster is finally subdued and buried in a massive ditch, another drop of Ami's blood brings him back to life. With Pulgasari in the lead, a huge peasant army launches an assault on the king's palace; they overrun the king's army, and Pulgasari, after destroying the palace, squashes the tyrant under his massive foot. However, the villagers' troubles do not end with the coup; Pulgasari's insatiable appetite has left them without the tools to tend their farms. In a bizarre series of events, Ami climbs inside a bronze temple bell and tricks Pulgasari into eating her, causing the monster to self-destruct. In the film's closing scene, a once again tiny Pulgasari zaps himself into Ami's lifeless body, presumably bringing her back to life.

In terms of its overall narrative, *Pulgasari* actually owes less to the *Godzilla* pictures than to the ancient Jewish golem tale in its depiction of a monster culled from humble materials (rice for mud), turning (at least figuratively) on its creators once the task of defense is complete. Further, while Godzilla is often figured as the incarnation of the atomic attacks on Japan or, alternatively, as the return of the repressed in genteel and effeminate modern Japan, *Pulgasari* is, at least ostensibly, a more straightforward allegorization of anti-feudal (and by implication anticolonial and anticapitalist) history. Pulgasari is the incarnation of the spirit of *inmin* resistance, a fantasy of agrarian revolt against aristocratic tyranny, carried through to a gruesomely logical conclusion in the crushing of the king. That he consumes metal is, presumably, the monster's revolt against the instruments of suppression—a point driven home when he eats a cannonball, chews it up, and spits it back at the king's guard. The thesis of the allegorization is made clear when, after Pulgasari has smashed the palace and killed the king, the village (and the peasant insurgents), gathers for a raucous party to celebrate their liberation.

Yet the allegory is nowhere near seamless, just as the golem story celebrates Jewish resistance as much as it provides a lesson about hubris. In *Pulgasari*, the moral lesson is not for the peasants, but has more to do with the monster itself. For when the party is over, Pulgasari's hunger does not subside but rather drives him to eat up all of the villager's tools. It is only Ami's sacrifice—which is at the same time a more literal consumption of the *inmin*, and a sort of matricide—that stops the monster. This postrevolutionary exploitation of the *inmin*, of course, can easily be read as an attack on the ruling elite in North Korea (i.e., a revolutionary force born of the masses but one that becomes a cannibalistic and even suicidal exploitation of its labor, livelihood, and spirit).[20] This is precisely how Sin Sang-ok would characterize Kim Il Sung's regime in his "letters," published in two of his memoirs, to Kim Jong Il and Kim Dae Jung. In fact, the tenor of Sin's memoirs (i.e., the suggestively titled *The Kingdom of Kim*) encourages another reading of the film wherein the despotic though ultimately helpless king stands in for the Supreme Leader himself. This is suggested within the film by the long, wide shots of the tyrant's palace, filmed at least partly in the Forbidden City, uncannily, if deviously, reminiscent of the monumental architecture of contemporary Pyongyang.

The two allegorical interpretations do not, of course, mesh in any logical manner—the monstrous subject of revolution cannot squash the feudal tyrant of mass dictatorship. And to a certain extent the true or deep structural meaning of *Pulgasari*, relying as it would on the assumption of a reluctant and slyly defiant author, is unavailable, if not irrelevant. In its stead is the agency of the cinematic apparatus itself, radically open to alternative analyses and resistant to discursive closure, in spite of authority, repetitiveness, or command of theory and criticism. For as in the enlightenment films and the remakes, Sin produced an ostensibly politically correct film with *Pulgasari*; its danger arose in the play and extravagance of its unique pleasures as a monster film. And there is perhaps no need to assume that any of its spectators were duped by the duplicity of Sin's works. When Sin finally met Kim Jong Il upon his release from prison, the future leader apparently took his hand and, pointing at a performance praising the regime, declared, "it's all fake." Sin, of course, was "invited" to the North not to make something real, but to bring everything he had learned in Japan, and the South, and America, and make the best possible fakes around.

7. Out to the World

North Korea experienced a number of significant transitions from the late 1970s through the late 1980s. The steady economic growth that had been built on the back of a vestigial colonial industrial infrastructure, strategic trade arrangements with the USSR and the People's Republic of China (PRC), and a series of carefully managed economic master plans had reached a plateau, and it was becoming apparent that South Korea was poised to surpass the North, both in terms of economic strength and international standing. The regime more actively sought the support and assistance of the USSR and the PRC, convening a number of talks throughout the early 1980s, many of which Kim Il Sung himself would secretly attend. But while the forthcoming cooperation was more symbolic than material, the two ostensible allies were certainly more receptive than in the Khrushchev era or the immediate aftermath of the Nixon talks. The North also began to cultivate relationships with a series of Third-World or "nonaligned" nations, receiving the heads of Libya, Egypt, Congo, and even Palestine in elaborate ceremonies throughout the 1980s. The state came to be seen as a model for the postcolonial version of the "Socialism in one country" thesis and Kim Il Sung seen as a highly respected figure of sovereign strength, an (albeit limited) international prestige the regime energetically worked to amplify through orchestrated cultural and ritual exchange. But perhaps the most substantial development of the period was the rise to visibility of Kim Jong Il, culminating in his official designation as successor in 1980. Taking on the "Dear Leader" and "Party" designations, Kim moved through a series of vital posts in the Politburo and Military Commission in the process of consolidating his image and power. The 1980s was for the DPRK a period of postrevolutionary internationalism—perhaps the last such light it would see for decades.

It is essential to view Sin Sang-ok's performance in North Korea through this political history. The very fact of his border crossing, regardless of whether it was voluntary or coerced, was enabled by North Korea's efforts to resituate itself geopolitically and by the need to consolidate symbolically the power that had been conferred officially to the heir to the throne. The regime's relationships with Japan, Hong Kong, or even China and the USSR were far from being normalized; nevertheless, the 1980s witnessed the spinning of tenuous networks of communication and exchange on which Sin's internationalism would be authorized to travel. And despite the looming fact of South Korea's ascendance and the decline of Communist power, the DPRK, after two decades of economic growth and the formalization of *juche* discourse, was by the 1980s relatively self-assured and open to moderate social change and novelty as well as the influx of foreign cultural capital. Sin Sang-ok proved to be an apt fit, both in his political flexibility and the facility with which he commanded the full apparatus of the cinema. He did not, of course, bring mass culture to North Korea; rather, he helped to develop, on an extant industrial infrastructure, a kind of production system that met but then exceeded the bounds of the existing cultural-ideological machine. Sin's work was not that of a radical auteur, but the kinds of films he produced—high(er) quality, entertaining films that could perform well on the international circuit and that aimed explicitly at mass pleasure and enjoyment—sometimes bore an implicit critique of the cultural-political practices of the regime. It was a critique, however, that the regime not only absorbed but also flaunted in its controlled flirtation with the outside world.

Notes

1. While many of the films were screened at film festivals and special events in parts of the old Communist bloc, only a handful were screened after 1986. A number were shown at a 1988 film festival in Paris, while *Salt* and *Record of an Escape* were slated for screening for a retrospective of Sin's films at the 2001 Pusan International Film Festival (though they were ultimately barred via a citation of the National Security Law). A commercial copy of *Pulgasari* was produced in 2001. Access to the films for

the purposes of the present research was gained primarily through the Koryo General Trade Company in Gardena, California, a small firm dedicated to the dissemination of North Korean materials, though many of the films are now available for viewing at the Research Institute at the Ministry of Unification in Seoul, South Korea.

2. The volume of writing on North Korea has increased rapidly with the greater access to North Korean films and materials following the sudden thawing of the Kim Dae Jung presidency. See Min Byeong-uk, ed., *Bukhan yeonghwa eui yeoksajeok ihae* [A Historical Understanding of North Korean Cinema] (Seoul, SK: Yeoknak, 2005); and Jeong Jae-hyeong, *Bukhan yeonghwa e daehae algo sipeun daseot gaji* [Five Things You Wanted to Know about North Korean Film] (Gyeonggi-do, SK: Jimmundang, 2004) for the development of North Korean film. Seo Jeong-nam, *Seo Jeong-nam ui bukhan yeonghwa tamsa* [Seo Jeong-nam's Look at North Korean Film] (Seoul, SK: Saenggak ui namu, 2002); and Yi Myeong-ja, *Bukhan yeonghwa wa geundaeseong: Kim Jeong-il sigi gajok mello deurama* [Modernity and North Korean Film: Family Melodrama in the Kim Jong Il Era] (Seoul, SK: Yeognak, 2005) offer analyses of filmmaking from the late 1980s onward. Interestingly, very little mention is made of Sin Sang-ok or the mid-1980s period in any of these studies.

3. Park Myung-jin, "Motion Pictures in North Korea," *Korea Journal* (Autumn, 1991): 95–103.

4. *Yeonghwa yesul ron* [Film Arts] was first published in 1973 and has been the *sine qua non* of film theory and criticism since. As with the rest of the massive volume of writing attributed to Kim Jong Il (and the even greater volume attributed to Kim Il Sung), the actual authorship is certainly in question, but largely irrelevant. These were clearly authorized texts and as such represent the official position. Nevertheless, it is tempting to see *Yeonghwa yesul ron* as Kim Jong Il's own work, given that he headed the Ministry of Information and Propaganda and that he was a reputed cinephile. The text was translated into English and published as *On the Art of the Cinema* (Honolulu: University Press of the Pacific, 2001).

5. An Jeong-suk and Kim So-hui, "Interview with Sin Sang-ok," *Cine21* 8, no. 4 (1998).

6. While this claim is often made in informal conversation, the only published mention of this found for the purposes of the present research is in John Gorenfeld's entertaining and surprisingly informative article "The Producer From Hell" in *The Guardian* (April 4, 2003).

7. Interview with Sin Sang-ok by Yi Yeon-ho, "Sin Sang-ok: Who Are You?" *Kino* 10 (1997): 120–27.

8. Choe Eun-hui and Sin Sang-ok, *Kim Jeong-il wang-guk* [The Kingdom of Kim Jong-il] (Seoul, SK: Donga Ilbosa, 1988); *Nae re Kim Jeong-il imneda* [My Name Is Kim Jong-il] (Seoul, SK: Haengnim Chulpan, 1994); *Uri ui talchuleun kkeutnaji anatta* [We Haven't Escaped Yet] (Seoul, SK: Weolgan joseonsa, 2001).

9. Choe and Sin, *We Haven't Escaped Yet*, 256.

10. Yi Hyo-in et al, *Tongil hangukin i boaya hal bukhan yeonghwa 50-seon* [Fifty Must-See North Korean Films for Unification] (Seoul, SK: KOFIC, 2002).

11. Anonymous, "Uri ga buk eseo bon Sin Sang-ok gamdok eui yeonghwa" [Sin Sang-ok Films We Saw in the North], *Daily NK*, April 13, 2006.

12. While allusions to and brief synopses of this film are scattered throughout Sin's memoirs and in North Korean cinema catalogues, it is the one film that was not available for the present study. Sin left North Korea before the postproduction process was completed, and it is not clear whether it was taken up by remaining staff.

13. These were part of a larger tradition of "national policy" (*jeongchaek yeonghwa*), or "enlightenment films" (*gyemong yeonghwa*), that has its most recognizable roots in the national policy and German-inspired "kultur" films produced in Japan and Korea in the later colonial and war mobilization periods.

14. Interview with Sin Sang-ok, *Kino*, 125.

15. See Yi Jae-seon, *Hanguk soseolsa: geun hyeondae pyeon* [The Korean Novel, Modern and Contemporary Volume] (Seoul, SK: Sol, 2000); and, recently in English, Kim Yun-sik, "KAPF Literature in Modern Korean Literary History," in *positions: east asia cultures critique* 14, no. 2 (Fall 2006).

16. See Baek Mun-im, *Chunhyang ui ddaldeul: Hanguk yeoseong ui panjjok jjari gyebohak* [Chunhyang's Daughters: An Incomplete Genealogy of Korean Women] (Seoul, SK: Chaek sesang, 2001) for a cultural history of the tale and its adaptations to film.

17. The literal translation of Sin's film, *Sarang sarang nae sarang* would be "Love, Love, My Love," but it is rendered here as it was in the catalogue for the 2001 Pusan retrospective, primarily because that translation is less unwieldy.

18. Hyangjin Lee, *Contemporary Korean Cinema: Identity, Culture, Politics* (Manchester, UK: Manchester University Press, 2000), 100. Wang Sun-nyeo. "Nambukhan chunhyangjeon eui bigyo" [Comparison of North and South Korea Chunhyang Tales] in *Bukhan yeonghwa eui yeoksajeok ihae*, ed. Min, 299–324.

19. Lee, *Contemporary Korean Cinema*, 88.

20. Another more complex but more easily accommodated approach would be to see the monster as a personification of capitalism itself (i.e., that which breaks the back of feudal hegemony and which must itself be broken for true freedom).

5

The Politics of Unification and Neoliberal Democracy: Economic Cooperation and North Korean Human Rights

Hyun Ok Park

T HE PHENOMENON OF KOREAN unification denotes the integration of territory, state, economy, and separated families. Its normative imperative resides in its assumption of ethnic rights to national sovereignty. With nationalism embedded in the socioeconomic and political order, the national politics of unification have gotten a radical makeover. The Minjung democracy movement of the 1980s considered the task of unification immanent to other democratic and national objectives, mainly the protection of rights of labor and other alienated masses, the elimination of authoritarian rule, and the liberation of the nation from colonizing forces, including American military power, international capital, and the legacy of Japanese colonization. For the national division was being sown by the synergy of the superpowers' vested interests in Korea and Koreans' own struggle over socioeconomic reforms, and it was reproduced at least in South Korea by the state's domination and export-led industrialization in the name of strengthening the nation and ultimately absorbing the North. This previous problematic of unification amounted to a national utopia, where national unification was expected to instantaneously realize justice and democracy at all societal, national, and international levels. In the post–Cold War era, the utopian politics of unification has been infused with a transnational market expansion accompanied by a new moralism and democracy. Unification in the neoliberal capitalist era is pursued less in the form of territorial and familial union than in forms of transnational market integration that espouse freedom as a human right. Moreover, the often opposed processes of unification—"economic cooperation" (*Kyeonghyeop*) and "North Korean human rights"—are informed by competing visions for the new global capitalist order in Asia.

In this chapter, I discuss a new social consensus on the market-driven politics of unification, which I argue is a form of neoliberal democracy. The new politics of unification in the post–Cold War era is striking for its radical amnesia of the previous utopian politics, which is joined by the readymade acceptance of the market as the mechanism of unification. Unification is distilled into the quests of realizing neoliberal market expansion and its new ideals of democracy—national reconciliation, a global peace, and human freedom. This new metamorphosis of unification is marked by an extreme collective amnesia about the historical origins of the national division and processes of reproduction since the division. Removed from this process are the binding ties of unification with the tasks of decolonization, critique of capitalist domination, and social justice. I argue that a neoliberal metamorphosis of the two Koreas' relations works as a value form that reconfigures the history and everyday experience of the regime of national division into an ideological discourse that displaces a new contested capitalist hegemony in South Korea and East Asia. The perpetual wait for the return to the undivided whole obfuscates the new dynamics of unification in which ethnic sovereignty assumes not a fatigued form of the singular nation-state but a new global form of transnational community that integrates the two Koreas and Korean diasporic communities in two ways: in uneven integration and by the forces of neoliberal democracy.

South Korea's sweeping consensus on neoliberal democracy has faced criticism in recent years from South Koreans. For Choi Jang Jip, a leading critic of the current process of democratization since 1987, the failure of South Korea's democratic system has resulted from the lag between the development of political society and the rise of technocratic rule.[1] The incomplete separation of executive and legislative power within the state and the authoritarian political party structure failed to make elected officials accountable for their actions. Despite its self-identity as a participatory regime, the Roh Moo Hyun government (2003–2007) relies on the rule of technocrats, lawyers, scholars, and other experts in the name of fostering efficiency and economic growth, leading to the establishment of various research institutes tied to the administration. For Choi, the values of efficiency and growth have more affinity with authoritarianism than with popular democracy, even when the state and progressives believe that economic growth and technological advances foster democracy. Choi's analysis of expert-led rule is in alignment with the critique of neoliberal democracy by philosophers such as Ranciere and Badiou.[2]

Drawing on theories of globalization and global democracy, Cho Hee Yon, another well-known critic of democracy in South Korea, observes that globalization fundamentally transforms the relationship among neoliberal capitalism, nationalism, and democracy. In a chorus to reconceptualize democracy on a global scale, David Held, Negri and Hardt, and Iris Young advocate respectively a new global representative system as a institutional mechanism of democracy, as global governance for public participation, and as "inclusive democracy" capable of implementing justice beyond the nation-state.[3] Similarly, Cho locates new tasks for reconstructing democracy in South Korea at two levels: one is to join the effort to create a global democracy by protecting the rights of (foreign) migrant workers; and the other is to expand citizenship to socially marginalized groups—homosexuals and persons with disabilities—and to create a security net at the national level combating the negative effects of globalization on the nation-state, such as the flexible labor law.

Whether imagined within the boundary of the nation-state or at the global level, the relationship of democracy, nationalism, and global capitalism begs the question of the relationship between the national, the local, and the global. I argue that an adequate analysis of the relationship of democracy, nationalism, and global capitalism needs to go beyond a popular trend of defining global capitalism in ethical terms. In the literature of globalization and global democracy, global capitalism is explored in terms of ethics or values—free market principles, deregulation, smaller government as a public good, the reduction of social security, and the emphasis on efficiency, leading to the implementation of renewed developmentalism and flexible labor laws. In fact, the characterization of global capitalism as value, that is, globalization confounded with tendentious homogenization of the world, is routine in the literature of globalization. Encompassing global capitalism within a value system obfuscates its concrete forces that construct uneven linkages between the nation and the state. Confounding global capitalist dynamics with homogenization belies uneven integration of local places, as well as unequal effects on people within the nation and the state. Global capitalism instead needs to be understood as a concrete force that reorganizes not only social dynamics but also the state, the nation, and relationships among states.

I discuss this new politics of unification with a dual focus: to describe their constitutive effects on the neoliberal capitalist order in South Korea and Northeast Asia; and to regard them as a form of democratic politics in which a historical consciousness mediates their experiences and political responses to the neoliberal capitalist order. First I shall analyze the discourses of unification and their spectacular roles in creating a new social consensus about capitalist democracy. In situating the politics of unification in the historical context of social movement, I then discuss the discontinuous historical consciousness of social movement groups, with which they disremember elementary problematics of unification.

1. *Kyeonghyeop*: Economic Cooperation of the Two Koreas

The notion of economic cooperation between the two Koreas, or *Kyeonghyeop*, quickly became commonsense in crisis-stricken South Korea, especially after the International Monetary Fund (IMF) crisis in 1997. Even the conservative media welcomed it. Despite the occasional yet persistent critique that *Kyeonghyeop* equates with *peojugi* (unconditional giving without return, a violation of the principle of economic exchange), the public seems firm on this as a suitable policy for engaging with North Korea. *Kyeonghyeop* signifies a quintessential shift in the unification policy of the South Korean government from the once-and-for-all unification to a gradual and linear process of unification, and from territorial to market integration of the two Koreas. The previous South Korean unification policy, as much as its North Korean counterpart, was based on the idea of a total "re"-unification of territory, politics, economics, and culture, which would be possible only by the subsuming of one Korea by the other. In contrast, the *Kyeonghyeop* agreement rests on the new principle of reconciliation first and reunification later. The deepening of reconciliation between the two Koreas, as well as within each Korea over the Koreans' suffering of the national division, is conjectured to usher in reunification in the future, even though the discussion of the timing and form of unification is deferred to the future. The *Kyeonghyeop* stage is termed the confederate stage of unification in which the progression of economic unity fosters national unity while territory, state, and social and cultural systems remain divided. A well-known rationale for putting off reunification is the enormous cost of unification for South Korea, which would far exceed the cost to West Germany for German unification given that the economic gap between the two Koreas is far greater than that between two Germanys. *Kyeonghyeop* is projected to narrow the gap between the two Koreas, create a balanced development of the national economy, and foster economic community, all of which will reduce the cost of unification.

The progress of *Kyeonghyeop* is believed to be an index of the progress of unification. The increase in trade and other forms of economic exchange is imagined to foster appeasement of previous hostility. It is also expected to assist economic development in North Korea, steadily closing the gap between the two Korean economies and thus preparing a less costly passage to unification. The success of *Kyeonghyeop* is assessed by the increase in volume, types, and agents of economic exchange. Typical studies of *Kyeonghyeop* map its progress as follows: from indirect to direct trade; from the exchange of natural goods (fishery goods from the North to the South and agricultural products from the South to the North) to outsourcing of manufacturing goods in the North; and from trade-centered exchange to direct investment in North Korea and joint-venture in the development of infrastructure, tourism, and manufacturing. Progress is also assessed by the expansion in both the number of firms invested in North Korea and the number of areas of the economic exchange.[4] With about 23.6 percent of North Korea's foreign trade, South Korea is second only to China, which has 33.4 percent of North Korea's trade.[5]

Under the Kim Dae Jung government, in my view, the South Korean state has established an unprecedented hegemony over policy toward North Korea. Since then, the *Kyeonghyeop* policy has become the foundation for the state, social movement sectors, and flourishing NGOs to develop a consensus on economic and social exchanges with North Korea. *Kyeonghyeop* organizes a consensus on unification policy among capital, the social movements, and the public. Following the official discourse of *Kyeonghyeop*, the South Korean economic community assesses that *Kyeonghyeop* plays an important role in political, military, and sociocultural relations with North Korea that far exceeds its role in the economic domain and it is a link that builds trust between the two Koreas through the exchange of people and goods despite continued strain in military and political relations. *Kyeonghyeop* has been hailed by economists and businesses as a "win-win" exchange for both Koreas: Outsourcing and investment in North Korea by small South Korean firms yield increased competitiveness and relief from high wages, shortages of labor and natural resources, and high land prices; and investment supplies North Korea with capital, technology, and management expertise. A shared view among business sectors is that *Kyeonghyeop* promotes South Korean economic interests since it not only helps South Korea reconfigure its industrial structure by first moving labor-intensive and declining industries to North Korea and then transferring other industries including electric-electronic, chemical, automobile, and other hi-tech industries. *Kyeonghyeop* also could create a new market for South Korean companies by reviving the North Korean economy and increasing income in North Korea.[6] Companies are known to focus their decisions about joining *Kyeonghyeop* on the basis of scrupulous assessment of profitability, especially after they experienced the 1997 financial crisis that partly had resulted from unbridled borrowing.[7]

2. Neoliberal Democracy: Market, Reconciliation, and Peace

The idea of neoliberal democracy is at the heart of state hegemony over unification politics in South Korea. The consensus is constituted by four principles of liberalism that accompany capitalist expansion: the separation of politics and economics (*cheonggyeong pulli*), rationalization, the market as peacemaker, and modernization theory of democracy. The separation of politics and economics is framed as "economic pragmatism" in establishing national reconciliation. Primarily the separation of economics and politics is presented as an immediately imperative utilitarianism that prevents the economic process of building trust from being derailed by sporadic yet critical moments of heightened political and military tension. *Sindongbang*, a book that compares South Korean and German unification, describes it as follows.[8] The Kim Dae Jung government's Sunshine Policy recognizes the immanent dissolution of North Korea as being unrealistic. Instead it seeks to methodically prepare the conditions for unification: "The policy to embrace the North" declares the economic blockage and the principle of nonintervention—the two main approaches to North Korea—as being nonviable. The economic blockage, a key U.S. policy of sanction, not only would exacerbate the food crisis in North Korea, but also would be ineffective, as North Korea has not depended on trade and other economic exchange with the outside world, although they have grown rapidly since the 1990s. The noninterventionist approach is not desirable either, since North Korea's military capacity, combined with the widely believed spread of pessimism following economic crisis, could lead to its initiation of war. South Korea, however, requires a stable security environment suitable for foreign investment and economic growth all the more, especially after the IMF bailout of the financial crisis in the late 1990s.

The principle of separating politics and economics distinguishes the Kim Dae Jung government's *Kyeonghyeop* policy from the earlier one. This principle constitutes the kernel of Kim's Sunshine Policy, which favors the inducement of voluntary change in North Korea over the use of force as the method for resolving conflict in the Korean peninsula. According to Kim Dae Jung, "the solution" to the problem of the Korean division may be found in the fundamental changes in the Cold War structure to the degree that the U.S.-Soviet conflict brought the Korean division. With the end of the Cold War, Kim conjectures the trends of history that change from "confrontation to peace, from conflict and friction to reconciliation and cooperation, and from division to unification."[9] For him, North Korea not only confronts "inevitable" changes after the collapse of the Communist bloc but more importantly is not an exception to the post–Cold War trend of "democracy and market economy."[10]

Rationalization is another principle that constitutes the discourse of the market for the nation. Rationalization is considered a mechanism of building a national economy. The *Kyeonghyeop* policy constructs the two Koreas as a national economy. The rationalization of integration for mutual benefit is put forth by the state, economists, and other supporters of *Kyeonghyeop*. Kim Dae Jung's policy capitulates that South Korea and North Korea can transform their differences into mutual benefit: South Korean investors could export items cheaply produced by North Korean laborers as South Korean products; and North Korea could export their products through South Korea's established trade networks with the world. The *Kyeonghyeop* policy construes the exchange of South Korean capital and energy and North Korean labor and resources as a division of labor within the same society. To construct the national unity, South Korea would invest in free trade zones in North Korea, while both sides jointly develop tourism and agriculture. Moreover, with national unity, the two Koreas would invest jointly in foreign countries, especially the forestry industry in Siberia and fishing operations in the Far Eastern region, taking advantage of North Korea's fishing privileges in the sea of Schosth and Kampchaka. Laid out in the blueprint of *Three Stages of Korean Unification*—a book written by Kim Dae Jung, all of these plans are under way and being realized, except joint investment in foreign countries and the international recognition of the trade between the two Koreas as internal trade.[11]

Underlying the consensus on *Kyeonghyeop* is a renewed developmentalism. Capitalist enthusiasm of South Koreans for North Korea's immanent future is marked by a discontinuous time consciousness. Even as economic liberalization has failed to deliver on its long-promised redistribution of wealth, the trauma of the IMF crisis has reinvoked the specter of developmentalism, enabling it to creep back into the subjectivity of Koreans. Deregulated foreign capital performed the dirty work for South Korean capital in mobilizing diverse sectors of the society to rally again for national unity in support of capitalist expansion. In the current historical juncture, where the nation's cultural appeal is significantly reduced, the memory of the IMF crisis transports the radiant dream of the past into the future. Will the opening of the North Korean market alleviate the social crisis, taming the neoliberal capitalist drive, which since the 1990s has expanded the part-time labor force to more than half the total labor force, eliminated job security, and reduced the size of the middle class? When neoliberal reforms have emptied out the meaning of democracy in the economic space, will the capitalist dream for North Korea help to reconcile democratization and economic growth? While South Koreans have condemned American imperialism, they are oblivious to their own fascination with North Korea, which may not be as imperialistic as America's but is just as inequitable. The construction of the American Other—whether in the form of enchantment (the antiwar movement or internationalism of NGOs) or denunciation (anti-Americanism)—deters Koreans from recognizing and confronting their own social reality in the present.

In the advocacy of *Kyeonghyeop* no voice challenges the capitalist logic of the new South Korean (and North Korea) politics. Thus, when the capital discloses that the economic interest of earning profits is the principle structuring participation in *Kyeonghyeop*, the state's policy of deregulation loses its authority for orienting economic activities to the purpose of the nation, which encapsulates the meaning of the public good, or mutual benefit of people in the two Koreas. Furthermore, the absence of social forces capable of influencing, if not constraining, the investment decisions of the capital leaves the future of the nation to be determined in terms of capitalist logic. Without such command over the capital, the state's policy of *Kyeonghyeop* and the social consensus on it render *Kyeonghyeop* as the mechanism to remove barriers to the global expansion of South Korean capital. Unless a mechanism tames the flow of capital, *Kyeonghyeop* risks turning North Korea into the frontier for South Korean capital. The nationalist discourse conceals the capitalist interests and forces that are dominating economic exchange with North Korea.

According to Kim Dae Jung's critique of the previous *Kyeonghyeop* policy, the absence of reference to peace is a critical flaw in President Roh Tae Woo's July 7, 2007, Declaration of Reconciliation with North Korea. Peaceful coexistence requires a profound change in military and political orientations, such as the nonaggression treaty, arms control, the withdrawal of forces from the DMZ, and mutual recognition by joining the UN together. In the policy and politics of *Kyeonghyeop*, peace is simplified into the reconciliation of former enemies and the cessation of the Cold War conflicts that persist in the Korean peninsula. The construction of peace as the resolution of the past hinders recognition of the actuality of the post–Cold War era. The notion of "peace through trade" is not a new ethic. According to Karl Polanyi, this formula must be reversed into "trade through peace."[12] Trade demanded peace in the nineteenth century because nations became dependent on an international monetary system that could not function in a time of war. One century later, the market is once again invoked as a putatively self-regulating institution, this time on a global scale. Korea is not an exception. The *Kyeonghyeop* politics embody the ethos of liberal capitalism as a new social consensus. The attribution of the market to the project of nation building and peacemaking obliterates the new neoliberal capitalist order in the post–Cold War era.

Kyeonghyeop projects a linear historical change from the coexistence of the two Koreas, to the construction of peace in Asia, and eventually to unification in a federal form. In my view, this linear time displaces the crisis-ridden, repetitious time of capital. The new global capitalist system is experienced by South Korean capital and the state as a crisis of the nation-state-bound economy and as an urgent need to create a regional bloc. Global capitalist forces are reified by the discourse of *Kyeonghyeop* as the new utopian promise of peace, undergoing a dialectical reversal: In representing capitalist exchange as the mechanism of peacemaking in Asia by alleviating military tension, the unification's goals of establishing decolonization, independent national sovereignty, and social justice and equality are disremembered; and unification is only understood as a quantity market expansion that measures the progress of peace. While the notion of human rights were firmly bound to social rights to work and just distribution of wealth, not merely to the democratization of political processes, it has now become abstracted with the "rigor mortis" of universalism.

The semantics of *Kyeonghyeop* proffers its unmediated identification of capitalist exchange with reconciliation and trust. The imagery of market exchange is seen as synonymous with peace. As Walter Benjamin saw "megalomania" in the monument that "equaled both capitalist and imperialist expansion with the progressive consequence of history," a similar megalomania of recognizing market expansion as the force of modernization is also welcomed by Koreans who see *Kyeonghyeop* as the sign of the new progressive era of peace.[13] However, nothing about economic cooperation guarantees the resolution of the social antagonism that is entwined with the roles played by the superpowers' Cold War in the Korean peninsula, which led to the national division in the first place, has continued since then, and has been transformed by changes in the global capitalist system in which both Koreas participate. When economic cooperation is represented as a panacea for bringing trust, the fateful effect of forgetting on an unconscious collective scale is the espousal of abstract notions of peace as the goal of unification. Capitalist dynamics prescribe the mode of the national reconciliation by which the market becomes the fetish. It wipes out the traces of unification problematics that stoked the fire of the Minjung democracy movement in the past. It does not register the repetition of capitalist time—its uneven integration and crisis-embedded expansion. Yet peace could be a floating signifier, like nationalism or cosmopolitanism, which can be mobilized as the unifying idea of various groups across social sectors. It is up to movement activists or politicians to give it precise content. A challenge for those interested in creating new politics capable of challenging the new global capitalist system is to distinguish themselves and their leadership from capital-led unification.

The appeal to peace represents the utopian dream of democracy—social equality and unalienated social life. Unification is a utopian quest for democracy, which congeals the desire for decolonization, social justice, and sovereignty confounded with national sovereignty: it is a recognition that democracy is not an institutional change but a realization of democracy in everyday life—not in the fetishized way that it is being used but rather as a problematic that the new social relations capable of abolishing alienation and commodified relations require a fundamental change of the global capitalist system. The official discourses of national division and unification, and the social movement groups in the post–Cold War era, reduce the Cold War to military and ideological confrontation, separating national division from its capitalist (and colonialist) underpinnings.

Despite its teleological and totalizing tendencies, the Minjung democracy movement prior to 1987 offered a somber awareness of the capitalist and international environment as a condition for the continued appeal to unification. Reunification is a utopian dream in the sense that it aims to return to the undivided past, but this past has been changed during the Cold War and the post–Cold War eras, transformed by the global capitalist system that includes military industries and is accompanied by its cultural and political underpinnings such as neoconservatism in the United States and cosmopolitanism in South Korea. The Minjung movement was flawed in its imposition of social unity at the expense of recognizing differences, diversity, and open-ended effects of political events. However, it recognized the importance of embedding the utopian unification ideal in the task of changing social relations and their sources in global capitalist (and military) systems. The current civil society movement in the post–Cold War era remains trapped by the ideology that pits the movement for structural change against issue-oriented, fragmented politics, disembedding the issue of unification from social and global problematics.

3. The Politics of North Korean Human Rights

Starting in 2001 nongovernmental organizations (NGOs) in South Korea began to tackle the issue of the human rights of North Korean migrants in China. Amnesty International set up a committee on human rights in North Korea in 2001, publishing reports on the deportation by the Chinese authorities of North Koreans to North Korea, criticizing Chinese policy, and on the violation of human rights of North Koreans. Four activists of the Good Friends, a Buddhist NGO, which conducted interviews of North Korean migrants in China and published research reports, were arrested and deported in May 2005. The former democracy movement activists, especially some of the former believers in the North Korean *juche* ideology called *Jusap'a*, renounced their commitment to socialism, radical social change, and the North Korean *juche* ideology. Founding the NKnet (Network for North Korean Democracy and Human Rights), they have established North Korean human rights as a key theme of the New Right in South Korea. Good Friends, another pioneer in the promotion of North Korean human rights, is run by a Buddhist circle of former university students once involved in the democracy movement but now focused on the issue of the refugees' human rights, and far less involved in the demonization of North Korea than the NKnet. The conservative Protestant Federation called Hangich'ong, which ran a program to protect North Korean refugees and played an instrumental role in attacking the North Korean record of human rights, has joined the New Right.

The NKnet is a think-tank of the New Right Network (NRN), formed in October 2005, which encompasses six organizations that pledge liberal reform (*Chayuchueui*) in various sectors, from healthcare, textbooks, education, and the church movement.[14] It distinguishes itself from another right-wing group, the National Federation of the New Right (New Right *cheonguk yeonhap*), which the NRN sees as serving the interests of individual politicians or political parties. The New Right distinguishes itself from the so-called Old Right. While the Old Right pursued state-led economic development, namely big government, on the basis of statism (*kukachueui*) and authoritarianism, the New Right pledges their support of market-based economic growth and small government. The New Right seeks to overcome the negative factors of both the Old Right and the Old Left: elitism, abuse of power and corruption of the former, and collectivism, egalitarianism, and obsession with change of the latter. The alternative philosophical basis of the New Right is liberal democracy that rests on private property rights and market principles. It reduces the state to the administration that serves the interests of society, which is itself reduced to market interaction. It condemns attempts to relieve economic disparity and create a new collective as threatening the private property system and individual rights.[15]

The advocates of North Korean human rights and *Kyeonghyeop* differ in their assessments of the food crisis, their definitions of displaced North Koreans, and their view of the DPRK's national sovereignty. Promoters of North Korean human rights regard the food crisis as an indisputable sign that North Korean dictatorship sacrifices the livelihood of its citizens for expansion of its military power. In contrast, the defenders of *Kyeonghyeop* attribute the food crisis in North Korea to natural, economic, and international conditions. These different assessments of the food crisis lead advocates of *Kyeonghyeop* and North Korean human rights to differ on the definition of displaced North Koreans: the Supporters of *Kyeonghyeop* regard them as economic migrants, while the advocates of North Korean human rights saw them as political refugees. In their joint strategy the NGOs organized the forced entry of North Koreans into foreign embassies and consulates in China to seek asylum, the United States legislated the North Korean Human Rights Act in 2004.

The controversy over North Korean "refugees" and their human rights is reflected in the contending notions of democracy in terms of state sovereignty, democratic subjects, and the concept of human rights, all of which are intertwined. The advocacy of human rights of the displaced North Koreans in China and elsewhere is entwined with the protection of human rights of those in North Korea. Those who came to China in search of food are said to be condemned by the North Korean state to be traitors of both their country and people, an act that, according to North Korean law, is punishable by forced labor for a maximum of seven years and, in serious cases, capital punishment. Advocates of the rights of North Koreans in China and North Korea regard the food crisis as being induced not just by floods and landslides but more importantly by an evil government that dispossesses North Koreans of their rights. Spectacles of the North Korean human rights crisis depict the scope of the calamity of the food crisis, the oppressive nature of the North Korean regime, and the moral responsibility and actions required of the global community. The North Korean Human Rights Act, passed by the U.S. Congress in 2004, combines the issue of the human rights of North Koreans in China and North Korea. Taking the displacement of North Koreans as the sign of North Korea's illegitimacy, the North Korean Human Rights Act aims at not just assisting displaced North Koreans to survive in China or migrate to South Korea but also to assist North Koreans to cross the borders. The North Korean Human Rights Act also authorizes the extension of monitoring of human rights violations by the North Korean state. It also pledges to bring market reforms to North Korea and democratize it. The Act further expands American financial support for the major South Korean NGOs that are instrumental in making North Korean human rights an international issue.

The advocates of North Korean human rights represent the protection of human rights as the central issue of global democracy. When many progressive organizations in South Korea charged the advocates of North Korean human rights of infringing on North Korea's national sovereignty, the NKnet defended the advocacy of North Korean human rights. According to Kim Soo Young,

> Under the concept of human rights, neither sovereignty nor interference can exist. Since the modern nation states emerged, national sovereignty seemed to be the highest priority of a nation in setting the international order. . . . (A)fter the Cold War, when the conflicts of Socialism vs. Capitalism had disappeared, there has been an increase of a new consensus on how international communist must handle the matter of human rights violations. The consensus is that widely accepted values gained from the modern history such as human rights and democracy must be respected under any circumstances, and these values are above the national sovereignty.[16]

In other words, the NKnet characterizes the protection of human rights as a transnational value. The advocates of North Korean rights represent the protection of human rights as the central issue of global democracy. Increased awareness of it is taken as evidence of the progress of mankind and global integration. In contrast, the South Korean government, the so-called progressive NGOs, and political parties except the largest minority party (the Grand National Party) have developed a consensus in the defense of the state sovereignty of North Korea. For them, the change for democracy must be in the hands of North Koreans themselves; and South Koreans must expand cooperation with the North to induce political and market liberalization. Calling its approach toward North Korean human rights "silent diplomacy," the South Korean government prioritizes the engagement with North Korea rather than elevating the issues of human rights of North Koreans as political and international issues.

The discourse of North Korean human rights is riding on cosmopolitanism—the promotion of human rights as universal rights, rather than rights tied to citizenship. Yet some of the cosmopolitan activists espouse a nationalism that demonizes the North Korean state and seeks to bring the dissolution of the regime as a means to achieving unification. The discourse of North Korean human rights therefore continues to be interlaced with nationalism. Although ignored by analysts and activists, market forces are also inseparable from the advocacy of North Korean human rights. Market forces drive North Korean migrants to embrace the discourse of North Korean human rights, commodifying both cosmopolitanism and nationalism. Some North Korean migrants, identified as refugees in China and defectors to South Korea, regard the passage to South Korea not as a return to the bosom of the nation but as a way to earn money. The indifference of the South Korean public toward North Korean migrants in South Korea is often taken as a sign of their preference for *Kyeonghyeop* over the flow of North Koreans into South Korea. This South Korean consciousness gives priority to economic growth over nation formation. Nationalism as an ideological mechanism of this uneven global capitalism and its commodifying forces is naturalized by policymakers, activists, and even critics of neoliberal global capitalism. A nation-state-based comparison is an ideological mechanism that represents the nation and nationalism as a natural, self-contained entity and conceals the changing relations between the market and nation/nationalism.

How does North Korean human rights advocacy serve the new order of neoliberal capitalism? The visual representation of human rights violations by activists and the linguistic representation in North Korean defectors' testimonies eliminate any ambiguity about the North Korean state's evil character. This, in turn, eliminates ambiguity about South Korean democracy in the phenomenological cognition and unconscious world of South Korean experience. The representation creates flashbacks to Cold War propaganda, which in the post–Cold War era strengthens consensus on the current social order in South Korea. Relegating human rights issues to moralism preempts the politics that are vital to revealing the causes leading to the food crisis and North Korean economic and political paralysis. Michael Rogin discusses forms of Cold War demonology that continue to be invoked and circulate in the postmodern American empire.[17] The advocates of North Korean human rights beckon Cold War images of totaltarian North Korea, obliterating the new global capitalist conditions.

4. Competing Capitalist Visions

Though often in opposition, the discourses of *Kyeonghyeop* and North Korean human rights both embody the variant ideas of neoliberal capitalist democracy in South Korea, which naturalize a liberal capitalist order as a truth and prescribe the market as the engine of democracy. In the discourse of economic cooperation, market integration is trusted to build peace in and beyond the Korean peninsula, while the discourse of North Korean human rights sees the abolition of the North Korean regime as a prerequisite for establishing the market and securing the liberty of individuals. The two sensationalized visions of unification mainly differ only on whether the North Korean state is allowed to continue. The opposition of economic cooperation and North Korean human rights derives from a political and ideological framework that removes nationalism and cosmopolitanism from their social and global underpinnings—the global capitalist system and its attendant social relations, which unevenly bind people of different local/national spaces. In other words, when the politics of North Korean human rights and the politics of *Kyeonghyeop* oppose global and local democracies, there is a material underpinning of such opposition. The politics of North Korean human rights and the politics of *Kyeonghyeop* share the desire to configure a new order in East Asia. These two modes of unification politics amount to competing inscriptions of post–Cold War configurations of Northeast Asia. The affairs of the Korean peninsula have become the center of competing ideas of the Northeast Asian regional order, which the two Koreas, their neighboring countries, and the United States aspire to create via crosscutting interactions of cooperation, competition, and conflict.

I analyze *Kyeonghyeop* as a national discourse, which articulates with global capitalist dynamics. According to the team of Han'guk cheongch'i yeonguhoe, the proposed breakthroughs with North Korea and the Socialist bloc in South Korea in the late 1980s resided at the contradiction in the world order: increased engagement of South Korea with the USSR and North Korea on the one hand, and renewed cooperation with U.S. military expansion on the other. This global structure posed an inherent limit to unification and Northern policies in the late 1980s. The United States determined the pace of South Korea's unification and Northern policies. The United States exhibited a lukewarm attitude, saying that "South Korea's Northern policy to improve relations with the USSR, China, and Eastern European countries is a good idea," but "the transfer of technology to the USSR and Eastern European countries requires caution."[18] It also warned that while improving its relations with South Korea, the USSR was still continuing to supply armaments to North Korea.

The dissolution of the Cold War tension between the United States and the USSR did not lead to world peace. Instead, the United States attempts to monopolize the term "peace" to describe actions that attempt to advance U.S. hegemony in the new world order of the post–Cold War era. The *Kyeonghyeop* policy signifies South Korea's departure from the binding submission to the Cold War economic structure—the U.S.-Japan-South Korea bloc—to create a new East Asian economic bloc. South Korea's attempt to reconfigure the East Asian regional order in the post–Cold War period began in the late 1980s, with the momentous change toward the special interest in creating a regional order based on neoliberal principles under the Kim Dae Jung government. The primary impetus in South Korea's new relations with the outside world is the economic force, which replaces the Cold War principle of anti-Communism. In the policy called Nordicpolitik, the Roh Tae Woo government (1988–1992) initiated economic exchanges with the Soviet Union and North Korea. As for its own groundwork for new relations with East Asia, the Soviet Union enacted arms reduction and held summits with China to relax its thirty-year-old conflict with China. Liberalization of the South Korean economy was furthered under the policy of *Segyehwa*, or globalization, under the Kim Young Sam government (1993–1997). As a new hegemonic ideology, the phrase *Segyehwa* replaced the old developmentalism. When liberalization, accompanied by the signing of the Uruguay Round and the GATT agreement, triggered fierce opposition from farmers and other sectors, the term *Segyehwa* became a new hegemonic ideology that treated the oppositional forces as parochial nationalists and collective egoists.[19]

In the aftermath of the 1997 financial crisis, the Kim Dae Jung government and its successor, the Roh Moo Hyun government, have taken liberalization to a different level. While the Kim Dae Jung government established firmly neoliberalism, the Roh Moo Hyun government interlaced neoliberal reforms with the aspiration to create a new regional bloc capable of replacing the U.S. hegemony in Asia. It has advanced liberalization by deploying it as the mechanism for creating a new Northeast bloc. It has represented *Kyeonghyeop* as the key to making South Korea the center of the Northeast hub, especially in the areas of trade, finance, and research and development. The chairman of the "Committee to Promote Northeast Economic Center" (*Tongbuka kyeongjechungshim chujin*), the presidential advisory committee, elaborates the facilitation of the Northeast hub as follows: To become a center of trade, Inchon, Pusan, and Kwangyang ports must be turned into international trade centers; as for becoming the financial center of Asia, deregulation and liberalization of foreign currencies are necessary to create the consolidation of foreign finance companies in Seoul, competing against Hong Kong and Singapore.[20]

North Korea constitutes the last link in the completion of the Northeast Asia economic bloc. Whereas China and Russia have steadily expanded their economic relations with South Korea throughout the post–Cold War era, they have begun to renormalize relations with North Korea only since the late 1990s, pledging aid to North Korea and further cooperation. Japan and North Korea have also attained a milestone in their process of normalization by reaching an agreement on compensation instead of reparation for the colonial occupation of Korea by Japan. Official normalization, however, is stalled momentarily because of Japan's fury over the abduction of Japanese nationals by North Korean security agents, and because of the new military alliance between Japan and the United States. A shared vision of a Northeast Asian bloc enabled each neighboring country to formulate a trilateral relation with the two Koreas. This vision foresees the trans-Siberian freight route linking the natural resources and manpower of Russia and North Korea with capital, technology, and surplus production of South Korea, Japan, and even China. The Asian community is projected not only to consolidate itself among Northeast Asia players but also to expand its power into Europe and Southeast Asia. The actualization of the Asian community is forestalled by other territorial disputes, competition for hegemony, and disagreement on the U.S. war against Iraq. Yet the capitalist crisis in Asian countries invigorates the aspiration for unity. These are favorable circumstances for South Korea, Japan, Russia, and China to oppose U.S. aggression against North Korea, which they regard as threatening the sovereignty of North Korea or the military power of China—often said to be the true target of the U.S. offensive in North Korea—and as threatening their common interests just when they are beginning to coalesce.

The politics of North Korean human rights are articulated to the American counter-strategy of reconfiguring East Asia in the post–Cold War era, as well as the South Korean partnership with the United States. The objective of the United States is to establish its hegemony in Asia, which, excluding Japan, Australia, and New Zealand, accounted for about one-quarter of world GDP by the mid-1990s and one-third by 2005. As Gowan writes about the importance of the Asian economy, the region, if Japan is counted, emerges as the center of the entire world economy, shifting out of the control of the Atlantic region for the first time in about five hundred years.[21] During the 1990s to 1997, the region accounted for some two-thirds of new global investment and for about half of total world GDP growth. The Asian economy has become the important stimulator of the economies of the Atlantic world. When the Cold War was over, the United States sought to revamp the old U.S.-Japan-South

Korea alliance—the building bloc of the Cold War—against the emergent power of China in East Asia, while creating new allies like India and Pakistan in other parts of Asia. The United States identifies China as the major threat to American hegemony in Asia.

The presidency of George W. Bush generated momentum for the U.S. strategy in Asia. Two primary moral discourses of the Bush government are defense of world peace from "rogue states" and protection of the human rights of all human beings, not just U.S. citizens. The redefined notion of human rights in the post–Cold War era endows the United States with the medium through which it reconstructs alliances with other states. As Gowan describes classic U.S. tactics during the Cold War, the United States invoked threats associated with Communism to persuade other countries that they faced external threats and that the United States had the resources to protect them from such threats.[22] Violation of human rights by Communist states was taken as a principal character of the menacing Communism. In the post–Cold War era, the rhetoric of defending world peace through the establishment of a market democracy and of protecting human rights of all human beings in the world continues to constitute the American moral discourse in claiming its leadership in the world. But this time, a newly identified threat to world peace is the rogue states, which, according to the Project for the New American Century, abuse their citizens, waste public resources for the interests of individual rulers, violate the basic value of human beings, and hate the United States and its ideals. The United States appeals to its pledged responsibility in protecting the universal value of human rights more strongly than before. It also propagates the principles of free market and free trade, which refer to the deregulation of economic activities, tax-reduction in financial policy, and the creation of free trade with other states. Naming North Korea as a rogue state and invoking the U.S. right to preemptive war against a state with weapons of mass destruction have served the United States in reconfiguring security and economic relations with Japan and South Korea.

The issue of North Korean human rights, in tandem with the issue of North Korean nuclear weapon and missile development, is a constituent of building a new U.S. hegemony in Asia. The U.S. strategy of "military global sourcing" and "strategic flexibility" has guided the new U.S.–South Korea–Japan security network. U.S. military global sourcing in South Korea consists of reducing U.S. infantry forces, relocating U.S. forces to South Korea's west coast facing China, relocating its Yongsan military installation, and changing strategic relations with South Korea, such as the heatedly debated transfer of the authority to control South Korean armed forces from the United States to the South Korean military. In pursing "strategic flexibility" of security, the United States aims not only to reduce its military expenditure by having South Korea take more financial responsibility but also to deploy U.S. weapons and armed forces at will. The threat from North Korea, together with the reopening of cases of Japanese abducted by North Korean security agents in the 1970s, has galvanized the drive in Japan to change its constitution and change its army from defensive to offensive units. It has also laid the ground for a new agreement between the United States and Japan.

5. Conclusion

The meaning of economic cooperation between the two Koreas is best understood by the urgent desire among social movement groups, after their embrace of the official policy of *Kyeonghyeop* as an emblem of the post–Cold War policy, to create a new social consensus on South Korea's approach to North Korea, unification, and, by extension, the Korean nation. During the presidential election in December 2007, social movement groups sought to create a broad coalition, regarding as largely futile the fragmentation of social movements that had been embraced as a means of enhancing specialization (*cheonmunhwa*) and rationality (*hapriseong*) since the late 1980s. The pressing impetus to reshuffle "unification" politics results from the social movement groups' perplexity over the inertia of the current unification movement in which the advocacy of *Kyeonghyeop* and the promotion of North Korean human rights are placed at the center. The decade-long practice of *Kyeonghyeop*, despite the misgivings of conservative voices in South Korea and the U.S. government, has significantly reduced the tension between the two Koreas, which the South Korean state and so-called progressive groups assess as the vital basis for creating Korean unification and constructing peace in Northeast Asia. Yet at the same time, activists within the unification movement identify the aimlessness of their movement as its fundamental problem. In a self-critique, the movement has been reduced to day-to-day hosting and management of events, such as exchanges of culture, youth, athletes, and delegates, and the commemoration of the June 15, 2000, declaration of mutual recognition of the two Koreas.

The fragmentation of the social movement and event making as an inclusive form of public participation are postmodern prescriptions for new popular politics. They are considered globally to be alternatives to the previous radical (Socialist) politics that have been criticized for sacrificing means to the ends and exerting force in the name of building revolutionary unity and creating a new collective. In my view, the recognized need for a full reshuffling of the social movement at the current moment in South Korea underscores the loosening grip of the democratic coalition of democratically elected officials and the social movement on popular support. The indisputable confidence of the South Korean public over the easing of tension with North Korea seems to remain stable even after North Korea's nuclear testing in October 9, 2006. The support for *Kyeonghyeop* among the public appears to be sustained. Taking into account the difficulty of sustaining the current unification movement, it is, however, difficult to characterize such reactions of South Koreans toward North Korea merely as the signs of increasing trust and reconciliation with North Korea, or the testimony of the success of the current democratization, at least from Kim Dae Jung's government. With deepening insecurity of employment, the real-estate bubble, and the new appetite for consumption as the backdrop, the disbelief of South Koreans over the North Korean threat can be also read as a growing indifference toward North Korea and the issue of unification. The crisis of the unification movement, thus, demonstrates the current crisis of democratization. The attempt to reorganize the social movement denotes an endeavor to create a new popular consensus on democracy.

Acknowledgments

This paper is part of a larger book project on the hierarchical Korean community, the research for which has been supported by the American Council of Learned Societies and the John D. and Catherine D. MacArthur Foundation.

Notes

1. Choi Jang Jip, *Minjuhwaihueui Minjujueui: Hangukminjujueui posujeok kiweonkwa wigi* [Democracy after Democratization: The Conservative Origins and the Crisis of the Korean Democracy) (Seoul: Humanitas, 2002).

2. Jacques Ranciere, *Disagreement* (Minneapolis: University of Minnesota Press, 1999); Jacques Ranciere, *Hatred of Democracy* (London: Verso, 2006); Alain Badiou, *Metapolitics* (London: Verso, 2005).

3. David Held, *Democracy and the Global Order: From the Modern State to Cosmopolitan Governance* (Stanford, Calif.: Stanford University Press, 1995); Antonio Negri and Michael Hardt, *Empire* (Cambridge, Mass.: Harvard University Press, 2000); Iris Young, *Inclusion and Democracy* (Oxford: Oxford University Press, 2002); and Cho Hee Yon, "Sinjayueui Sidae-post-minjuhwasidaeeui hanguk minjujueuieui saeroun kwajedeul" [New Tasks of Korean Democracy in the Age of Neoliberalism and Post-Democracy]. A paper presented at the Symposium: "Is Democracy Still a Language of Hope?" January 16, 2006, Seoul, South Korea.

4. For the statistical and graphic description of South Korean import and export volumes from 1989 to 2004, see Lim Won Hyeok, "Pukhaekkwa nambuk kyeonghyeop: Yongyeinga, pyonghaenginka?" [North Korean Nuclear Development and the

Economic Cooperation between the Two Koreas: Are They Entwined or in Parallel?],
in *Kukhoe nambuk kyoryuhyeopryeok euiwonmoim*, a paper presented in the symposium on The Peaceful Resolution of the Crisis in the Korean Peninsula and the Two
Koreas' Relationship, March 28, 2005, Seoul, South Korea.

5. Lim Won Hyeok, "Pukhaekkwa nambuk kyeonghyeop."

6. Hong Il Pyo, "Nambukkyeonghyeopeui hyeonjusowa hyanghu kwaje" [The
Current Conditions of the Two Koreas' Economic Cooperation and Future Agenda],
in 6.15 *Nambuk kongdong seoneon silhyeongwa hanbando pyeonghwareul wihan tongil
yeondae* [The Current Conditions of the Two Koreas' Economic Cooperation and
Future Agenda], a paper presented in the Tongil [Reunification] Symposium, July 22,
2004, Seoul, South Korea, at www.615tongil.org.

7. "Nambukkyeonghyeop chejilkaeson" [A Basic Change of the Economic Cooperation of the South and North Korea], *Hangyeore*, May 21, 2003, at h21.hani
.co.kr/section-021005000/2003.

8. Hwang Byongduk et al., *Sindongbang cheongchaekkwa taebuk poyong cheon-
gchaek: Brant wa Kim Daejungeui minjok tongil tagusang* [The New Eastern Policy
and the Policy to Embrace North Korea: The Great Vision for National Unification by
Brant and Kim Dae Jung] (Seoul: Turi, 2000), 79–82, 161–81.

9. Kim Dae Jung, *Kim Dae-jung's "Three-Stage" Approach to Korean Reunification:
Focusing on the South-North Confederal Stage* (Los Angeles: The Center for Multiethnic
and Transnational Studies, of the University of Southern California, 1997), 5.

10. Kim Dae Jung, *"Three-Stage" Approach*, 6.

11. Kim Dae Jung, *"Three-Stage" Approach*, 6.

12. Karl Polanyi, *The Great Transformation: The Political and Economic Origins of
Our Time* (Boston: Beacon Press, 1964).

13. Susan Buck-Morss, *Walter Benjamin and the Arcades Project* (Cambridge, Mass.:
MIT Press, 1991).

14. It includes organizations in various sectors, including healthcare (*Euiryowasa-
hoe*), textbook reform (*Kyogwaseo* forum), education reform (*Chayucheui kyoyuk
undong yeonhap*), and church reform (*Han'guk kidokkyo kaehyeok undong*).

15. For the critiques of neoliberalization and globalization as the causes of the
IMF crisis, see David Harvey, *The New Imperialism* (London: Oxford University Press,
2003); Neil Smith, *The Endgame of Globalization* (New York: Routledge, 2005).

16. Kim Soo Young, "The North Korean Human Rights Act in Comparison with
Other U.S. Legislation Concerning Foreign Countries," *KEYS* 18 (Autumn, 2004).

17. Michael Rogin, "'Make My Day!'; Spectacle as Amnesia in Imperial Politics,"
Representations, no. 29 (Winter, 1990): especially 114–16.

18. *Han'guk ilbo*, February 21, 1989.

19. Jongryn Mo and Chung-in Moon, "Democracy and the Origins of the 1997
Korean Economic Crisis," in Jongryn Mo and Chung-in Moon, eds., *Democracy and
the Korean Economy* (Stanford, Calif.: Hoover Institution Press, 1999).

20. Lee Sungcheol, July 25, 2003, *Economy 21*. Online: www.economy.21co.kr.

21. Peter Gowan, *The Global Gamble: Washington's Faustian Bid for World Dominance* (London: Verso, 1999).

22. Gowan, *The Global Gamble*.

6

Refugees, Abductees, "Returnees": Human Rights in Japan–North Korea Relations

Tessa Morris-Suzuki

1. From North Korea to Japan, 2007

AT FOUR O'CLOCK IN THE MORNING on June 2, 2007, a man out fishing near the port of Fukaura in Japan's Aomori Prefecture came upon a small boat with four people in it. The boat had left the North Korean port of Cheongjin one week earlier, and the people on board—a couple and their two adult sons—were North Korean refugees.[1] They were the first to appear on Japan's shores by boat since 1987, when eleven refugees from North Korea had arrived in Fukui on a boat called the *Zu-Dan 9082*. The events in the sleepy little town of Fukaura briefly became headline news in Japan, igniting media debate about a possible impending influx of displaced people from the Korean peninsula, and about the appropriate Japanese response to the North Korean refugee problem.

The four refugees told Japanese authorities that they had been heading from Cheongjin to Niigata (a route which, as we shall see, has an interesting historical resonance), but had been carried north to the coast of Aomori Prefecture by the currents. However, even though their intended landfall had been Niigata, they were apparently not seeking asylum in Japan, but were instead asking to be resettled in South Korea.[2] After a brief detention in Japan, and a flurry of negotiations between the Japanese and South Korean governments, on June 16 the four refugees were shipped out of Japan to South Korea,[3] and Japanese public interest in the incident subsided. In this chapter, I want to use the arrival of that small boat as a starting point for thinking about the North Korean refugee issue (particularly as it relates to Japan), and more broadly for considering some aspects of the contentious problem of North Korean human rights.

For anyone concerned with human rights in Asia, the North Korean case presents an intractable problem, above all because it is one of the cases where human rights and political calculations have become most inextricably enmeshed. There can be little doubt that, by almost any measure, the current regime in the Democratic People's Republic of Korea (DPRK) is among the world's worst violators of human rights. The problem is what the rest of the world can or should do about it.

For those (mostly on the right of the political spectrum) who advocate outside intervention to force regime change, the answer seems simple. North Korea's human rights violations are their chief justification for demanding the use of pressure, or even of military force, to overthrow the current regime. Such intervention, they claim, would save many lives—the lives of those incarcerated in labor camps or facing malnutrition and possible starvation. At one level, this claim is probably correct, but (as I shall try to show in this paper) one does not need to probe very far into this rhetoric of human rights to find that it is riddled with self-contradictions.

However, there are a large and growing number of people (among whom I would include myself) who believe that the use of outside threats or force to trigger regime change in North Korea would, in the long run, cause much more human suffering than it could relieve. Although the situations in North Korea and Iraq are in some ways very dissimilar, it is impossible to ignore the lessons of Iraq. There can be no doubt that the invasion of Iraq *did* save some—perhaps many—lives. There are people who would have died in Saddam Hussein's prisons, but who survived because of the invasion. At the same time, however, it is equally clear that the invasion caused an even larger number of deaths, terrible human suffering, and a mass of new human rights problems to which no solution is in sight. It is reasonable to suggest that outside-imposed regime change in North Korea would do the same, and that a gradual process of engaging North Korea in interaction with the region is the best way of allowing a lasting transition to a new and better social order.

The problem for those who take this view, though, is that the notion of promoting engagement leaves little scope for practical steps to address existing human rights violations in North Korea, and it therefore becomes all too tempting to ignore these violations or sweep them under the carpet. The task of identifying alternative responses to the North Korean human rights problem—responses not linked to a hawkish political agenda—is an urgent and difficult one. In the pages that follow, I shall use a critical analysis of some Japanese debates on North Korean human rights as a basis for considering some aspects of this problem.

Beginning from the arrival of the four boat people in June 2007, I shall work backwards through history to explore some of the factors influencing Japan's response to North Korean human rights issues. In the final section of the paper, I propose some possible new approaches that might at least help to address one practical problem: the plight of the small but growing number of people attempting or hoping to leave North Korea for Japan.

2. Victims or Secret Agents? Japan's Response to North Korean Refugees

The arrival of the four boatpeople in Fukaura evoked a mixed response from the Japanese mass media. Much of the comment was sympathetic. Newspapers and television commentators expressed astonishment that they had survived the dangerous voyage, and stressed the desperation that must have driven them to embark on their perilous journey. The *Yomiuri* newspaper's front-page article noted that the refugees had brought poison with them to drink if they were caught by the North Korean authorities, and quoted them as saying that they were fishermen, and that they had "left North Korea because life was so hard."[4] The *Asahi*'s editorial called for tighter border controls and for dialogue between the region's countries to develop a framework for receiving refugees. But it also reminded readers that more than one hundred North Korean refugees were already living in Japan and needed greater assistance and support than they had received so far.[5]

However, particularly after it was revealed that one of the two young men on the Fukaura boat had been carrying a small amount of amphetamines, some of the public commentary turned more hostile. In late June, the right-wing *Sankei* newspaper invited its readers to respond to a series of questions about Japan's policy toward North Korean refugees, one of which was "Should those who want to stay in Japan be recognized as economic refugees?" Sixty-eight percent of respondents to this question said "no" and only 32 percent, "yes." Since the respondents were a self-selected group of *Sankei* readers, their views cannot be seen as representing Japanese public opinion, but the comments they submitted to the newspaper shed an interesting light on the range of emotions evoked by the arrival of North Korean refugees. One self-employed man in his sixties posed the questions: "Are they really refugees? Are they really a family? Maybe they've been sent as secret agents [*kōsakuin*] posing as refugees. Has this been checked properly?" Others made a similar point: a white-collar worker in his thirties, for example, wrote: "On no account should they be accepted as economic refugees. There is a high probability that some of the people who claim to be refugees are really secret agents. Besides, the Japanese government and the Japanese people lack the mental space and preparedness [*seishinteki yoyū to kakugo*] to accept economic refugees."[6]

Repeated reference to "secret agents," of course, reflects the way in which the refugee issue is intertwined in the popular imagination with the abductions of at least thirteen Japanese citizens by North Korean agents during the 1970s and 1980s. (The North Korean government admits to thirteen; the Japanese government claims that the number is at least seventeen).[7] The wellsprings of the fear and suspicion expressed by the *Sankei* readers can better be understood if we consider an interesting commentary on the arrival of the four boat people by Araki Kazuhiro, a professor at Takushoku University who also heads the Investigation Commission on Missing Japanese Probably Connected to North Korea [*Tokubetsu Shissōsha Mondai Chōsakai*, commonly known in Japanese as *Chōsakai* for short]. The *Chōsakai* is one of a cluster of closely linked and highly influential lobby groups campaigning for action on the abduction issue. Its main role is to investigate hundreds of unsolved missing-person cases stretching back as far as 1948 in search of evidence that they were abductions by North Korean agents, and its energetic detective work has produced estimates of the number of kidnap victims that range as high as 470.[8]

Araki begins his report on the arrival of the refugees by pointing out that the stretch of Aomori coastline where the boat arrived is "a mecca for landings by secret agents":

> people from the mass media who visit the fishermen's houses that line the shore are surprised to find that houses everywhere contain letters of thanks from the police. As I discovered from experience, everyday conversations there are full of stories about such things as discovering radios or equipment bags belonging to [North Korean] secret agents, and handing these in to the police.[9]

Having set the scene with this image of sinister visitations, he goes on to concede that "it seems the four people are not secret agents, but even if they are refugees, I can't help feeling that something is afoot." Recalling a prediction he first reported fifteen years ago, Araki cites an estimate by the former head of the Tokyo Immigration Control Bureau, Sakanaka Hidenori, that economic and political crisis in North Korea might generate a wave of 300,000 refugees sweeping, tsunami like, onto Japan's shores. This prediction, as Araki explains, is based on the fact that, between 1959 and 1984, 93,340 people—mostly ethnic Koreans resident in Japan [*Zainchi* Koreans], but including over 6,000 Japanese spouses and dependents of Japan—took part in a mass "repatriation" from Japan to North Korea (the details of which are described in greater detail in a later section of this paper). The experience of these "repatriates" [*kikokusha*][10] has generally been very difficult, and it is reasonable to assume that a large number may now want to go back to Japan. Araki agrees that Japan should respond to demands from former repatriates who seek re-entry to Japan, but the overall message of his article is that "the only way to stop ordinary North Koreans from arriving as refugees is ultimately to replace the Kim Jong-Il system and create a better regime." He concludes by summarizing the *Chōsakai*'s view of the boat people as follows: "I imagine that there will be a growing number of people in Japan who will say, 'let's drive out all the refugees!' Of course, we are opposed to this view, but we hope that those who feel alarmed by the refugees will start saying 'in that case, let's bring about regime change as soon as possible!'"[11]

Araki's image of hundreds of thousands of North Korean refugees poised to descend on Japan is echoed in other quarters. A recent prediction by a government security think-tank came up with the slightly more modest estimate of 100,000 to 150,000.[12] These predictions seem to me extremely far-fetched. However, it is undoubtedly true that some of the Cold War era repatriates would like to return to Japan, where many still have relatives. The one hundred or more refugees already resettled in Japan, and alluded to in the *Asahi* editorial on the Fukaura incident, are in fact all people who took part in the Cold War migration from Japan to North Korea or dependents of these repatriates.[13] The arrival of these returnee-refugees [*dappoku kikokusha*], who have trickled into Japan over the past decade or so, has been almost entirely unheralded by the media, since they came not by boat but (in most cases) on flights from Beijing or other Asian cities arranged with the help of Japanese diplomatic missions. Their precise number is uncertain, because there is no official resettlement scheme and no figures are published by the government, but the best estimate as of mid-2007 was around 140.[14] It seems very possible that, with accelerating social and political change within North Korea, the number seeking resettlement in Japan may rise to several thousand, and this fact makes the question of Japan's response to the refugee problem an important and pressing one.[15]

Yet, as some commentators on the refugee issue pointed out, the Japanese government has yet to define any clear policy on the refugee issue. Of the 140 or so refugees already in the country, many are Japanese citizens, and those without Japanese nationality have not been granted asylum under the Geneva Convention on the Status of Refugees, nor under Japanese national law. Rather, they have been allowed to remain in Japan through a discretionary act of the Japanese Ministry of Justice. The government's response to arrival of the four boat people was likewise entirely *ad hoc*. Lawyer Ōhashi Tsuyoshi argues that the most appropriate course of action would have been to treat them as asylum seekers and assess their claims according to the norms of the Geneva Convention on the Status of Refugees, to which Japan is a signatory, but this did not happen. Instead, the four North Koreans were held in police "protection," using a law normally applied to runaway children, and then shipped out to South Korea.[16]

In fact, though a new law passed in 2006 (commonly referred to as "North Korea Human Rights Act") commits the Japanese government to developing a policy on the refugee issue, nothing has so far been done to put this intention into practice.[17] The arrival of the boat people indeed casts interesting light on the paradoxes inherent in the new law. The legislation's full title is "The Law on Countermeasures to the Abduction Problem and other Problems of Human Rights Violations by the North Korean Authorities" [*Rachi Mondai sono ta Kita Chōsen Tōkyoku ni yoru Jinken Shingai Mondai e no Taikō ni kansuru Hōritsu*]. It will be referred to subsequently as the North Korea Abduction and Human Rights Law. Although it is in some respects modeled on the U.S. North Korea Human Rights Act of 2004, the law's cumbersome title suggests just how much the Japanese version is driven by the agenda of the abduction problem, which has become the central issue in Japan's relationship with the DPRK.

The law focuses mainly on detailing the pressures to be placed on North Korea to resolve the abduction issue. Article Six commits the Japanese government to "endeavoring to establish measures related to the protection and support of North Korean refugees [*dappokusha*],"[18] but is very short on specifics. The only elaboration of this is a statement that Japan will cooperate closely with foreign governments, international organizations, and "non-governmental organizations [*minkan dantai*] both at home and abroad" to address the problems of abductees, refugees, and other victims of North Korean human rights abuses. The failure to come up with anything more concrete than this, despite massive criticism of North Korea's human rights record in Japanese media and political circles, reflects internal contradictions that we have already glimpsed in Araki Kazuhiro's commentary on the arrival of the boat people.

3. The North Korean Crisis and the Rise of "Human Rights" Nationalism in Japan

To understand these internal contradictions, it is necessary to look a little more closely at the political environment that framed the emergence of the Japanese media debate on the North Korean human rights issue. The language of human rights is of course protean, always pulled between one political pole and another, as each side seeks to claim it for its own. Throughout the 1970s and 1980s, though some Marxists discounted the notion as bourgeois window dressing, the concept of human rights can generally be said to have been more widely used as a political ideal by the Left than by the Right. Human rights activists in Japan, for example, battled for workplace equality for women and minorities, opposed the fingerprinting of foreign residents, and lobbied unsuccessfully for the abolition of capital punishment. In the process, they were sometimes criticized for attempting to impose an inappropriate alien ideology on Japanese society.

After the collapse of the Soviet Union, however, the language of human rights (not only in Japan but also elsewhere) came to be more widely used by the Right as well as the Left, and was increasingly used to justify military interventions in countries that were deemed to fail international humanitarian standards. German academic and politician Uwe-Jens Heuer described this trend as the rise of "human rights imperialism," which he saw as being characterized by an "instrumentalization of human rights." A key feature of this process, according to Heuer, was that the discourse of human rights became separated from international law. Rather than respecting and implementing the rights embodied in international charters, powerful countries used military force to punish weaker states that failed to respect human rights, with these rights themselves being unilaterally and selectively defined by the powerful.[19]

In the Japanese context, I want to trace a phenomenon related to, though somewhat different from, the trends discussed by Heuer. I call this phenomenon the rise of "human rights" nationalism. The phrase "human rights" is in quotation marks because, as I shall argue, although this ideology makes extensive use of the rhetoric of human rights, its recognition of rights is highly selective, and its underlying logic is in fact one of "protection" rather than of "rights." In "human rights" nationalism, the emotions of humanitarianism become instrumentalized in the service of national security. Anxiety about the destiny of one's own nation comes to be focused on a particular external force—a foreign nation, an alien ethnic group, and so on—which is seen both as radically threatening to national security and as violating key human rights. Thus nationalism and human rights are fused into a single ideology that has great emotional appeal.

But the problem is that (like Heuer's "human rights imperialism") this ideology is *not* based on respect for the international laws and institutions that (however imperfect they may be) provide the foundations for the long-term maintenance of human rights. Instead, "human rights" nationalism focuses selectively on particular humanitarian concerns that happen to overlap with national security concerns. Even more importantly, in this ideological fusion, it is always human rights that are made the instrument of the security of the nation-state, not the other way around. So, in any situation where the interests of human rights diverge from the interests of national security, it is always the former that are sacrificed to the latter.

"Human rights" nationalism is specific neither to Japan nor to the 1990s. It has existed ever since the concepts of nationalism and human rights first appeared. It should also be emphasized that other strands of human rights discourse in Japan have continued to flourish outside the restricting framework of "human rights" nationalism, as illustrated by the work of social movements like the Solidarity Network with Migrants Japan (SMJ), which supports the rights of foreign residents in Japan, and the Violence Against Women in War Network (VAWW-Net), which campaigns for redress to former victims of wartime sexual abuse by the Japanese military (the so-called comfort women). However, I shall argue that a particular form of "human rights" nationalism has become very influential in Japan since the mid-1990s and into the twenty-first century, and that this was focused on the threatening image of a destabilized North Korea. The continuing influence of this "human rights" nationalism is a crucial source of the difficulties that still beset public responses to the North Korean refugees today.

Several factors created the environment for the rise of this variant of nationalism in 1990s Japan. One, of course, was the collapse of the Communist bloc and the growing evidence of extreme poverty and political repression in the remaining Stalinist state, North Korea. But other factors were also at work, including the political fluidity in early 1990s Japan and the changing relationship between Japan and its other neighbors, particularly South Korea and China. Domestically, a major split in the long-dominant Liberal Democratic Party (LDP) led to the formation of a series of short-lived coalition governments, and created uncertainty about the directions of Japan's political development. Regionally, meanwhile, South Korea had become a highly industrialized country, and was in the midst of a rapid process of democratization, while China's embrace of economic liberalization was beginning to bear fruit. One important aspect of the changes in Japanese domestic politics and in the regional balance of power was the resurgence of debates about historical responsibility, which led to a series of significant apologies by prime ministers Hosokawa and Murayama for past wrongs committed by the Japanese state. The controversies surrounding these apologies can, in retrospect, be seen as having had an important effect on emerging perceptions of the abductions and the North Korean human rights issues.

The first people to put the abduction issue into the public arena were a group of researchers and politicians, many of them originally associated with the Democratic Socialist Party [*Minshatō*], a small party that was dissolved in 1994.[20] To give some sense of their human rights discourse, however, I shall focus particularly on three prominent North Korea human rights activists, all of whom are researchers and public commentators associated with the Modern Korea Institute [*Gendai Koria Kenkyūjo*]. This organization was originally established in 1961 under the title the Korea Research Institute [*Chōsen Kenkyūjo*]. The activists whose work I shall discuss here are Satō Katsumi, who has been a key figure in the Institute since 1964; Araki Kazuhiro, who became head of the research section of the Institute in 1993, and (as we have seen) subsequently also became director of the *Chōsakai*; and Miura Kotarō, who, with Satō, co-edited the Institute's flagship journal *Modern Korea*, while also heading a human rights NGO: the Society to Help Returnees to North Korea [*Kita Chōsen Kikokusha no Seimei to Jinken o Mamorukai*, or *Mamorukai* for short].

Satō and Araki come from very different intellectual and ideological backgrounds. Satō, who was already in his sixties by the 1990s, had been a well-known left-wing researcher and activist, and had spent much of his early life advocating closer ties between Japan and North Korea, as well as working to improve the human rights of the Korean community in Japan. As a Communist Party member and official of the Niigata Branch of the Japan-Korea Association [*Nicchō Kyōkai*], he was from 1960 to 1964 actively involved in promoting and organizing the mass repatriation of Koreans from Japan to North Korea.[21] He joined the *Chōsen Kenkyūjo* in 1965, and by the mid-1970s had become one of its leading members. By the late 1970s, however, Satō's political stance was changing, and growing splits were appearing in the ranks of the Institute.

Satō Katsumi's disillusionment with Communism began to become evident after a visit to China during the final stages of the Cultural Revolution.[22] By this time, he was also beginning to become aware of the fate of the repatriates, most of whom suffered great poverty and hardship after their arrival in the DPRK, and thousands of whom were ultimately sent to North Korean labor camps. This realization left Satō in the painful position of feeling himself to be both a betrayer (because he had sent others to a terrible fate) and betrayed (by Communism and by the North Korean *juche* ideology in which he had believed, but which had proved so desperately flawed). "Sadly," he wrote, "the substance of the first several decades of my involvement with Korean issues has been totally negated by reality."[23] Such experiences help to explain the intense personal anger toward North Korea that permeates much of Satō's writing.

From the 1980s on, his writings on North Korea came increasingly to highlight the violent and oppressive nature of the DPRK and the widening gaps between the comfortable life of the political elite and the sufferings of ordinary people.[24] At the same time, other aspects of the rightward shift in Satō's views became visible. For example, after the 1980 Kwangju Uprising against the Chun Doo-Hwan dictatorship in South Korea, whose suppression involved the massacre of an estimated one thousand to two thousand people by the South Korean military, Satō criticized human rights groups in Japan for circulating what he claimed were invented stories of military brutality in Kwangju. He condemned Japanese supporters of the imprisoned South Korean opposition politician (later to become president) Kim Dae Jung for in effect providing encouragement to North Korean ambitions.[25] The result was an irrevocable split between Satō and other members of the Korea Research Institute, which led to the demise of the old organization and its reappearance in 1984 as the Modern Korea Institute, led by Satō with the assistance of a small band of like-minded activists.

The transformation of Satō's ideology was not simply motivated by increasing awareness of economic collapse and political repression in North Korea, nor was it a simple extension of his earlier human rights concerns to abuses north of the thirty-eighth parallel. Rather, this ideological transformation was one that Satō himself explicitly linked to the emergence of a post–Cold War order. The collapse of Communism and the rapidly evolving political situation in South Korea, he argued, were resulting in a gradual political rapprochement between North and South Korea. Whereas Japan and South Korea had previously been able to unite against the "common enemy"—the DPRK—now North and South Korea were not only engaging in dialogue, but even joining in condemning Japan for issues such as its failure to address issues of historical responsibility, most notably, the "comfort women" issue.

In August 1993, Japan's coalition government completed an investigation into the institutionalized sexual abuse of women in military "comfort stations" [*ianjo*] during the Asia Pacific War. The report acknowledged that many thousands of women had experienced terrible suffering in the "comfort station" system, and that the Japanese military had been involved in their recruitment. In response to the findings of the report, Chief Cabinet Secretary Kōno Yōhei issued a public apology on behalf of the Japanese government.

The report and apology attracted impassioned criticism from Satō Katsumi, who viewed it as evidence of a dangerous shift in the power relationship between Japan and the two Koreas. Japan, Satō warned, was suffering from a dangerous "apology disease," and its statements of regret for the past were placing it in a "subordinate" position to North and South Korea. More alarmingly still, apologies (he warned) were likely to encourage both Koreas to join in demanding monetary compensation, re-opening issues that (in the South Korean case) were supposed to have been resolved by the payment made when Japan normalized relations with the Republic of Korea in 1965.[26]

Satō's vision of Japan's imperiled national prestige and security brought his views into close alignment with those of the much-younger Araki Kazuhiro, who joined the Modern Korea Institute in 1993. Araki's father had trained during the war in the Manchukuo Military Academy alongside a man then known as Takaki Masao, who (under his real name, Park Chung-Hee) was later to become president of the Republic of Korea (ROK). This connection had a lasting influence on the younger Araki, who wrote his graduation thesis on Park, visited South Korea on a number of occasions during the last years of the Park dictatorship, and still cites Park as one of the two people whom he most admires.[27]

Araki initially seemed to be headed for a career in politics. He joined the Democratic Socialist Party in 1979 and became secretary-general of its youth branch, before running as an independent for a seat in the Lower House of Parliament in 1993.[28] Thereafter he embarked on a career as a researcher in the Modern Korea Institute and at Takushoku University, while pursuing political activism through a variety of groups including the *Chōsakai*—created in 2003 as a "sister organization" of the better-known *Rachi Higaishi o Sukuukai* (National Association for the Rescue of Japanese Kidnapped by North Korea, generally known in Japanese by the abbreviation *Sukuukai*). Araki has also established his personal security think-tank, the Strategic Intelligence Institute Inc. [*Senryaku Jōhō Kenkyūjo KK*], and lists one of his current positions as "Opinion Leader for the Office of the Inspector General, Eastern Section, Ground Self-Defense Forces" [*Rikugun Jieitai Tōbu Hōmen Sōkanbu Opinionrīdā*],[29] a role that could be regarded as somewhat alarming, given that one of the *Chōsakai*'s current objectives is to "seek to foment outside opinion and create the conditions within the Self-Defense Force" for direct intervention by the Japanese armed forces to rescue Japanese abductees in North Korea.[30]

By the mid-1990s, Araki had become a fairly high-profile public commentator on Korean affairs, and particularly on the increasingly dire state of affairs in North Korea. After the death of Kim Il Sung in 1994, there was much speculation about the future of the DPRK. Amidst uncertainty about the succession of Kim Jong Il, and growing evidence of economic collapse and impending famine, Araki published a book and a series of articles predicting not only the impending collapse of the regime but also an armed attack on South Korea by a desperate North Korean military. This attack, he suggested, would take the form of a blitzkrieg strike on Seoul, the main aim of which would be to destroy South Korea's political and economic infrastructure and take hostage large numbers of South Koreans and foreign residents. The South Korean military and U.S. troops based in the South, he believed, would probably be unable to respond effectively because South Korean student and opposition groups had been infiltrated by tens of thousands of North Korean agents, who were waiting to act on orders from Pyongyang "as they did during the Kwangju Incident."[31]

Meanwhile, from about 1996 onward both Araki and Satō, together with a group of politicians including Ōguchi Hideo and Nishimura Shingo, had also taken up the cause of a number of Japanese citizens who had mysteriously disappeared, and were believed to have been kidnapped by North Korea. In the early stages, Araki's writings particularly highlighted the cases of two thirteen-year-olds—Yokota Megumi, who had vanished while returning home from badminton practice in the city of Niigata in 1977, and Terakoshi Takeshi, who together with his two uncles Terakoshi Sotoo and Shōji, had disappeared while on a fishing trip off the coast of Ishikawa Prefecture in 1963.[32] Takeshi Sotoo and Shōji were actually known to be in North Korea, because fourteen years after their disappearance, their family in Japan had finally received a letter from Sotoo, informing them that Shōji had died, but that he and Takeshi were living in the DPRK.

While the story of Yokota Megumi was to became the most internationally notorious of all the abduction incidents, the Terakoshi case subsequently disappeared from most public accounts of the abductions, in part at least because the victim failed to behave in the way that the Japanese media and support groups expected an abductee to act. Despite considerable circumstantial evidence that he was indeed taken to North Korea against his own will,[33] Terakoshi Takeshi, who had since become a senior union official in North Korea and changed his name to Kim Yeong-Heo, has consistently denied that he was abducted. He made a short visit to his old home in Japan soon after Koizumi's trip to Pyongyang in 2002, but has remained living in Pyongyang, while his mother, who has visited him in Pyongyang on numerous occasions, has insisted that his name not be included on official Japanese government lists of abductees.[34] Meanwhile, however, the Modern Korea Institute had begun to investigate other possible abductions by North Korea. By the late 1990s the issue came to prominence, and public interest reached fever pitch in 2002, after the Kim Jong Il regime admitted to having kidnapped thirteen Japanese, but stated that eight (including Yokota Megumi, who was claimed to have committed suicide) were now dead.

In other circumstances, the "human rights" nationalism developed by figures like Satō and Araki in the 1990s might have remained just one of many contesting streams in Japanese political discourse. But the shockwaves created by the revelations about the abductions gave the views of the Modern Korea Institute, *Sukuukai*, and their associates an extraordinary influence both on media debate and on Japanese diplomacy: an influence further inflated as a growing number of ruling LDP politicians, including Abe Shinzō, made the abduction issue a central plank of their political agendas.

The abduction issue had an unprecedented influence on public opinion. Many ordinary people who had never been involved in politics or NGO activism before rallied to the cause because they were genuinely moved at the terrible plight of the abductees and their families: particularly of Yokota Megumi's parents, who had experienced a particularly bizarre and agonizing version of every parent's worst nightmare. This was, par excellence, an issue where concern for human rights and for national security coincided. As Satō Katsumi stressed, in carrying out the abductions, North Korea had violated both Japanese sovereignty and the most fundamental of human rights.[35] However, the Modern Korea Institute's passion for human rights was now wholly focused on those human rights abuses that were simultaneously threats to national security. In the process, its commitment to human rights suffered a strange bifurcation. Satō's pursuit of justice for the abductees, for example, went hand-in-hand with his equally vocal *opposition* to compensation for former "comfort women," while Araki's went hand-in-hand with his active involvement in the campaign to *prevent* Japanese local governments from granting voting rights to foreigners.[36]

4. "Human Rights" Nationalism and the Refugee Issue

But it is in relation to the issue of North Korean refugees that the internal contradictions of "human rights" nationalism become most evident. The critique of North Korea's human rights record, after all, demands sympathy toward those who flee the country in search of a better life elsewhere. But national security (as envisaged by nationalist commentators) demands tight border controls and a wary, if not hostile, attitude to outsiders who seek entry into Japanese society.

During the 1990s, in his commentaries on the North Korean military threat, Araki Kazuhiro began to cite the suggestion from "a senior Ministry of Justice Official" (whom he later identified as Sakanaka Hidenori) that a possible 300,000 former "repatriates" from Japan and their families might flee a collapsing North Korea and arrive in waves on Japan's shores.[37] As time went on, Araki's predictions on the subject became more alarming. In March 1999, following an incident when the body of a dead North Korean soldier was washed ashore in Japan, he wrote an article in which he recalled the arrival of the North Korean refugee boat the *Zu-Dan 9082* in 1987:

> It is said that, if the North Korean system should collapse, possibly as many as 300,000 refugees would eventually flow into Japan. If the political instability within North Korea continues, some of them will arrive on Japan's shores not as dead bodies but as second and third *Zu-Dans*. In the worst case scenario, they may arrive carrying weapons.[38]

The Japanese state (he insisted) should make urgent preparations for this alarming scenario; but it was entirely unclear whether the preparations Araki had in mind were plans to receive and help these victims of North Korean oppression, or defensive measures to drive armed intruders back into the sea.

Other members of the Modern Korea Institute, however, have over the years developed much more specific visions for a positive Japanese policy toward North Korean refugees. These visions stress the need for tight border controls, while also proposing—as part of a vision of Japan's cultural uniqueness—measures to accept and assimilate certain types of refugee. In other words, they place acceptance of returnee-refugees, alongside rescue of abductees, at the center of an explicitly nationalist agenda. One of the most enthusiastic proponents of this vision is Miura Kotarō, chief representative of the *Mamorukai*, a group set up in 1994 to help those 93,340 ethnic Koreans and their Japanese spouses who were repatriated to North Korea during the Cold War era. Miura is also a key figure in the Tokyo branch of RENK (Rescue the North Korean People), the best-known of the Japanese NGOs involved in the North Korean human rights issues.

From the late 1990s onward, the *Mamorukai* has become increasingly active in supporting returnee refugees. Together with other groups such as the *Sukuukai* and *Chōsakai*, it lobbied the government to include support for refugees (as well as investigation of suspected abduction cases and tough sanctions against the DPRK) in the 2006 North Korea Abduction and Human Rights Law. Shortly after the law was passed, and again immediately after the arrival of the four North Korean boat people in June 2007, Miura Kotarō published articles spelling out his thoughts on the future of Japanese policy toward North Korean refugees.

In the first of these articles, Miura begins by making a clear distinction between returnee-refugees, whom Japan should accept for resettlement, and other North Korean refugees, to whom Japan (he believes) does not have a responsibility. Miura's argument is that returnee-refugees should be accepted and helped, above all, because they perceive Japan as their true homeland [*kokyō*]. Indeed, he emphasizes that the homeland for which they long is not so much the real Japan of the twenty-first century as the long-lost and more innocent Japan they left in the early 1960s. In this sense, the returnee-refugees are depicted not only as true Japanese at heart, but also as embodiments of a pure Japaneseness that some young Japanese of today have lost: "Surely we should welcome as Japanese nationals the returnee-refugees, who are demanding to return, settle and be 'assimilated' into Japan or more precisely, are demanding to 'return' to the Japan of the early 1960s, the age when Japan still retained its local and family communities."[39]

This desire for "assimilation" into a vanishing traditional Japan seems to make the returnee-refugees an ideal test case for what Miura (borrowing a term from French historian Emmanuel Todd) calls "open assimilationism."[40] Rejecting the multiculturalist notion of "the right to difference," which (he argues) has only caused social division and inter-ethnic tension, Miura proposes that Japan should develop its own unique brand of "open assimilationism," which may serve as a model for other nations currently beset by ethnic conflicts.

To realize this vision, Miura proposes a series of practical steps, which begin at the point where former returnees and their families make the dangerous crossing of the border out of North Korea and into China. At present, the refugees are generally forced to remain in hiding in China for months while they contact relatives in Japan to obtain papers, make contact with Japanese diplomatic missions in China, and wait for permission to leave China and enter Japan. This wait is a time of great anxiety, since discovery would mean being returned across the border to probable incarceration in a grim North Korean prison.

Miura's first proposal, then, is that Japanese consulates in the relevant parts of China should create facilities where refugees can live for several months while their claims to be former returnees are checked. The checking, Miura emphasizes, should be extremely rigorous, so as to weed out "bogus returnee-refugees" and secret agents, and should include DNA tests to ensure that those who claim to be families are actually related to one another. While in the consulate, refugees should be given information and advice about Japan, to be provided in part by Japanese NGOs. This should include warnings that life will be difficult, and that they will receive greater material support if they choose to resettle in South Korea rather than Japan.

Those who nonetheless choose to go to Japan should be accepted and given various forms of assistance, including government-supported help in finding work and housing. They could also be granted livelihood protection payments (the relatively small welfare payments available to the destitute in Japan) for up to a year or a year and a half. However, Miura emphasizes the dangers of welfare dependence, and therefore believes that these payments should be made only on condition that the refugees initially live in a closed training facility, which Miura calls a "Japanese-style *Hanawon*." The controversial *Hanawon* in Anseong, south of Seoul, is a South Korean processing and resettlement center, where refugees from North Korea are kept separated from the rest of society for two months while they are trained in work and social skills.[41] Miura's proposed "Japanese *Hanawon*" seems a more far-reaching project, since he envisages refugees remaining there for at least six months, while NGOs (supported by the government) provide them with language and skill training, counseling, and education in "the rules of life in a democratic society."[42]

Language training is particularly strongly emphasized, not simply for practical reasons, but because Miura sees language as the vehicle through which the refugees will acquire a knowledge of Japanese "rules, customs, behavior patterns, social relationship structures, etc." Therefore, "study and mastery of the Japanese language" [*Nihongo gakushū to shūtoku*] is defined as a duty for all refugees, and as a prerequisite that they must fulfill if they are to receive Japanese citizenship or permanent resident rights.[43]

Miura concludes his essay on the subject by quoting from the postwar Shintoist writer Ashizu Uzuhiko, who called for a revival of Japanese ethnic tradition centered on the emperor, and on a positive reevaluation of Japan's prewar and wartime pan-Asianism. Unlike many nationalists, Ashizu saw the acceptance of immigrants as part of Japan's imperial tradition. Reviving the phrase (much used in the wartime empire) "All the Four Corners of the World Under One Roof" [*hakkō ichiu*], he presented migration as a way of enhancing Japan's international status and gathering people from around the world under the protection of the emperor, and he claimed that "ever since the Meiji period Japan has led the world in emphasizing racial equality and freedom of migration." "When the issue of allowing the entry of returnee-refugees faces various difficulties," comments Miura, "I always think of these words."[44]

The practical activities of the *Mamorukai* have doubtless provided many returnee-refugees in Japan with much-needed and welcomed practical support. Indeed, the limited support available to the 140 or so already in Japan comes mainly from NGOs like the *Mamorukai* and the more recently created Japan Aid Association for North Korean Returnees [*Kikoku Dappokusha Shien Kikō*], established in 2005 by former Tokyo Immigration Bureau head Sakanaka Hidenori. For Sakanaka, as for Miura, support for the repatriate-refugees is part of a more ambitious political agenda. Sakanaka sees this as the final remaining issue in his lifework—"solving the problem of *Zainichi* society" [*"Zainichi shakai" no mondai kaiketsu*].[45] Both as a senior official of Japan's Immigration Control Bureau and since his retirement in 2005, Sakanaka has argued energetically for a more open Japanese policy toward immigrants, and for measures to make it easier for Korean and other foreigners in Japan to become Japanese nationals. Although Sakanaka does not share Miura's enthusiasm for evoking memories of the wartime empire, he does explicitly place this openness to foreigners in a wider nationalist agenda, arguing that large-scale future immigration is the only way to maintain Japan's economic, cultural, and political strength in an age of falling birthrates.

In terms that in some ways echo Miura's notion of "open assimilationism," Sakanaka calls for "Japanese-style multicultural coexistence" as the only way to maintain a "big Japan" (as opposed to the "small Japan" threatened by population decline).[46] Many of the practical measures he proposes (such as changes to the nationality to make naturalization easier, and the creation of an antidiscrimination commission) would in practice enhance the rights of migrants to Japan. But this vision, too, is not underpinned by a logic of the *rights* of migrants, but rather by a logic of *national security*. Implicitly at least, "desirable foreigners" [*nozomashii gaikokujin*][47] are to be welcomed and protected as long as they serve the aim of promoting a strong Japan, but are in danger of becoming "undesirable" the moment they cease to serve that aim.

Since the North Korea Abduction and Human Rights Law stresses government cooperation with NGOs in dealing with the refugee issue, future refugee support policies are also likely to involve a large role for these NGOs. However, the political ideals behind the NGOs we have examined raise important concerns, for reasons that are best explained by going back the late 1950s and considering the origins and nature of the repatriation that took Korean and Japanese migrants from Japan to North Korea in the first place.

5. From Japan to North Korea, c. 1960

Recalling his own involvement in the mass relocation of ethnic Koreans from Japan to North Korea, Satō Katsumi has described how a movement demanding repatriation emerged from within the Korean community in August 1958, clearly promoted by the North Korean government itself. The movement, however, spread quickly, and was soon also taken up by the mainstream Japanese media, public intellectuals, and some of Japan's leading politicians.[48]

There is, in fact, an ironic similarity between the wave of media emotion generated by the repatriation movement in 1958–1959 and the even greater emotion evoked by the story of the abductions from 2002 onward. Both issues involved powerful stories of human suffering. In 1958 and 1959, for the first time since the end of the Asia-Pacific War, Japanese national newspapers were full of accounts of the individual hardships faced by Koreans in Japan, and (as the date for the departure of the first repatriation ship approached) media reports repeatedly highlighted the deep desire of the departing Koreans to see their native land again.[49] As in the case of the abductions (though for different reasons), there were genuine problems of human rights at stake. Also, as in the case of the abductions, the human rights dimensions of the issue happened precisely to coincide with a widely accepted understanding of the interests of Japanese national security. Many media articles at the time pointed out that repatriation to North Korea, while satisfying the heartfelt longing of Koreans to "go home," would simultaneously remove from Japan a group of people who were widely viewed as being left wing and a source of social disruption.

Satō argues that the originators of the scheme were the government of the DPRK and the Pro-North Korean General Association of Korean Residents in Japan [*Chongryun*], and that Japanese politicians were lured into supporting this disastrous plan by the enthusiasm and skillful propaganda of its North Korean proponents.[50] However, recently declassified documents show that the background to the repatriation movement was much more complex than had previously been realized by most people—even by those like Satō who had been personally involved in the events of the time. In fact, as early as 1955, some senior bureaucrats and politicians in the ruling LDP had quietly taken up the idea of promoting a mass exodus of ethnic Koreans from Japan to North Korea. They sought to promote this migration via the intermediary of the international Red Cross movement, so as to avoid the political repercussions that might ensue if it was seen as being a Japanese-promoted scheme.[51] A major motive for their support of a mass migration to North Korea was the perception of Koreans in Japan as being potentially subversive and a burden on the welfare system.[52] On the Japanese side, a combination of carrots and sticks helped to make the prospect of migration appear attractive to *Zainichi* Koreans. The sticks included a clamp down on the very limited forms of welfare available to Koreans in Japan, and the explicit exclusion of all foreigners from newly created national pension and health insurance schemes. The carrots included complex secret negotiations to ensure international acceptance of the "repatriation" scheme, and a nationwide campaign by a *Zainichi* Korean Repatriation Assistance Association [*Zainichi Chōsenjin Kikoku Kyōryoku Kai*], whose leading members included prominent politicians from across the Japanese political spectrum.

The North Korean government was initially reluctant to accept a large inflow of Koreans from Japan, but in mid-1958 decided to promote the "repatriation" scheme for its own strategic interests, which included a need for labor power and technological know-how, and a desire to disrupt moves toward normalization of relations between Japan and South Korea.[53] From then on, the Kim Il Sung regime used a massive propaganda campaign to persuade Koreans in Japan that a better life awaited them in the DPRK. *Chongryun*, together with Japanese local government offices and the Japan Red Cross Society, became the main agent in carrying out the repatriation, and appears to have used pressure both to persuade some of the undecided to leave for North Korea and to prevent the departure of those whose repatriation did not suit the North Korean government's strategy. Meanwhile the United States, although concerned about this mass migration from the "free world" to a Communist nation at the height of the Cold War, did nothing to prevent it because the Eisenhower administration was more concerned with maintaining good relations with the Japanese government, with whom it was then negotiating the revision of the U.S. Security Treaty with Japan.[54]

It was against the background of these complex Cold War political maneuvers that tens of thousands of Koreans in Japan were persuaded to volunteer for resettlement in North Korea where, they were led to believe, a happier and more secure future awaited them. Elsewhere I have looked in more detail at the political forces behind the repatriation, and at its human consequences.[55] Here, however, I would like to consider just three aspects of the Cold War repatriation story that seem to me to have particular relevance to the refugee issue today.

6. Lessons from the Cold War Repatriation Project

One of the forces that helped turn the repatriation into a tragedy was, I believe, the fact that both Japanese and North Korean authorities tended to view the Korean "returnees" as an undifferentiated mass, and attributed to them certain stereotypical characteristics that fitted the strategic objectives of the governments concerned. To many Japanese politicians and bureaucrats, the repatriation project was aimed at "certain Koreans" whom they viewed as impoverished, left wing, disruptive, and criminally inclined. To North Korean politicians and bureaucrats, on the contrary, they were oppressed compatriots whose terrible experiences in Japan had given them a burning desire to help build the Socialist homeland. Needless to say, neither of these stereotypes even began to capture the diversity of personalities, experiences, hopes, and motivations that characterized the 93,340 people who ultimately left Japan for North Korea.

Some were certainly poor, some had criminal records, some had experienced great hardship in Japan, a fair number were indeed filled with hope for the future possibilities of Socialism. But they also included the rich and successful, the utterly apolitical, and huge numbers of people whose main motive was the tentative hope that life in North Korea might be a little more secure than life in Japan. The homogenizing images imposed on returnees by both sides had far-reaching consequences. The stereotype held by Japanese officials explains the enthusiasm that some of them (including some senior officials of the Japanese Red Cross Society) showed for maximizing the number of Koreans leaving Japan.

The stereotype propagated on the North Korean side, meanwhile, helps explain the increasing mistrust and prejudice with which returnees came to be viewed as it became evident that they did not fit the expected model. Such misplaced expectations were undoubtedly one factor behind the increasingly repressive approach of the North Korean authorities to the people whom they had invited to "return to the Socialist homeland."

In the light of this experience, it seems particularly important that the same mistake should not be made again in relation to North Korean refugees (including returnee-refugees) today. If the returnees themselves were an extremely diverse group, so too are returnee-refugees. Though all have suffered as a result of the collapse of the North Korean economy, some had nevertheless managed to live relatively stable lives in North Korea, while others have been victims of terrible political persecution. Some undoubtedly feel a sense of nostalgia for the Japan they left in the 1960s or 1970s, but others (particularly the younger generation) have no memories of Japan at all. Some speak perfect Japanese and need no language training, while others (particularly the older groups of returnee-refugees, who are now in their forties) may never be able to acquire really high levels of Japanese-language competence. Some are filled with passionate anger toward the North Korean regime because of their tragic experiences, while others have no interest in politics. Some, meanwhile, also feel that the Japanese government bears a large measure of responsibility for their fate.[56] Any effective response to the needs of refugees, then, must be able to encompass and respond to this diversity. Surely the last thing that the returnee-refugees need is to become the test-case in yet another scheme for nationalist social engineering.

Another fundamental cause of the repatriation tragedy was the absence of legally enshrined rights for Koreans in postwar Japan. This in turn was a product of lacunae in both national and international law. Within Japan, ethnic Koreans, who had held Japanese nationality during the colonial period, were arbitrarily deprived of the right to that nationality in April 1952, when the San Francisco Peace Treaty came into effect. Since no alternative law was introduced to provide them with clearly defined permanent residence rights in Japan, they were left in a legal limbo that lasted for more than a decade. The normalization of relations between Japan and South Korea in 1965 provided some clarity to the position for those who registered and for citizens of the Republic of Korea, but failed to resolve the problem for other Koreans in Japan. Testimony by returnees to North Korea, both at that time and since, shows that this sense of uncertainty was a key factor for many in determining their decision to leave Japan.

The sense of uncertainty was particularly great for the substantial group of Koreans in Japan (possibly in the region of 100,000 people or more) who were or had become "illegal entrants": that is, Koreans who had entered (or re-entered) Japan in the period after 1945. One aspect of this uncertainty was the fact that there was no reliable way for Koreans in Japan to obtain re-entry rights if they left the country, for example, to visit relatives in Korea. As a result, many made undocumented journeys out of and back into Japan, thereby becoming "illegal entrants" who, if discovered, were liable to internment in Ōmura Migrant Detention Center and repatriation to South Korea.

This history is a reminder of the fact that rights enshrined in national and international law play a key role in protecting minorities, migrants, and refugees. The problem with the current Japanese system for accepting returnee-refugees is that it continues to rely on official discretion. Those re-entering Japan have no legally defined right to claim resettlement in Japan, or to claim support services when they arrive there. Meanwhile, the Chinese government refuses to accept the application of the Geneva Convention to North Korean refugees on its soil.

The approach to the refugee problem set out by Miura Kotarō includes some worthwhile proposals. It does seem important that Japanese diplomatic missions should be better prepared to respond to the needs of returnee-refugees, and that those being resettled in Japan should be offered language classes, skill-training, counseling, and help in finding housing and employment (though Miura's vision of a "Japanese-style *Hanawon*" is problematic).

Miura's approach, however, is in essence not a "human rights" approach at all, but rather a "state protection" approach. The concept of human rights is based on a belief in certain fundamental and universal rights, which exist in nature but can be effectively implemented only when they are enshrined in law. By contrast, the "state protection" approach is wary of the concept of rights, but encourages a benevolent state to give its protection to groups of people who fulfill particular criteria consistent with the aims of state security and power. State protection can indeed save lives, and make existence happier and easier for those whom the state defines as "good" immigrants or refugees.[57] But, as the history of Koreans in postwar Japan shows, it can also leave those who fail to serve the purposes of the state in a desperately vulnerable position, with tragic results.

In twenty-first-century Japan, what will become, for example, of returnee-refugees who do *not* feel nostalgia for the family values of 1960s Japan, and who find it difficult or impossible to master fluent Japanese? What will become of those who blame not only North Korea and *Chongryun* but also the Japanese government for their experiences over the past four decades? What of those who fail to fit the accepted image of the patriotic Japanese citizen or the "desirable alien"? What will become of refugees who may wish to come to Japan because their closest friends are there, but who fail to fit the definition of "returnee-refugee"? All these questions point to the need for a new approach to the refugee issue, one that goes beyond the restrictive bounds of "human rights" nationalism.

7. Beyond "Human Rights" Nationalism: Rethinking the Refugee Issue

The political situation on the Korean peninsula is, as I write, fluid and uncertain. It is impossible to predict the outcome of current movements toward the denuclearization of North Korea, the normalization of relations between North Korea and the United States, and the signing of a peace treaty. But, however events unfold, it is very likely that the outflow of people across the border between North Korea and China will continue, and may increase in the next five to ten years. Though parallels with the end of the Cold War in Europe should be treated with caution, it would also be unwise to ignore the European experience of the large-scale documented and undocumented migration out of the former "Communist bloc" that accompanied the reintegration of East and West. If North Korea becomes more closely reintegrated into the region—both politically and economically—there seems a real likelihood that emigration will increase, adding to other expanding regional migration flows.

In Northeast Asia, much of the cross-border movement will surely continue to be (as it is today) short-term movement back-and-forth between the DPRK and China. Others leaving North Korea will seek short-term or long-term settlement in South Korea. But it is likely that a number of former "returnees" and others will seek to reach Japan, while some of those leaving the DPRK may find it difficult to settle in any of the immediately neighboring regions, and may seek a new home further afield. So far, the region is very poorly prepared to deal with this migration. By way of conclusion, I shall suggest some steps that urgently need to be taken in the Japanese and regional contexts to prevent the outflow of migrants from North Korea from becoming a source of extreme human suffering, rising xenophobia, and social conflict.

These steps relate specifically to Japan's role in receiving North Korean emigrants. The information now available on the 1959–1984 repatriation makes it clear that the Japanese government, together with the North Korean government, has a deep moral responsibility to address the problems of those who migrated from Japan to the DPRK. The most obvious way to fulfill this responsibility is to make a clear official commitment that Japan will accept all those former "returnees" and their immediate family who wish to resettle in Japan. This commitment should include provision of permanent residence rights to those who do not have Japanese citizenship, as well as measures to ensure that returnee-refugees have access to government-supported welfare, language classes, skills training, and counseling services. All other North Korean refugees who arrive on Japan's shores should have their claims for asylum assessed under the rules of the Geneva Convention. In order to prevent this issue from becoming a source of fear and xenophobia, it is important that the Japanese government should prepare the ground for the acceptance of an inflow of returnee-refugees and other asylum-seekers from North Korea through reasoned public debate.

A further essential step is for a wider range of Japanese and international NGOs to become involved in the process of supporting North Korean refugees (including returnee-refugees) in Japan. At present, reliance on discretionary government decisions and on a small number of NGOs with highly politicized agendas leaves returnee-refugees in an extraordinarily vulnerable position. The issue here is a delicate one. My aim is not to deny the value of the practical help that groups like the *Mamorukai* or the Japan Aid Association for North Korean Returnees provide to refugees. On the contrary, they are to be commended for giving vital assistance when others were not willing to do so. The problem is rather that other groups whose ideas are more firmly based on universalist human rights principles, rather than "human rights" nationalism, have failed to take up the issue. To put it simply, in the political environment of post-2002 Japan, issues related to the abductees and to North Korean refugees have come to be seen as part of the agenda of the "right," and more liberal or left-leaning social movements have become reluctant to engage with them. The experience of the 1959–1984 repatriation reveals how dangerous it can be for those with few legal rights to be placed in a position of reliance on the humanitarianism of groups with strongly nationalist agendas. For this reason, it is particularly important for a wide range of civil society groups with diverse approaches and perspectives to become engaged with this issue, offering their expertise, skills, and financial support to programs that support North Korean refugees in Japan.

Finally, the North Korean refugee issue has reached a point where isolated and uncoordinated national responses are increasingly inadequate. A regional approach is needed, and governments and NGOs should engage in informal consultation on practical and flexible responses to the needs of emigrants from North Korea. Although South Korea, China, Japan, as well as countries like Thailand, Laos, and Mongolia (through which many North Korean refugees pass) are most obviously affected, there is also potentially a significant role to be played by other nations of the region like Australia and New Zealand, which have long been migrant-receiving countries. Wealthy nations with large immigration programs should be prepared to develop programs for accepting emigrants from North Korea who seek resettlement outside the Northeast Asian region. These programs should not simply be targeted at emigrants with high levels of technical skills, but should include a strong humanitarian component.

In a rapidly changing Northeast Asia, the movement of people across borders, and particularly emigration from North Korea, is likely to emerge as a major political and social challenge to national governments. But a new

human rights–based response to this problem—one that goes beyond the
limits of "human rights" nationalism—could also become one element in the
emerging regional collaboration that will link the countries of Northeast Asia
(and more widely of East Asia and its southern neighbors Australia and New
Zealand) as the Cold War in our region finally comes to end.

Notes

1. *Asahi shinbun*, June 4, 2007, 1; *Yomiuri shinbun* (Tokyo), June 3, 2007, 1; *Sankei shinbun*, June 3, 2007, 1.
2. *Asahi shinbun*, June 4, 2007, 1.
3. *Tokyo shinbun*, June 17, 2007, 3.
4. *Yomiuri shinbun* (Tokyo), June 3, 2007, 1.
5. *Asahi shinbun*, June 4, 2007, 3.
6. *Sankei shinbun*, June 30, 2007, 17.
7. Statement by Mr. Masayoshi Hamada, Vice Minister for Foreign Affairs of Japan at the Preview of "Abduction: The Megumi Yokota Story," February 6, 2007, at www.mofa.go.jp/region/asia-paci/n_korea/abduction/state0702.html (accessed September 2, 2007).
8. See figures provided on the *Chōsakai* website, chosa-kai.jp/listsyukei.html (accessed September 2, 2007).
9. *Chōsakai nyūsu*, no. 511 (June 2, 2007).
10. For the sake of simplicity, I use the term "repatriate" in this article. However, it should be emphasized that the vast majority of those who migrated from Japan to North Korea in the Cold War years came from the southern rather than the northern half of Korea, and that for this reason the term "migration" or "resettlement" is probably more strictly accurate than the term "repatriation."
11. *Chōsakai nyūsu*, no. 511 (June 2, 2007).
12. *Asahi shinbun*, January 5, 2007.
13. *Asahi shinbun*, June 4, 2007, 3.
14. *Yomiuri shinbun* (Tokyo), June 12, 2007, 1.
15. A similar estimate is put forward by a well-informed observer of the refugee issue, Ishimaru Jirō of Asia Press, who discounts predictions of hundreds of thousands of refugees, but says "it is possible that the numbers crossing the sea could be in the thousands"; *Tokyo shinbun*, July 22, 2007, 29.
16. *Tokyo shinbun*, July 22, 2007, 28.
17. See, for example, *Tokyo shinbun*, June 17, 2007, 3.
18. Text of the North Korea Abduction and Human Rights Law, at law.e-gov.go.jp/htmldata/H18/H18HO096.html (accessed September 2, 2007).
19. Uwe-Jens Heuer, "Human Rights Imperialism," *Monthly Review* 49, no. 10 (March 1998).
20. The politicians included Ōguchi Hideo (now an opposition Democratic Party parliamentarian and prominent member of the National Association for the Rescue of Japanese Kidnapped by North Korea, NARKN, known in Japanese as *Rachi Higaishi*

o Sukuu Kai, or just *Sukuu Kai* for short) and Nishimura Shingo (who was forced to resign from a junior ministerial post in 1999 after advocating Japan acquisition of nuclear weapons, and is currently a Democratic Party parliamentarian).

21. Satō Katsumi, "Waga tsūkon no chōsen hantō" [The Korean Peninsula that Pains Us], *Seiron* (September 1995). As he explains in this article, Satō was expelled from the Japanese Communist Party in 1966.

22. See Wada Haruki and Takasaki Sōji, *Kenshō: nitchō kankei 60-nenshi* [A 60-Year History of Japan-North Korea Relations] (Tokyo: Akashi shoten, 2005), 71.

23. Satō, "Waga tsūkon no chōsen hantō."

24. See, for example, *Sankei shinbun,* September 23, 1992, 5; *Mainichi shinbun,* February 23, 1992, 4.

25. Wada and Takasaki, *Kenshō: nitchō kankei 60-nenshi,* 78–79.

26. *Sankei shinbun,* August 11, 1993, 4; *Mainichi shinbun,* February 23, 1992, 4.

27. See *Ehime shinbun,* April 18, 1999, 8; on Park's training in the academy, see Kim Hyung-A, *Korea's Development under Park Chung Hee: Rapid Industrialization, 1961–1979* (London and New York: RoutledgeCurzon, 2004), 20–21.

28. *Sankei shinbun,* July 13, 1993, 24; rather surprisingly, Araki chose to run not only as an independent, but also for the seat held by the highly popular Kan Naoto, and he was unsurprisingly defeated.

29. See Araki's homepage, araki.way-nifty.com/about.html (accessed September 3, 2007).

30. *Chōsakai nyūsu,* no. 507 (May 23, 2007).

31. Araki Kazuhiro, "Kita chōsen sangatsu shokuryō kiki setsu: bōhatsu ga uchi ni baai, soto ni mukau" [A Theory on March Food Crisis in North Korea: When the Eruption is Inward, [It Will] Explode Outward], *Ekonomisuto* (January 30, 1996), 72.

32. See, for example, *Chūnichi shinbun,* February 12, 1997, 11; *Sankei shinbun,* May 9, 1997, 29; *Hokkoku toyama shinbun,* January 29, 1998, 32.

33. The most plausible explanation put forward for the Terakoshi incident is that their fishing boat collided with a North Korean military or spy vessel engaged in secret maneuvers, and that they were rescued by North Korean forces, but not allowed to return to Japan for fear that they would report what they had witnessed.

34. On the Terakoshi case, see *Yomiuri shinbun* (Tokyo), June 17, 1987, 26; *Mainichi shinbun* (Osaka), October 16, 2002, 1; *Asahi shinbun,* September 18, 2003, 28; *Hokkoku shinbun,* September 19, 2003, 46; *Yomiuri shinbun* (Tokyo), May 21, 2005, 31.

35. *Sankei shinbun,* February 13, 1997.

36. See, for example, *Sankei shinbun,* May 28, 1999.

37. Araki Kazuhiro, "Kita chōsen hōkai de nihon no futan, 14" [Japan's Burden in Case of North Korea's Collapse, 14], *Ekonomisuto* (March 11, 1997), 52.

38. Araki Kazuhiro, "Nihonkai-gawa ni nagaretsuku kita chōsen heishi no shitai wa sakana ni shippai shita hitotachi" [Corpses of North Korean Soldiers that Float into the Japan Sea Side are those of People that Failed to Fish], *Ekonomisuto* (March 30, 1999).

39. Miura Kotarō, "Dappoku kikokusha no nihon ukeire no tame ni" [Toward Japan's Acceptance of Former Returnees Who Escaped North Korea], *Shokun* (September 2006), 92–101.

40. It should be noted that Todd's support for assimilation is argued specifically in the context of a French legal system that grants citizenship to all foreigners born on French soil, a situation very different from the one that prevails in Japan.

41. See, for example, Ma Seok-Hun, "Talbuk cheongsonyeon e daehan namhan sahwoeui daeeung bangsik" [The Treatment of South Korean Society toward North Korean Young Defectors], in *Welkeom tu koria: bukjoseon saramdeul eui namhan sari* [Welcome to Korea: Lives of North Koreans in South Korea], Jeong Byeong-Ho, ed. (Seoul: Hanyang University Press, 2006).

42. Miura Kotarō, "Dappokusha 4-nin no nihon tōchaku," June 2007, at www.ocn .ne.jp/~rachi/miura2.htm.

43. Miura, "Dappoku kikokusha no nihon ukeire no tame ni," 101.

44. Miura, "Dappoku kikokusha no nihon ukeire no tame ni," 101; on Ashizu, see Curtis Anderson Gayle, *Marxist History and Postwar Japanese Nationalism* (London and New York: RoutledgeCurzon, 2003), 158–60.

45. Sakanaka Hidenori, *Nyūkan senki* [The Battle Record of Immigration Control] (Tokyo: Kōdansha, 2005), 139.

46. Sakanaka Hidenori, *Nyūkan senki*, chap. 10.

47. See Sakanaka Hidenori, *Nyūkan senki*, 151–54; for an analysis of Sakanaka's ideas, see Song Ahn-Jong, "Korean-Japanese Identity and Neoliberal Multiculturalism in Australia," paper presented at the workshop "Northeast Asia: Re-Imagining the Future," Australian National University, July 4–6, 2007.

48. Satō, "Waga tsūkon no chōsen hantō"; see also Satō and Kojima, *Seiron* (2003). Sato Katsumi and Kojima Harunori, "Tojisha ga kaikon komete shidan suru 'shiturakuen' kita chōsen kikoku jigyō no suishinsha [The Promoters of Repatriation to North Korea Who Remosefully Scorn the 'Paradise Lose']" *Seiron* May 2003, 50–67.

49. For example, *Sankei shinbun*, February 2, 1959; "Jindō mondai ni natta hokusen sōkan," *Yomiuri shinbun* (evening edition), February 5, 1959.

50. Satō, "Waga tsūkon no chōsen hantō."

51. See Tessa Morris-Suzuki, *Exodus to North Korea: Shadows from Japan's Cold War* (Lanham, Md.: Rowman & Littlefield, 2007).

52. Morris-Suzuki, *Exodus to North Korea*; see also Inoue Masutarō, *Fundamental Conditions of Livelihood of Certain Koreans Residing in Japan* (Japanese Red Cross Society, November 1956), copy held in the Archives of the International Committee of the Red Cross (ICRC Archives), Geneva, B AG 232 105-002; letter from William Michel to ICRC, "Mission Michel et de Weck," May 23, 1956, 2, in ICRC Archives, B AG 232 105-002; Telegram from U.S. Ambassador MacArthur to Secretary of State, Washington, February 7, 1959, in NARA, RG95, CFDF 1955–1959, box 2722, document no. 694.95B/759, parts 1 and 2.

53. See Morris-Suzuki, *Exodus to North Korea*, chap. 14; see also "Record of Conversation with Comrade Kim Il-Sung, 14 and 15 July 1958," in *Dnevnik V. I Pelishenko*, July 23, 1958, Foreign Policy Archives of the Russian Federation, archive 0102, collection 14, file 8, folder 95.

54. Morris-Suzuki, *Exodus to North Korea*, chap. 16; see also "The Korean Minority in Japan and the Repatriation Problem," report attached to confidential memo from Parsons to Herter, "Korean Repatriation Problem," July 10, 1959, 3, DOS, FE Files Lot

61 D6 "Japan-ROK Repatriation Dispute," reproduced as document no. 786 in micro-fiche supplement to Madeline Chi, Louis J. Smith, and Robert J. McMahon, eds., *Foreign Relations of the United States 1958–1960*, vols. 17–18; telegram from Ambassador Watt, Australian Embassy Tokyo, to Department of Foreign Affairs, Canberra, July 15, 1959, "Repatriation of Koreans," in Australian National Archives, Canberra, series no. A1838/325, control symbol 3103/11/91, Part 1 "Japan—Relations with North Korea"; Department of State Memorandum of Conversation, "Problems Relating to the Republic of Korea," January 19, 1960, reproduced as document no. 142, in Chi, Smith, and McMahon, *Foreign Relations*, vol. 18, 275.

55. Morris-Suzuki, *Exodus to North Korea*.

56. See Jung Gunheon, "Nihon no sekinin o tou hokusō higaisha" [Victims of North Korean Repatriation Are Questioning Japan's Responsibilities], *Chosun Online* (Japanese edition), June 16, 2005.

57. See Abe Kohki, "Are You a Good Refugee or a Bad Refugee? Security Concerns and Dehumanization of Immigration Policies in Japan," *AsiaRights*, no. 6, rspas.anu.edu.au/asiarightsjournal/Abe.pdf (accessed October 2, 2007).

Index

About the Contributors

Charles K. Armstrong is associate professor of history and director of the Center for Korean Research at Columbia University. A specialist in the modern history of Korea and East Asia, he has published widely on modern Korean history, the international history of East Asia, and U.S.-Korean relations. He is the author of *The Koreas* (2007) and *The North Korean Revolution, 1945–1950* (2003), and the editor of *Korea at the Center: Dynamics of Regionalism in Northeast Asia* (2006) and *Korean Society: Civil Society, Democracy, and the State*, 2nd ed. (2006). His current book projects include a study of North Korean foreign relations in the Cold War era and a history of modern East Asia.

Steven Chung is an assistant professor in the Department of East Asian Studies at Princeton University, where he teaches courses in Korean and East Asian cinema and modern Korean literature. He is currently working on a book manuscript, tentatively entitled *Sin Sang-ok and Postwar Korean Mass Cultures*, which examines the filmmaker's turbulent career against the forces of postcoloniality, authoritarianism, and ideological division.

Gavan McCormack is emeritus professor in the Research School of Pacific and Asian Studies, Australian National University (ANU). A graduate of the universities of Melbourne and London (Ph.D. from London in 1974), he taught at the universities of Leeds (UK), La Trobe (Melbourne), and Adelaide, before joining the ANU as a professor in 1990. He has lived and worked in Japan on many occasions since first visiting it as a student in 1962, and has been a visiting professor at Kobe, Kyoto, Ritsumeikan, Tsukuba, and International Christian Universities. He was elected a Fellow of the Academy of Humanities of Australia in 1992 and was awarded a Centennial Medal for Service to the Humanities in Australia in 2002. His work has been translated and published in Japanese, Chinese, Korean, Thai, Arabic, and the main European languages. His recent books include *The Emptiness of Japanese Affluence* (2001, translated into Japanese, Korean, and Chinese), the jointly edited volume *Japanese Multiculturalism: From Paleolithic to Post-Modern* (1996), *Japan's Contested Constitution—Rethinking the National Role* (with Glenn Hook, 2001), and *Target North Korea: Pushing North Korea to the Brink of Nuclear Catastrophe* (2004, translated into Japanese and Korean). In July 2007 he published his latest book, *Client State: Japan in the American Embrace.* Korean, Chinese, Japanese, and Spanish translations are forthcoming.

Tessa Morris-Suzuki is professor of Japanese history and convenor of the Division of Pacific and Asian History in the College of Asia and the Pacific, Australian National University. She also convenes the Asia Civic Rights Network, and co-edits its online journal, *AsiaRights.* Her books include *Re-inventing Japan: Time, Space, Nation* (1998); *The Past Within Us: Media, Memory, History* (2005); and *Exodus to North Korea: Shadows from Japan's Cold War* (2007).

Hyun Ok Park joined the Department of Sociology at York University in 2007 after receiving a Ph.D. in sociology from the University of California at Berkeley and teaching at New York University. Hyun Ok Park is the author of *Two Dreams in One Bed: Empire, Social Life, and the Origins of the North Korean Revolution in Manchuria* (2005). She is completing a book tentatively entitled *Neoliberal Democracy: Transnational Migration, History, and Post–Cold War Asia.* She was co-editor of *Boundary 2: Problems of Comparability/Possibilities for Comparative Studies,* Vol. 32, No. 2 (2005). Park has published widely on Korean nationalism, colonial migration, diasporic movements, and anti-Americanism in South Korea. She was a fellow at the Institute for Advanced Study in Princeton from 2005 to 2007.

Sonia Ryang is associate professor of anthropology and international studies, C. Maxwell and Elizabeth M. Stanley Family and the Korea Foundation Scholar of Korean Studies, and director of the Center for Asian and Pacific Studies at the University of Iowa. Her publications include *North Koreans in Japan: Language, Ideology, and Identity* (1997); *Koreans in Japan: Critical Voices from the Margin* (2000, editor); *Japan and National Anthropology: A Critique* (2004); *Love in Modern Japan: Its Estrangement from Self, Sex, and Society* (2006); and *Writing Selves in Diaspora: Ethnography of Autobiographics of Korean Women in Japan* (2008).

Made in the USA
San Bernardino, CA
19 October 2013